University of Cambridge

Department of Applied Economics

OCCASIONAL PAPER 18

POVERTY IN BRITAIN AND
THE REFORM OF SOCIAL SECURITY

University of Cambridge

Department of Applied Economics

Occasional Papers

Poverty in Britain and the Reform of Social Security

by A. B. ATKINSON

CAMBRIDGE

AT THE UNIVERSITY PRESS

1969

PUBLISHED BY

THE SYNDICS OF THE CAMBRIDGE UNIVERSITY PRESS

Bentley House, 200 Euston Road, London N.W.1

American Branch: 32 East 57th Street, New York, N.Y. 10022

© Department of Applied Economics University of Cambridge 1969

Library of Congress Catalogue Card Number: 76-85711

Standard Book Numbers 521 07522 X cloth
521 09607 3 paper

Printed in Great Britain at The Alden Press, Osney Mead, Oxford

Contents

List of Text Tables and Figures

TABLES

Tables *Page*

9

10

Preface

I should like first of all to thank the many people who have helped me in writing this Occasional Paper.

Chronologically, I must begin with Professor J.E. Meade, who first encouraged me to become interested in this field, and who has been a constant source of advice. Secondly, I am indebted to the Director of the Department of Applied Economics, Professor W.B. Reddaway, not only for allowing the publication of this study in the Department's series, but also for his invaluable criticism of the first draft, which led to great improvement in the argument and presentation.

The first draft of the paper was read in full by P.S. Albin, J.M. Atkinson, K.D. George, R.F. Henderson, D.E. Moggridge, Z.A. Silberston, C. Spencer, D. Wedderburn and J.H. Williamson. A number of people also read parts of the original version — F. Field, I. Gough, D.S. Lees, T. Lynes, T. Stark and A. Walsh. I am most grateful to all these people for their comments and suggestions, which have helped me considerably in preparing the final version. I also very much appreciate the comments made on the first draft by the Economic Advisor's Office of the Department of Health and Social Security.

In addition, I was greatly helped by all the people who supplied me with information of one kind or another. I must particularly mention here the Department of Employment and Productivity, the Department of Health and Social Security, T. Stark, and R. Agarwala.

Secondly, I should point out that although I have tried in preparing the final version to take account of new developments up to June 1969, this has not been altogether possible. This may perhaps be excused by the speed with which events have happened in this field in the past few months. Between the writing of the first draft and its final version, new Government proposals for sickness and unemployment benefits have appeared, the results of an enquiry into national minimum wage have been published, increases in National Insurance benefits and contributions have been announced, and the Budget made a number of changes in the income tax! More changes will doubtless have taken place before this paper finally appears.

A. B. Atkinson

August 1969

Introduction

In this book I have two principal aims: to examine the available evidence about poverty in Britain today, and to evaluate the various proposals that have been made for reforming the social security system. This is an ambitious undertaking, particularly in a study of this length, but I feel that it is important to consider the problem as a whole and to take an overall view of the possible solutions.

My primary concern throughout is with the effectiveness of the social security system in helping low income households. Part I of the study is concerned with the present situation and with the contribution of the present social security provisions. Part II deals with the possible reforms and the extent to which they would provide greater benefit to those with low incomes.

In Part I, I begin by discussing the problems involved in defining poverty and explain the approach adopted in this study, which is based on the concept of a national minimum income guaranteed through the social security system. In Chapter 1, I describe the development of the present provisions from the Beveridge Report of 1942, with particular emphasis on the role of National Assistance/ Supplementary Benefits. In Chapter 2, I examine the evidence about poverty in Britain at present, drawing heavily on the work of others, as well as presenting my own estimate for 1967. In this chapter, I explore some of the principal characteristics of people with low incomes; and in the remainder of Part I, I consider in more detail the position of two particular groups — old people and households supported by a man in full-time work. In the case of old people, I discuss in Chapter 3 the present state pension provisions, the importance of income from other sources and the role of National Assistance. In Chapter 4, I have tried to analyse in detail the effect of the 1966 Ministry of Social Security Act, which replaced National Assistance by Supplementary Benefits. In considering the position of people in work, I examine the importance of family size as a cause of poverty and the benefit from Family Allowances (including the substantial increase in 1968), and explore the problem of low earnings and of the wage stop.

The second part of the book has its own introductory chapter (Chapter 6), which summarises the findings of Part I and describes the ground to be covered in Part II. Here it is sufficient to say that I discuss measures to help old people (including the proposed National Superannuation scheme) in Chapter 7, new child benefits, minimum wages and new social security contributions in Chapter 8, and negative income tax and social dividend schemes in Chapter 9. The results of this discussion are brought together in the concluding chapter (Chapter 10).

In view of the fact that many readers will not have the time (nor perhaps the inclination) to read the analysis in detail, I have included a short summary at the end of most chapters. It should be stressed, however, that these summaries do not incorporate all the qualifications mentioned in the text and should be read with this in mind. Also it was suggested to me by a number of people who read the book in manuscript that it would be useful to include a short summary of the present social security provisions. I have accordingly given a brief description of the most important features of the National Insurance and Supplementary Benefit schemes in Appendix A.

Finally, I should emphasise at the outset that I have not tried to cover the field comprehensively. There are many problems which I have left undiscussed — such as those of fatherless families and of disabled — and there are certain very relevant reforms which I have not considered — such as those relating to housing policy. In addition I have concentrated on the cash social security benefits and have taken no account of benefits in kind such as those from the health services or education.

Note: National Assistance/ Supplementary Benefits

To prevent any possible confusion about these schemes, which play a central role in this study, it may be helpful to note here that Supplementary Benefits *replaced* National Assistance with effect from November 1966 and fulfills essentially the same function.

In the course of the book there are many occasions on which I refer to them both and to avoid repetition of the cumbersome term National Assistance/Supplementary Benefits, I use the shorthand 'assistance'. When reference is made to a person receiving assistance, this should be taken to mean National Assistance over the period 1948 – November 1966 and Supplementary Benefits thereafter. I have tried not to use the word 'assistance' in any but this specific sense.

PART I   POVERTY IN BRITAIN

1   Poverty and the National Minimum

The aim of this chapter is to explain the approach adopted in this study to the definition of poverty, and to describe the broad features of the development of the social security system since the Beveridge Report, with particular emphasis on the role of the National Assistance and Supplementary Benefit schemes.

1.   THE DEFINITION OF POVERTY

The first attempts to measure the extent of poverty in any very scientific way were those of Charles Booth and Seebohm Rowntree at the turn of the century. Rowntree's work was particularly significant in that he was the first person to face up to the problems involved in defining poverty. His solution was to consider a family to be living in poverty if its 'total earnings were insufficient to obtain the minimum necessaries for the maintenance of merely physical efficiency.'[1] The 'minimum necessaries' were calculated by estimating the nutritional needs of families of different sizes, translating these needs into quantities of different foods and hence into money terms, and adding the rent paid and certain 'minimum' amounts for clothing, fuel and sundries. This method was used by Rowntree in his first survey of York in 1899 and in his subsequent surveys in 1936 and 1950, although in each of the later years the list of 'minimum necessaries' grew longer.

In this study, I have adopted a rather different approach to the definition of poverty. Unlike Rowntree, I have not used a standard based on the minimum expenditure thought necessary for the maintenance of health, but have taken instead the standard applied by the Government in determining eligibility for Supplementary Benefits. In other words, I consider a person to be living in 'poverty' if his income is below that at which he would qualify for Supplementary Benefits.

There are two principal reasons for adopting this approach. The first is that my primary concern is to examine the effectiveness of the present social security provisions *in the light of the objectives of Government policy*, objectives which can be best expressed in terms of a 'national minimum' standard of living. This concept of a national minimum played a fundamental role in the Beveridge Plan and although the Government did not implement the Beveridge recommendations in

---

[1] B.S. Rowntree, *Poverty — A Study of Town Life* (Macmillan, 1901). This definition relates to Rowntree's 'primary' poverty. (In this study I make no use of the concept of 'secondary' poverty as defined by Rowntree).

full, the essential idea was embodied in the post-war legislation.[1] Through the National Assistance scheme (and now through Supplementary Benefits) the Government has set a minimum standard below which it feels that no household should fall. To quote from a recent publication of the Ministry of Social Security, 'the purpose of the Supplementary Benefit scheme is to bring the resources of each person up to the appropriate level of requirements approved by Parliament.'[2] For this reason, it seems logical to take as the standard for assessing the effectiveness of the present provisions the minimum income guaranteed by Supplementary Benefits. In this way, the success of Government policy is being judged in the light of its own minimum standards.

This approach is very similar to that adopted by Professors B. Abel-Smith and P. Townsend in their study *The Poor and the Poorest*, where they argue that:[3]
> 'Whatever may be said about the adequacy of the National Assistance Board level of living as a just or publicly approved measure of 'poverty', it has at least the advantage of being in a sense the 'official' operational definition of the minimum level of living at any particular time.'

The same approach was also followed in the recent enquiry by the Ministry of Social Security into the circumstances of families. In her foreword to the report, Miss Herbison pointed out that:[4]
> 'The number of people in the country whose incomes can be said to be below their needs, ..., will also vary according to the standard by which the adequacy of incomes in relation to needs is judged. The supplementary benefit scheme sets such a standard which has been approved by Parliament.'

It is in this sense of an 'official' operational standard of adequacy approved by Parliament that the Supplementary Benefit scale is used in this study.

The second reason for adopting a different approach from Rowntree is that his absolute subsistence standard involves a number of serious conceptual difficulties, which were recognised by him and which have been discussed in detail by Townsend.[5] The basic problem is that, despite Rowntree's pioneering efforts, it is just not possible to define an absolute subsistence level as a basis for the poverty line. Even in the case of food, it is difficult to determine requirements with any precision, and rather than any one absolute level of

---

1 For a discussion of the development of the idea of a 'national minimum', see M. Bruce, *The Coming of the Welfare State*, Fourth Edition (Batsford, 1968), p. 26—7.

2 Department of Health and Social Security, *The Right to Help* (H.M.S.O., 1969).

3 B. Abel-Smith and P. Townsend, *The Poor and the Poorest*, Occasional Papers on Social Administration Number 17 (G. Bell and Sons, 1965).

4 Ministry of Social Security, *Circumstances of Families* (H.M.S.O., 1967).

5 P. Townsend, 'Measuring Poverty', *British Journal of Sociology*, 1954. See also P. Townsend, 'The Meaning of Poverty', *British Journal of Sociology*, 1962. This paragraph draws heavily on Professor Townsend's analysis.

subsistence requirements, there is a broad range where physical efficiency declines with a falling intake of calories, proteins, etc. Where precisely we draw the line depends on the judgement of the investigator, and the idea of a purely physiological basis to the poverty criterion is lost. It must be recognised that any subsistence standard is inevitably influenced by current living standards, and that we cannot define a poverty line in a vacuum but only in relation to the living standards of a particular society at a particular date — a point well appreciated by Adam Smith: [1]

> 'By necessities I understand not only the commodities which are indispensably necessary for the support of life, but whatever the custom of the country renders it indecent for creditable people, even of the lowest order, to be without.'

The Rowntree standard does therefore convey a false impression of concreteness and rather than calculate any present day equivalent, it seems to me preferable to recognise the relative nature of poverty explicitly in our definition. This relative nature is well reflected in the National Assistance/Supplementary Benefit standard. When the National Assistance scale was introduced in 1948 it was set at a level roughly equivalent in terms of purchasing power to the poverty line used by Rowntree in his 1936 survey of York. Since then the scale has risen in real terms (if somewhat erratically) and over the period as a whole it has increased more or less in line with the average level of earnings (see below).

Since the Supplementary Benefit standard plays a central role in the analysis, it may be helpful to describe its operation in more detail. Before doing so, however, I should emphasise that its use as the basis for a definition of poverty is subject to a number of qualifications and that the results based on this definition should not be interpreted out of their context. Firstly, this approach does not imply any judgement about the adequacy or otherwise of the Supplementary Benefit scale. This applies not only to the overall level, but also to the relative treatment of households of different composition (for example, the relationship between the scales for children and those for adults) and to the inclusion of a separate allowance for housing expenditure.

Secondly, the very nature of the definition means that any attempt by the Government to help low income families by raising the Supplementary Benefit scale will have the effect of *increasing* the number defined as living in poverty. As was pointed out by Miss Herbison 'It follows paradoxically that any increase in benefit designed to relieve the distress caused by inadequacies of income enlarges the number of people whose incomes are regarded as inadequate.'[2] This must, of course, be borne firmly in mind, particularly when making comparisons over time. However, it should be remembered that our aim, like that of the Ministry enquiry, is not to make any absolute statements about adequacy, but

---

1 A. Smith, *The Wealth of Nations*, Book 5, Chapter 2, Part II (Although it should be noted that this passage relates to the question of commodity taxation rather than to that of defining poverty).

2 *Circumstances of Families*, op. cit. p. iii.

rather 'to concentrate attention on those families having incomes which are below the current level of supplementary benefit as approved by Parliament'.[1]

The Supplementary Benefit Scale

Supplementary Benefits are payable to anyone over 16 who is not in full-time work.[2] A person with dependants receives a supplement related to their requirements as well as his own: for example where a husband and wife are both pensioners, a single supplement is paid. The scale of requirements is based on two principal components: a basic scale rate (which depends on the number of dependents and the ages of any children) and an allowance for housing expenditure.

The basic scale in force in June 1969 is set out in Table 1.1. These rates came into effect in October 1968, and are due to be increased in November 1969. The higher scale for long-term cases includes a long-term addition of 10s. It applies to pensioners and others under pension age who have received Supplementary Benefits for a continuous period of 2 years and who are not required to register at a labour exchange.

Table 1.1.   Supplementary Benefit basic scale — June 1969

	Long-term cases			Other		
	£	s	d	£	s	d
Householders:						
Single person	5	1	0	4	11	0
Married couple	7	19	0	7	9	0
Children:						
Aged — under 5				1	7	0
5 — 10				1	12	0
11 — 12				1	19	0
13 — 15				2	1	0

Source: *Annual Report of the Department of Health and Social Security for the year 1968*, (H.M.S.O., 1969), p. 273.

To this basic scale we have to add the allowance for housing expenditure. For people paying rent, this is usually paid in full (together with rates), although it may be reduced if there are non-dependent members of the household or if it is considered 'unreasonable'; in the case of an owner—occupier the addition covers rates, an allowance for repairs and insurance plus any mortgage interest which is being paid. The actual level of the Supplementary Benefit scale will therefore

---

1 ibid.

2 Persons involved in a trade dispute are also excluded (although Supplementary Benefits may be paid to their dependants). For further details of the Supplementary Benefits scheme, see Appendix A.

vary from household to household. For ease of exposition, I have estimated what might be considered 'average' housing expenditure for households of different types and I shall refer to the total scale including this average rent as the Supplementary Benefit Scale (I.A.R.) — Including Average Rent. (The details of the calculation of the estimated average rent are described in Appendix B). The resulting Supplementary Benefit scales (I.A.R.) for certain representative households in June 1969 are shown in Table 1.2.

Table 1.2. Supplementary Benefit Scale (I.A.R.) for Certain Representative Households — June 1969

	Supplementary Benefit Scale (I.A.R.) £ s d	As % of take-home pay for manual worker with average earnings[b] %
Single pensioner[a]	6 11 0	38
Pensioner couple[a]	9 14 0	52
Unemployed man with wife and:		
2 children (aged 4 and 7)	12 12 0	60
4 children (aged 4, 7, 10, and 12)	16 3 0	67
6 children (aged 2, 4, 7, 10, 12 and 14)	19 11 0	72

Notes: a Including the long-term addition.

b Based on earnings of adult male manual workers in manufacturing and certain other industries, as published by the Department of Employment and Productivity (estimated at £24 for June 1969) adjusted for income tax, National Insurance contributions and Family Allowances. The income tax and Family Allowances are those applicable to a man with the dependants shown.

The second column in Table 1.2 compares the Supplementary Benefit scale (I.A.R.) with the take-home pay of a person whose earnings are equal to the average for adult male manual workers. This provides some indication of the relationship of the poverty line adopted here to the general level of incomes. For a pensioner couple it is only a half and even for a family with 6 children it reaches less than three-quarters of the income of the average manual worker (with that number of children).

As mentioned earlier, the National Assistance scale introduced in 1948 was based broadly on the recommendations of Beveridge, which in turn were derived from the 1936 enquiry of Rowntree. Since 1948 the scale has risen considerably in real terms. The June 1969 scale for a married couple (not including the long-term addition) is over three times that applicable in 1948, and if we deflate this by the

19

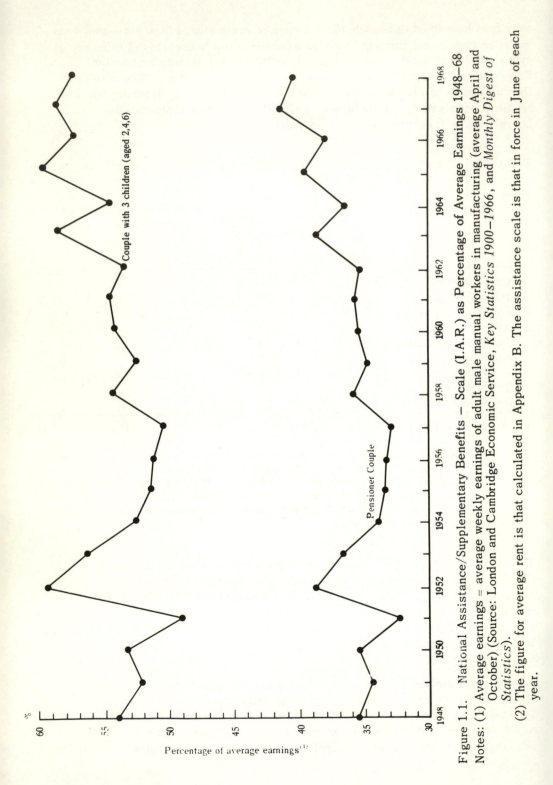

Figure 1.1. National Assistance/Supplementary Benefits – Scale (I.A.R.) as Percentage of Average Earnings 1948–68

Notes: (1) Average earnings = average weekly earnings of adult male manual workers in manufacturing (average April and October) (Source: London and Cambridge Economic Service, *Key Statistics 1900–1966*, and *Monthly Digest of Statistics*).
(2) The figure for average rent is that calculated in Appendix B. The assistance scale is that in force in June of each year.

retail price index, the real value has risen by some 70%.[1] The assistance scale has in fact kept more or less in line with the average level of earnings – see Figure 1.1. There have been marked fluctuations but over the period as a whole the Supplementary Benefit scale (I.A.R.) has remained approximately the same proportion of gross weekly earnings for adult male manual workers. In the past few years there has perhaps been a tendency for the Supplementary Benefit scale to rise faster, but even so the 1968 figure is only a few percentage points higher than twenty years earlier.[2]

Finally, it should be noted that many people receiving Supplementary Benefits have incomes which are in fact higher than the scale described above. There are provisions for disregarding certain amounts of income (for example, earnings up to £2 – see Appendix A). Secondly, there are circumstances in which additions may be made to the basic scale to cover exceptional expenses (such as for a special diet or extra fuel). In their study, Abel-Smith and Townsend adopted for this reason a poverty criterion of the National Assistance scale + 40%, although I shall not follow them in doing this.

2. SOCIAL SECURITY IN THE WELFARE STATE – BEVERIDGE AND AFTER

The Beveridge Plan

The fundamental objective of the Plan was described by Beveridge as being 'to abolish want by ensuring that every citizen willing to serve according to his powers has at all times an income sufficient to meet his responsibilities.'[3] The aim was 'to ensure at all times to all men a subsistence income for themselves and their families as of right.'[4] As P.E.P. afterwards described it, it was to be a Plimsoll Line for incomes – a line below which no household need fall. The actual subsistence standard recommended by Beveridge was based principally on that used by Rowntree in his 1936 enquiry, but he fully appreciated that 'determination of what is required for reasonable human subsistence is to some

---

1 As has been pointed out by Professor R.G.D. Allen, T. Lynes and others, the prices of necessities have tended to rise faster than other prices and the retail price index may not be appropriate. For discussion of special price indices for low income groups, see R.G.D. Allen, 'Movements in Retail Prices since 1953', *Economica,* 1958 and T. Lynes, *National Assistance and National Prosperity,* Occasional Paper on Social Administration Number 5 (Codicote Press, 1962).

2 For a much more detailed analysis of the increases in the National Assistance scale over the period 1948–61, see Lynes, *National Assistance and National Prosperity,* op. cit.

3 Lord Beveridge, *Social Insurance and Allied Services* (H.M.S.O., 1942) – the 'Beveridge Report' – para. 444.

4 Lord Beveridge, House of Lords, *Hansard,* vol. 182, cols. 675–6.

extent a matter of judgement; estimates on this point change with time.'[1]

This 'national minimum' level of income was to be guaranteed through social insurance covering all major risks of loss or interruption of earnings and through Family Allowances for families with 2 or more children. (Beveridge assumed that earnings would be sufficient to meet the needs of households with only 1 child or no children). The scheme of social insurance was to be formed by the unification of existing provisions and the addition of new benefits where necessary, so that it covered sickness, industrial injuries, unemployment, and widowhood as well as providing guardians' benefits, grants for marriage, maternity and death, and retirement pensions for those no longer working. The scheme was to cover everyone irrespective of income or personal risk, and the benefits were to be paid at the same flat rate for all. The Plan was to be financed by contributions from employers, the Exchequer, and employees, the latter being at a flat-rate and not related to income.

Central to the Plan was the condition that these social insurance benefits should be provided 'as a right' without any means test and Beveridge laid considerable stress on the 'strength of popular objection to any kind of means test'. He did, however, recognise that there would still be some need for public assistance: since, for example, the insurance benefits were conditional on the contribution record, some people would be bound to fall through the insurance net. He also envisaged that full pensions would not be paid immediately, but would be built up over a twenty year transition period, so that there would be a temporary need for assistance to old persons. The role of the assistance system was, however, expected to be minimal, and it was essential to the Plan that people should not be forced to rely on assistance because the social insurance benefits were not sufficient to bring them up to subsistence level. To quote from the Introduction to the Report,[2]

'National assistance is an essential subsidiary method in the whole Plan for Social Security, and the work of the Assistance Board shows that assistance subject to means test can be administered with sympathetic justice and discretion taking full account of individual circumstances. But the scope of assistance will be narrowed from the beginning and will diminish throughout the transition period for pensions. The scheme of social insurance is designed of itself when in full operation to guarantee the income needed for subsistence in all normal cases.'

The Post-War Legislation

The Beveridge Plan was accepted in principle by the Government in 1943, and the post-war legislation followed its proposals in broad outline if not in precise detail. The first to be enacted was the Family Allowances Act of 1945, under which cash allowances were paid for each child in a family except the first —

---

1 *Social Insurance and Allied Services*, op. cit., para. 27.

2 ibid. p. 12.

although at a considerably lower rate than that recommended by Beveridge. After this followed the National Insurance Acts of 1946, which established flat-rate benefits for the unemployed, sick, widows and those involved in industrial injuries. Under the same acts, the existing contributory old age pension was replaced by a universal, flat-rate pension conditional on retirement (referred to below as the *Retirement Pension*).

The final part of the immediate post-war legislation was the National Assistance Act of 1948. This Act opened dramatically with the statement that 'the existing poor law shall cease to have effect'. In terms of administration the break with the past was indeed dramatic: the National Assistance Board now took over responsibility for the provision of assistance from the local authorities which in one guise or another had been responsible for its administration since *The Acte for the Reliefe of the Poore* of 1598, and a uniform national scale replaced the previously widely different scales paid by local authorities.[1] But while the method of administration was very different, the underlying principle was unchanged: the National Assistance Board provided cash payments to people satisfying a means test and certain other conditions. The only major change of principle was that the pre-war 'household means test' was abolished and assistance was based instead on a personal means test in which no account was to be taken of the income of non-dependent members of a person's household. (Children were no longer expected to support their aged parents).

Since 1948, there have been three major changes in the social security system. Firstly, the graduated pension scheme was introduced in 1961. This new scheme, which is in addition to the existing Retirement Pension, discards two of the fundamental principles of the Beveridge Plan. Under the graduated scheme, benefits and contributions are not flat-rate but graduated according to income, and the scheme allows contracting out where the employer provides an occupational pension scheme with comparable benefits. Secondly, earnings-related benefits were also introduced in 1966 for unemployment, sickness, industrial injuries and widowhood. This benefit is again additional to the flat-rate benefit, but in this case there is no contracting out. Finally, under the Ministry of Social Security Act of 1966, National Assistance was abolished and replaced by the present Supplementary Benefit scheme. This involved a number of changes, including the incorporation in the regulations of a specific entitlement to benefit, and the merging of its administration with that of the contributory benefits in the new Ministry of Social Security. The underlying principle, however, was again unchanged. (The introduction of Supplementary Benefits is discussed in more detail in Chapter 4).[2]

---

1 Although this process had already begun with the Unemployment Assistance Board and supplementary pensions.

2 For further discussion of the historical development of social security in this country, see (among others) *The Coming of the Welfare State*, op. cit., T.H. Marshall, *Social Policy* (Hutchinson, 1965), and B.B. Gilbert, *The Evolution of National Insurance in Great Britain* (Michael Joseph, 1966).

3.   THE ROLE OF NATIONAL ASSISTANCE/SUPPLEMENTARY BENEFITS

As we have seen, one of the fundamental principles of the Beveridge Plan was that insurance benefits should be sufficient to guarantee subsistence and that people should not have to resort to National Assistance because the insurance benefits were inadequate. The role of National Assistance was to be a minimal one, with the number of recipients diminishing steadily over time.

In this respect, however, there has been a major departure from the principles of Beveridge. For the National Insurance benefits have in fact been consistently below the subsistence standard set for National Assistance. In 1948, the National Insurance benefit for a married couple was £2 2s, whereas the National Assistance scale which came into effect in that year was £2 plus housing expenditure, so that a couple with no other income and average rent would have to rely on National Assistance to reach the Government's own definition of subsistence. For a family with 3 children the National Insurance benefit in 1948 fell below the National Assistance scale even before allowing for any rent. This situation continued throughout the 1950s and 1960s. For a married couple, the National Insurance benefit has never been more than 4s. 6d. above the National Assistance/ Supplementary Benefit level (before housing expenditure) and for much of the period it actually fell below. Throughout this period, a household with an average level of housing expenditure would fallen below the assistance scale if it had relied on the flat-rate National Insurance benefits alone.

The Government has therefore failed to satisfy one of the fundamental assumptions of the Beveridge Plan and has since 1948 provided insurance benefits which fall below its own definition of subsistence as embodied in the National Assistance provisions. The national minimum level of income has been provided not through social insurance as proposed by Beveridge, but by the means-tested National Assistance.

The natural result has been that National Assistance has played a very much more important role in the social security system than was envisaged by Beveridge. The number receiving assistance has not died away and has in fact increased quite substantially over the period 1948–68 – see Figure 1.2. The increase has been such that in December 1968 there were two and a half times as many households receiving assistance as in December 1948.

If we examine the types of household receiving National Assistance/ Supplementary Benefits, we can see that for a large number it was being paid as supplement to National Insurance benefits – see Table 1.3. In December 1948, nearly half of the households receiving National Assistance were also receiving Retirement Pensions, and two thirds were receiving some kind of National Insurance benefit. In November 1968, the proportion receiving Supplementary Benefits as a supplement to insurance benefits was even higher – only a minority of those receiving assistance were in fact people who had fallen through the insurance net; the remainder were people who had to rely on assistance because their insurance benefits were insufficient.

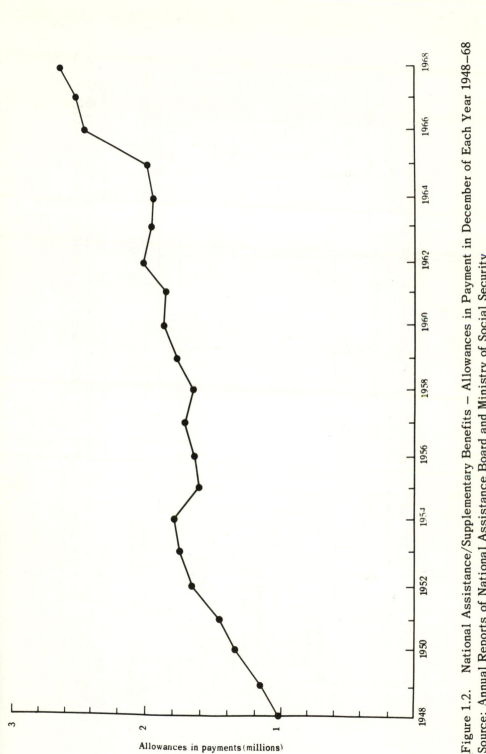

Figure 1.2. National Assistance/Supplementary Benefits – Allowances in Payment in December of Each Year 1948–68
Source: Annual Reports of National Assistance Board and Ministry of Social Security

Allowances in payments (millions)

Table 1.3.   Households Receiving National Assistance/Supplementary Benefits – 1948 and 1968

	Numbers of Weekly Payments ('000's)		Percentage of Total	
	Dec. 1948	Nov. 1968	Dec. 1948	Nov. 1968
Receiving National Insurance benefits:				
Retirement Pensioners	495	1620	49	61
Sickness and injury benefits	80	169	8	6
Unemployment pay	19	a	2	a
Widows' benefits	81	121	8	5
Total	675	1910	67	72
Not Receiving National Insurance Benefits	336	727	33	28
Overall Total	1011	2637	100	100

Source: *Report of the National Assistance Board for the year ended 31st December 1949*, (H.M.S.O., 1950), Appendix II, and *Annual Report of the Department of Health and Social Security for the year 1968*, op. cit., p. 313.

Note: a   Since September 1966 it has no longer been possible to distinguish between unemployed receiving National Insurance benefit and those who are not. I have included all the unemployed receiving Supplementary Benefits in November 1968 in the group not receiving National Insurance, which will lead to an under-statement of the total number receiving Supplementary Benefits as a supplement to National Insurance.

The extent to which Supplementary Benefit now acts as a supplement to the National Insurance benefits can also be seen from Table 1.4 which shows the proportion of those receiving National Insurance benefits in December 1968 who were also receiving Supplementary Benefits. Approximately a quarter of those receiving Retirement Pensions, unemployment benefit or widows' benefits had to rely on Supplementary Benefits — which is a far cry from the Beveridge objective.

Table 1.4.   Proportion of Households Receiving National Insurance Benefits which also Received Supplementary Benefits — December 1968[a]

Households receiving:	Percentage receiving Supplementary Benefits
Retirement Pension	28.6
Unemployment benefit	20.2
Sickness benefit	14.5
Widows' benefits [b]	21.9

Source: *Annual Report of the Department of Health and Social Security for the year 1968*, op. cit., page 330.

Notes: [a] These figures are provisional.

[b] Excluding widow's basic pensions.

See also notes to original source.

SUMMARY OF CHAPTER 1

The definition of poverty adopted in this study is based on the Supplementary Benefit (previously National Assistance) scale of requirements. The primary reason for adopting this definition is that it is my concern to judge the effectiveness of the present social security provisions (and proposed reforms) in the light of the Government's own minimum standards.

These minimum standards derive from the concept of a 'national minimum' which was central to the Beveridge Plan. As envisaged by Beveridge, this minimum was to be guaranteed by social insurance, with National Assistance providing for only a small (and diminishing) number of people. However, the National Insurance benefits have been below the assistance scale throughout the post-war period, and the Government has in fact relied on National Assistance/Supplementary Benefits to fulfil the role of a national minimum. As a result their importance has increased rather than diminished over the period.

Through the National Assistance/Supplementary Benefit schemes, the Government has tried to provide a 'safety net' below which it feels that no one should fall — a Plimsoll line for incomes. As we have seen, a large number of people are in fact at the Plimsoll line, but the important question is whether anyone still falls below. Has the combination of National Insurance and National Assistance/Supplementary Benefits successfully ensured that no one has an income below the assistance scale? In the next chapter, I examine the available evidence about people with low incomes in an attempt to answer this question.

2 Low Incomes in Britain

This chapter has two chief aims: to examine the available evidence about poverty in Britain and to consider the principal reasons why people fall below the poverty line.

In the first section, I discuss the main sources of information about people with low incomes and the estimates that have been made of the number of people with incomes below the National Assistance/Supplementary Benefit standard.

In the second section, I then examine some of the most important characteristics of the people falling below this poverty line and the reasons why National Assistance and Supplementary Benefits have failed to provide an adequate 'safety net'.

1. LOW INCOMES – THE EVIDENCE

In this study, a person is considered to be living in 'poverty' if his total income is less than his requirements assessed according to the Supplementary Benefit scale. As explained in Chapter 1, the primary reason for adopting this approach is that I want to judge the success of Government policy by its own subsistence standards. However, the use of the assistance scale as a criterion of poverty has a number of implications which should be discussed before we turn to the evidence.

The Definition of Poverty

Any definition of poverty must be based on certain important elements. These obviously include the income level below which the term is to be applied and the treatment of people living in families of different sizes, both of which have been discussed in Chapter 1. Equally important is the question of defining the 'unit' with which we are concerned. Is, for example, a household consisting of a family with 3 children and a grandmother to be treated as a whole (taking their total income and requirements), or is the grandmother to be treated as a separate 'unit'? A second question concerns the period of assessment, which could be weekly, monthly or annual. Since the answers to these questions are important for interpreting the evidence and for reconciling information from different sources, a brief outline of the treatment under National Assistance and Supplementary

Benefits is given below.[1]

The 'Unit' One of the major features of the 1948 National Assistance Act was its final abandonment of the household means test and its adoption of a narrower family unit for purposes of determining eligibility for assistance. Eligibility for National Assistance/Supplementary Benefits is now based on the income and requirements of the applicant and his dependents (wife and children) and does not allow for any income of non-dependent members of the same household. This means that in the example given above the family with 3 children would be treated separately from the grandmother, who could apply for assistance in her own right.

The implications for the measurement of poverty of adopting this narrower definition are obvious. Firstly, it means that we shall find a higher proportion of people with low recorded incomes than if we were considering the household as a whole. The total income of the family with 3 children and a grandmother might exceed the sum of their requirements calculated according to the assistance scale, but the grandmother's income taken by itself may not be enough to raise her alone to the assistance scale. At the same time, the narrower definition may over-state the number of people with *actual* living standards below the poverty line, because it takes no account of income sharing within the household. The grandmother may in fact be better off than many old people living on their own with higher recorded incomes, if the family shares its income with her.[2] (This income sharing is probably important at both ends of the age scale — both grandparents and young adults may be supported to a considerable extent by their families.)

The difference between estimates of poverty based on a household definition and those based on the narrower assistance scale definition may be best seen in terms of the degree of income sharing. The narrower definition allows for no sharing of recorded income, whereas the household definition assumes that income is shared according to needs (on the assistance scale). We may expect, therefore, that the number of persons with low *actual* incomes (allowing for income sharing) will be under-stated by an estimate based on a household definition and over-stated by an estimate on the narrower assistance scale definition. (Nonetheless, we must bear in mind that it is with the narrower National Assistance/Supplementary Benefit definition that we are concerned in assessing the impact of Government policy).

Period of Assessment The assistance scale is applied to income and requirements in a particular week. This means in effect that it allows for a minimum of averaging and it seems likely that we shall find a larger proportion of

---

1 For further discussion of the conceptual problems involved in measuring poverty, see J.N. Morgan, 'Measuring the Economic Status of the Aged', *International Economic Review*, January 1965, and L.A. Epstein, 'Measuring the Size of the Low-Income Population, in L. Soltow (ed.), *Six Papers on Size Distribution of Wealth and Income* (National Bureau of Economic Research, 1969).

2 Although old people living on their own may well also receive support from relatives.

people with low incomes on this basis than if we adopted an annual assessment period as under the income tax. At the lower end of the income distribution, there will in any one week be a larger number of people whose income in that week is *below* their average income than there are people whose income is *above* average.[1]

The Evidence

In order to estimate how many people do fall below the National Assistance/ Supplementary Benefit scale, we would need information from a sample of the whole population covering their income in a particular week, the number of people in the family unit, the ages of any children, and their housing expenditure. Unfortunately, this information is not available, and we have to rely on sources which are not ideally suited to our purpose. These sources are the Inland Revenue survey of personal incomes and the Family Expenditure Survey. In what follows I discuss the results obtained from these surveys, drawing heavily on the work of other writers in the field, and in addition consider the evidence from two recent Government enquiries into the financial position of Retirement Pensioners and families receiving Family Allowances. (The results obtained from these different sources are summarised on page 37).

(a) *Inland Revenue Survey of Personal Incomes*

In its Annual Reports the Inland Revenue publishes estimates of the distribution of income by family size, based on their annual survey of personal incomes reported for tax purposes.[2] Unfortunately, the inadequacy of the figures relating to low incomes is almost as striking (if less well documented) as the deficiencies at the upper end of the scale.[3] Most importantly, the tables published in the Annual Report exclude incomes below the effective exemption limit (at present £275 per year) and the income reported excludes all social security benefits apart from Retirement Pensions and Family Allowances.

This difficulty does not occur in the adjusted estimate of the distribution of income (based on the same source) provided by the Central Statistical Office in the National Income Blue Book. This includes both the social security benefits excluded from the Inland Revenue figures and incomes below the effective exemption limit (down to £50 per year). There is, however, the serious problem for our purposes that the distribution is not broken down according to family size.

---

1 This point has received particular attention in the literature on the consumption function. See, for example, M.R. Fisher, 'Exploration in Saving Behaviour', *Bulletin of the Oxford University Institute of Statistics*, 1956.

2 The most recent is that for 1966—7 reported in the *Report of the Commissioners of Her Majesty's Inland Revenue for the year ended 31st March 1968* (H.M.S.O., 1969). This survey covered some 120,000 out of 21,690,000 incomes over £275. The larger Quinquennial Survey was most recently carried out in 1964—5.

3 See R.M. Titmuss, *Income Distribution and Social Change* (George Allen and Unwin, 1962).

There are also a number of other well-known difficulties, applying to both the Inland Revenue and the Central Statistical Office estimates, such as cases where a person appears twice (for instance a woman marrying in the course of the year), cases where a person is only present for part of the year (deaths, school-leavers, etc.), and cases where the income of a child may not be aggregated with that of the family.

It does not, therefore, seem possible to use the published figures as they stand to estimate the proportion of the population living below the poverty line. However, a recent study by Prest and Stark has combined the Central Statistical Office estimates with the original Inland Revenue distribution to give a more complete distribution of income by family size.[1] In the course of this they also correct for the most important deficiencies in the figures. Using this adjusted distribution, Gough and Stark have then estimated the number of people with incomes below the National Assistance scale in 1954, 1959 and 1963.[2]

The estimates of Gough and Stark are reproduced in Table 2.1. Since the original source provided no information about the ages of children or about housing expenditure, they had to assume that the allowance for children could be taken as the average of that for 5—10 year olds and for 11—15 year olds, and that each family paid an average amount of rent. (The assumptions about average rent were very similar to those made in the construction of our Supplementary Benefit scale (I.A.R.) — see Appendix B). They also adjusted for the uneven rise in the National Assistance scale over the period by taking the trend value between 1949 and 1965.

Table 2.1. Persons with Incomes below the National Assistance Scale — Estimates of Gough and Stark

Year	Persons in income tax units with incomes below National Assistance scale ('000's)	Percentage of Total Population %
1954	6 300	12.3
1959	4 600	8.8
1963	5 100	9.4

Source: Gough and Stark, op. cit., Table IV

From the estimates presented in Table 2.1, it appears that a large number of people had incomes below the assistance scale (I.A.R.). In the most recent year (1963), over 5 million people fell below the poverty line — nearly 10% of the whole

---

[1] A.R. Prest and T. Stark, 'Some Aspects of Income Distribution in the U.K. Since World War II', *The Manchester School*, September 1967.

[2] I. Gough and T. Stark, 'Low Incomes in the United Kingdom', *The Manchester School*, June, 1968.

population. It should be emphasised that these figures relate to incomes *including* all National Insurance benefits and National Assistance; so that 10% of the population fell below the poverty line even allowing for the effects of social security. Moreover, there would have been people above the poverty line on Gough and Stark's estimates who were in fact worse off than many of those receiving National Assistance. This would have been so for two reasons: (i) in the case of people in work, we have not allowed for working expenses, National Insurance contributions, and (possibly) income tax, which would not be paid by someone receiving National Assistance, and (ii) under National Assistance, certain kinds of income are disregarded and additional allowances are paid to people with special needs.[1] Finally, we must bear in mind that the income tax figures are based on a yearly assessment period, so that they will under-state the number with low incomes on a weekly assessment.

While the figures on which Gough and Stark base their estimates have been corrected for the most serious deficiencies, there remain a number of reasons why their estimate may tend to over-estimate the number falling below the poverty line. These include cases where the married person dies in the course of the year, where the wife has earnings below the deduction limit which are not aggregated with the income of the family, and where children and adults with small convenants appear as separate units. It seems likely, however, that the error involved is fairly small. Allowing for the deaths of married persons, for example, could at the outside reduce the proportion of the population falling below by 0.8% and a more realistic estimate would be 0.3–0.4%.[2]

(b) *Family Expenditure Survey*

The alternative source of information about the whole population is the Family Expenditure Survey, which has been carried out annually since 1957.[3] The chief object of the Survey is to collect details of household budgets as a basis for calculating the retail price index; but it also provides information about the distribution of income for households of different types.

For our purposes, the information provided by the Family Expenditure Survey has two clear advantages. Firstly, the nature of the survey is such that there is no possibility of a person's appearing twice and thus inflating the number with low incomes. Secondly, the information relates to one particular week, so that there

---

1 The present provisions for disregarding income under Supplementary Benefits are described in Appendix A. For details of the provisions effective in 1963, see *Report of the National Assistance Board for the Year Ended 31st December 1963* (H.M.S.O., 1964), page 24. Additional allowances for special needs are paid chiefly to the sick and the old to cover extra fuel, special diet, laundering, domestic help, etc. At the end of 1963, these additions were being paid to 52% of the households receiving National Assistance.

2 I am very grateful to Dr. Stark for providing me with these figures.

3 Department of Employment and Productivity, *Family Expenditure Survey — Report for 1967* (H.M.S.O., 1968).

33

is no need to adjust for marriages, deaths, etc. as in the case of the Inland Revenue survey. Nonetheless, the Family Expenditure Survey involves difficulties all of its own. Most importantly, the basic unit is the *household* and the information provided does not allow us to adjust this to the narrower unit adopted in assessing eligibility for assistance. The estimates based on the Family Expenditure Survey will therefore under-state the number of people with incomes below the assistance scale. There are also a number of technical difficulties in using the Family Expenditure Survey:

(i) The earnings reported are 'normal' take-home earnings, which means that a man away from work for 13 weeks or less is regarded as continuing to receive his normal earnings when at work. This will lead to an under-statement of the number of households with low *actual* income since a man's income when sick or unemployed will almost certainly be less than his normal earnings.

(ii) Participation in the Survey is voluntary and the response is far from complete (71% in 1967). There is evidence that certain groups are under-represented — particularly the aged and sick, and this again will lead to an under-statement of the number with low incomes. On the other hand, families with children tend to be over-represented which will probably work in the opposite direction.[1]

(iii) There is a well-established tendency for income to be under-stated in the Survey. This obviously leads to an *over*-statement of the number with low incomes, although a recent study suggests that in the case of earned income the overall discrepancy is relatively small.[2]

(iv) The Survey is based on a substantially smaller sample than the Inland Revenue Survey. In the 1967 Survey, which was very much larger than in previous years, the number of co-operating households was only 7,386. This means that when we are considering low income families, the numbers in certain cells may be very small and the sampling error quite substantial.

In addition to these difficulties, there is the same problem as with the Inland Revenue figures that we have no information about the ages of children or about housing expenditure. To allow for these, I make the same assumptions as Gough and Stark: that the allowance for children can be taken as the average of that for 5–10 year olds and 11–15 year olds and that all households pay 'average' rent as defined in Appendix B.

On these assumptions, we can estimate from the Family Expenditure Survey for

---

[1] This point is discussed by Abel-Smith and Townsend in *The Poor and the Poorest*, op. cit. pp. 20–1. They argue that on balance the Family Expenditure Survey figures would tend to under-state the true number of households with low incomes.

[2] A.R. Thatcher, 'The Distribution of Earnings of Employees in Great Britain', *Journal of the Royal Statistical Society*, Series A, 1968.

1967 the proportion of *households* that then had incomes below the Supplementary Benefit level (I.A.R.). (The method of estimation and the detailed calculations are described in Appendix C). The results are summarised in Table 2.2, which shows that 4.9% of all households in the Survey had incomes below the Supplementary Benefit scale. These households contained 3.5% of the people in the Survey, so that if we extrapolate from this to the population as a whole, there would be something like 2 million people living in households below the poverty line.[1] Moreover, the detailed assumptions made in the construction of this estimate are such that it is likely to be an under-estimate rather than an over-estimate (see Appendix C): for instance, the Supplementary Benefit scale used was that in force for the first part of the year, but if we had used the new scale introduced in October 1967 the figure would have been noticeably higher.

Since the Family Expenditure Survey includes information about housing expenditure, it would be possible if we had access to the raw returns to obtain a more accurate estimate of the number of low income households. By retabulating the original data we could dispense with the assumption that each household pays an average amount of rent (as well as that with regard to the ages of the children). Such a retabulation is outside the scope of this study, but it has been carried out for the 1960 Survey by Professors Abel-Smith and Townsend in their book *The Poor and the Poorest*. From their retabulated data, they estimate that 4.7% of all households in 1960 had incomes below the National Assistance scale — a figure very close to that obtained from the 1967 Survey using cruder methods. These households contained 3.8% of the persons in the Survey, which for the population as a whole would mean nearly 2 million people below the poverty line — the same figure as that obtained for 1967. Table 2.3 gives their results in more detail. These show that nearly half a million people were living at a level more than 20% below the National Assistance scale, and that nearly a million were more than 10% below. Moreover, almost 1 household in 5 was within 40% of the National Assistance scale.[2] It should be stressed that these results are based on a small sample (the 1960 Survey was half the size of the 1967 Survey and the total number of households below the National Assistance scale was only 167).

(c) A Third 'Minimum' Estimate

The Inland Revenue personal incomes survey and the Family Expenditure Survey are the only sources of information covering the whole population. However, there have recently been two Government enquiries, which, while not providing an overall picture, do form the basis for a third 'minimum' estimate of the number of people below the poverty line.

---

[1] The method used to 'blow up' the Family Expenditure Survey results (see Appendix C) is only crude and the resulting figure for the population as a whole may not be very reliable. In order to make a more accurate estimate, independent control totals would be necessary.

[2] As mentioned in Chapter 1, Abel-Smith and Townsend adopt as their basic poverty standard the National Assistance scale + 40%. Since the figure of 40% is essentially arbitrary (and there is no reason why there should be a larger margin for those with higher rents), I have not followed their procedure.

Table 2.2. Households with Incomes below the Supplementary Benefit Scale
(I.A.R.) in 1967 — Estimates based on Family Expenditure Survey

Household Type:	Percentage of Households of that Type below Supplementary Benefit level (I.A.R.)
Single Person	16.8
Married Couple	4.6
Couple with:	
1 child	0.4
2 children	1.0
3 children	3.1
4 or more children	9.4
All other	2.1
Percentage of all households below Supplementary Benefit level (I.A.R.)	4.9
Percentage of all persons below Supplementary Benefit level (I.A.R.)	3.5

Note: For details of the construction of this estimate, see Appendix C.

Table 2.3. Households with Low Incomes in 1960 — Estimate of Abel-Smith
and Townsend

Total Income	Households %	Persons %	Estimated total number of persons in U.K. ('000's)
Below 80% of N.A. Scale	1.3	0.9	471
Below 90% of N.A. Scale	2.3	1.8	942
Below N.A. Scale	4.7	3.8	1 990
Below 120% of N.A. Scale	12.5	9.0	4 714
Below 140% of N.A. Scale	18.0	14.2	7 438

Source: *The Poor and the Poorest*, Table 15.

Note: N.A. = National Assistance (including allowance for housing
expenditure for each household).

These are the Ministry of Pensions and National Insurance enquiry in 1965 into the financial circumstances of Retirement Pensioners,[1] and the 1966 Ministry of Social Security enquiry into the circumstances of families receiving Family Allowances.[2] These enquiries are particularly useful to us because they cover 'high risk' groups of the population and because their express objective was to determine the number of households with incomes below the National Assistance level (which means that they are likely to provide a more accurate estimate than those given earlier).[3]

The first of these enquiries showed that in June 1965 around 1 million Retirement Pensioners had incomes (after allowing for any National Assistance in payment) which were below the National Assistance scale then in force — nearly 1 in 5 of all Retirement Pensioners. From the second enquiry, we can estimate that in June 1966 there were 155,000 families containing 535,000 children with incomes below the National Assistance scale (again after allowing for any National Assistance in payment). Combining these figures, we can estimate that within these two groups alone — Retirement Pensioners and families receiving Family Allowances — nearly 2 million people would have had incomes below the National Assistance scale in June 1966.[4] This means that at least 3.7% of the population were living below the poverty line in 1966 — not counting those outside these two groups whose income also fell below.

Low Incomes in Britain — Summary

The evidence from the different sources is summarised below:

Source	Year	Percentage of population with incomes below National Assistance/Supplementary Benefit Level
Gough and Stark	1963	9.4%
Abel-Smith and Townsend	1960	3.8%
Own Estimate	1967	3.5%
'Minimum' Estimate	1966	3.7%

In trying to draw conclusions from these figures, it must be borne in mind that the

1 Ministry of Pensions and National Insurance, *Financial and other circumstances of Retirement Pensioners* (H.M.S.O., 1966).

2 *Circumstances of Families*, op. cit.

3 In particular, no assumption about 'average rent' was required, since each household's own housing expenditure was taken into account.

4 The figure for Retirement Pensioners is adjusted to June 1966 by allowing for the increase in total Retirement Pensioners between June 1965 and June 1966.

Gough and Stark estimate and the 'Minimum' estimate were both based on the narrower family unit adopted in determining eligibility for National Assistance, but the other two estimates followed the household unit used in the Family Expenditure Survey. As we have seen at the beginning of this section, we should expect the proportion of the population found to be living in poverty to be higher on the basis of the National Assistance unit than on a household basis, and this must explain at least part of the difference between the estimates. (The 'Minimum' estimate certainly suggests that those derived from the Family Expenditure Surveys would be too low on a National Assistance unit basis). It also means that if we are concerned with the strict National Assistance definition, then it is the higher figure of 9% that is relevant. In addition, we have seen that the estimates from the Family Expenditure Survey may be biased downwards (because, for example, they relate to normal rather than actual earnings), and similarly the Gough-Stark estimates may be rather too high (although this might be offset by the fact that they relate to annual rather than weekly income).

It seems fair to conclude that the proportion of the population with incomes below the National Assistance/Supplementary Benefit scale lies towards the upper end of the range 4%–9%. In other words, around 5 million people are living below the standard which the Government feels to be the national minimum. If we allow for the sharing of income among the members of a household, then the number whose actual living standard is below the poverty line is probably rather smaller, although not less than 2 million.

2. THE CAUSES OF POVERTY

One of the Charity Organisation Society representatives on the Royal Commission on the Poor Law of 1905–9, Helen Bosanquet, commented later that 'Of course there have not been wanting witnesses who have regarded the question from a political point of view, and have assigned the existence of pauperism to such causes as Capitalism, Free Trade, and the system of Land Tenure. The Commission felt it to be beyond their reference either to endorse or to controvert such suggestions'.[1] Although not sharing Mrs. Bosanquet's own political views, I shall equally limit the discussion of this section to what were called by Rowntree the 'immediate' causes of poverty. In it I discuss some of the principal characteristics of the 5 million or so people we have found to be living below the assistance scale, and the reasons why National Assistance and Supplementary Benefits have failed to keep them above the national minimum.

The information that can be obtained from the Inland Revenue Survey and from the published results of the Family Expenditure Survey about the characteristics of people with low incomes is only very limited. For this reason, I rely principally on the results derived by Abel-Smith and Townsend from their retabulation of the 1960 Family Expenditure Survey.

---

1 H. Bosanquet, *The Poor Law Report of 1909* (Macmillan, 1909), p. 42.

Table 2.4. Composition of Households with Incomes Below Assistance Scale

Household Type:	Percentage of Total Households with Incomes Below Assistance Scale		
	1960%[a][d]	1963%[b][d]	1967%[c]
Single Person	41	72	50
Couple	29	13	25
Couple with			
1 child	9	6	1
2 children	7	3	2
3 children	5	3	3
4 or more children	9	3	6
Other	–	–	12
Total:	100	100	100

Notes:
[a] The 1960 figures are those from *The Poor and the Poorest* and relate to households with incomes below the National Assistance scale + 40%.

[b] The 1963 figures are from Gough and Stark, op. cit., Table V, and relate to assistance units rather than households.

[c] The 1967 figures are estimated on the basis of the 1967 Family Expenditure Survey — see Appendix C.

[d] The figures for 1960 and 1963 are only approximate since the original data relate to households with 1, 2, 3, 4, 5, 6 plus people and do not distinguish between, for example, 3 adults and a couple and 1 child. I have assumed for the purposes of this Table that a household with x persons consists of a couple and $x - 2$ children ($x > 2$).

One piece of information that can be obtained from all three surveys is the breakdown of low income households by household composition shown in Table 2.4 (although even this is not fully satisfactory — see the notes to the table). This table brings out very clearly the differences between the 1963 figures (based on the narrower unit as defined for assistance purposes) and those for 1960 and 1967 (using the household definition). As we should expect, the proportion of single person units is very much higher in 1963 — reflecting the separate treatment in this estimate of people who would be included in another household in the Family Expenditure Survey. On the other hand, the household composition for 1960 and 1967 is more or less the same. In 1967, single person households accounted for half of those with low incomes, and couples without children for a further quarter. Couples with children made up only 12% of low income households, but accounted for nearly a third (31%) of all *people* living in households with low incomes. Abel-Smith and Townsend found in 1960 that a third of all persons living in low income households were aged under 16.

In their analysis of the 1960 Family Expenditure Survey, Abel-Smith and Townsend classified the low income households according to their primary source of income — see Table 2.5. This shows that over a third of the persons living in households with low incomes were primarily dependent on pensions, and that nearly a half were primarily dependent on other state benefits (e.g. unemployment or sickness benefit, National Assistance). While we should expect these two groups to be strongly represented among those with low incomes, one of the surprising features of Abel-Smith and Townsend's results is the number who fell below where earnings were the primary source of income. This was true of nearly 1 in 5 of the people in low income households and in very few of these cases was there any secondary source of income. This important finding was later confirmed by the Ministry of Social Security enquiry in 1966 into the circumstances of families receiving Family Allowances. This showed that 70,000 families containing 255,000 children had incomes below the National Assistance scale even though the father was in full-time work.

Table 2.5. Primary Source of Income for Households with Incomes below the National Assistance Scale — 1960

Primary Source of Income [a]	% of Total Persons Living in Households with Incomes below National Assistance	Estimated total persons in U.K. ('000's)
Pensions [b]	37	740
Other State Social Security Benefits [c]	44	876
Earnings and Other Private Income	18	365

Source: *The Poor and the Poorest*, Tables 21 and 22

Notes: [a] A primary source is defined as one providing half or more of income

[b] Pensions include Retirement Pension, widow's pension and the non-contributory old age pension (since abolished).

[c] Including National Assistance, National Insurance benefits apart from pensions and Family Allowances.

It may be interesting to compare these findings with those of Rowntree's original survey of poverty in York in 1899. In this he found that 'The life of a labourer is marked by five alternating periods of want and comparative plenty.'[1] The periods of want were those of childhood, when he himself had children, and when he was too old to work. The evidence from Abel-Smith and Townsend suggests that the

[1] *Poverty*, op. cit., p. 136.

picture today is not very different. Their figures show that over a third of the people falling below the poverty line were primarily dependent on pensions, and that a further third were children. Although the relative importance of old age as a cause of poverty has increased since 1899, it still seems to be true that poverty is particularly associated with these three stages in a person's life cycle. As was emphasised by Rowntree, this implies that the proportion of the population who are in poverty *at some time in their lives* is very much higher than the proportion found to be in poverty at a particular moment of time.

Supplementary Benefits and Those with Low Incomes

The aim of Supplementary Benefits is to ensure that no-one falls below the national minimum level; yet from the evidence presented in this section it is quite clear that this aim is not at present being achieved. While those in families supported by a man in full-time work are not eligible, those primarily dependent on social security would in general qualify for Supplementary Benefits. Abel-Smith and Townsend's analysis for 1960 showed, however, that only 40% of those in these two groups were receiving National Assistance — 21% of those primarily dependent on pensions and 58% of those dependent on other state benefits. This raises two important questions:

(a) Why did people receiving National Assistance still appear to fall below the National Assistance scale?

(b) Why did people apparently eligible for National Assistance not receive it?

There are two principal answers to the first of these questions. There may, quite simply, be errors in recording income or needs. I have already mentioned, for example, the tendency for income to be under-stated in the Family Expenditure Survey. Abel-Smith and Townsend refer to the possibility that they may have over-estimated housing expenditure.[1] In this context it is worth pointing out that 3 out of 4 of the households falling below the National Assistance scale although receiving assistance had incomes between 95% and 100% of the scale.

There is, however, a second, quite genuine reason why the income of households receiving National Assistance may in fact be below the National Assistance scale. Under the National Assistance (and Supplementary Benefit) regulations, the amount of assistance that can be paid to a man who is unemployed or temporarily sick is restricted to the amount of his net weekly earnings when at work. This regulation, described officially as 'an adjustment to normal earnings' but better known as the *wage stop*, means that if a person has normal net earnings below the assistance scale, he will not receive the full assistance allowance if he is out of work. For example, a man with 3 children under 5 would receive £13 10s. on the June 1969 Supplementary Benefit scale (including £2 rent), but if his normal earnings in a full-time job were £12 (after allowing for Family Allowances, income tax, National Insurance contributions and working expenses),

---

[1] *The Poor and the Poorest*, op. cit., p. 44.

£1 10s. will be deducted from his Supplementary Benefit payment. This is one major reason why families receiving assistance may still fall below the assistance scale. Abel-Smith and Townsend do in fact refer to a number of wage-stopped families – including one family of 6 children whose income was only 76% of the National Assistance scale! (The role of the wage stop is discussed further in Chapter 5.)

The second problem is that a large proportion of those apparently eligible for Supplementary Benefits are not in fact receiving it, particularly in the case of pensioners. Assuming that these households had reported their income correctly, they could only not have qualified had their savings been in excess of the maximum permitted under the National Assistance regulations. It seems unlikely that this would be true of many cases, [1] and we may reasonably conclude that a substantial number of people are not getting the assistance to which they are entitled.

This conclusion has received support from a number of other enquiries. In the next chapter, I discuss those relating to old people (including the 1965 Ministry of Pensions and National Insurance enquiry). For those below pension age, the Ministry of Social Security enquiry in 1966 into the circumstances of families receiving Family Allowances provides further evidence. This enquiry shows that in the case of fatherless families, nearly all of those eligible for National Assistance were in fact receiving it, but that in families where the father was sick or unemployed, the proportion of those eligible who were receiving National Assistance was lower (60%). It should be noted, however, that in the case of those receiving sickness benefit, there was a marked contrast between those who had been out of work for less than 3 months and the longer-term sick; only 1 in 6 of the latter was not receiving National Assistance. From this it appears that the problem of people's not claiming the assistance to which they are entitled is somewhat less serious among those below pension age than among those above, although the problem does definitely exist among the sick and unemployed.

SUMMARY OF CHAPTER 2

In this chapter I have estimated that between 4% and 9% of the population have incomes below the Supplementary Benefit scale. It seems likely that the figure is nearer the upper rather than the lower end of the range, which would mean that around 5 million people fall below the level which the Government considers to be the national minimum.

The majority of the people below the poverty line are single persons or married couples without children, but nearly a third are children. Most of the people with

---

[1] In 1960 a person could have savings up to £600 plus an owner-occupied house plus 'war savings' of up to £375 per person. For further details, see *Report of the National Assistance Board for the Year Ended 31 December 1959* (H.M.S.O., 1960), p. 17.

low incomes depend chiefly on pensions or other social security benefits, but for about 20% earnings are their primary source of income.

This evidence suggests that the present social security provisions are far from fully successful in guaranteeing a minimum income at the Supplementary Benefit level. There are three main reasons for this:

(a) People are not claiming the Supplementary Benefits to which they are entitled.

(b) For some people their earnings are not sufficient to bring them to the Supplementary Benefit level even when working full-time.

(c) The amount of Supplementary Benefits paid may be restricted through the operation of the wage stop.

These problems will be discussed further in the following chapters. The first is taken up in Chapters 3 and 4, where I examine the position of old people in more detail. The second and third problems, which are clearly intimately related, are examined in Chapter 5.

3   Poverty and Old People

A comparison of the results of Rowntree's original survey of York in 1899 with those of his third survey in 1951 is striking evidence of how the importance of old age as a cause of poverty has increased in the course of this century. In 1899, he found that old age was the chief cause of poverty for fewer than 5% of the households living below his poverty line; but in 1951 old age was the chief factor in two thirds of the cases. As Rowntree pointed out,[1] there are a number of reasons for this dramatic change – the increase in the proportion of the population aged over 65, the reduction of poverty among other groups, and the fact that old age pensions now allow old people to live on their own rather than having to choose between living with their children and the workhouse.

Since poverty among old people is so important, I have devoted this chapter to a more detailed examination of the problem. The first section deals with the income of old people and the relative importance of different sources – particularly the state pension (including the graduated pension), occupational pensions, income from savings, and earnings. In the course of this I examine how many old people have sufficient income from these sources to reach the Supplementary Benefit level without having to rely on Supplementary Benefits, and whether particular groups of old people are more likely to fall below than others. The second section discusses the role of Supplementary Benefits and the reasons why many pensioners do not claim the assistance to which they are entitled.

Before embarking on the analysis, it may be helpful to give a brief sketch of the present pension provisions. The basic state pension is the flat-rate Retirement Pension. The minimum age at which this can be paid is 65 for a man and 60 for a woman, but up to the age of 70 for a man and 65 for a woman it is only paid if a person has retired from regular work. Above those ages it is paid regardless of whether a person has retired. In other words, for the 5 years after the minimum retirement age it is a *retirement* pension, but after that it becomes an *old age* pension. The pension is paid subject to a person satisfying the contribution conditions. In addition to the flat-rate Retirement Pension, a person may receive a graduated pension. Under this a person not contracted out of the scheme receives an additional pension related to his earnings over his life (or since the scheme came into operation in April 1961). Employers who provide an adequate occupational pension scheme can contract their employees out of the graduated scheme. (For further details of the pension provisions, see Appendix A).

---

1   B. Seebohm Rowntree, *Poverty and Progress* (Longmans, 1941), pp. 113–5.

1.   LOW INCOMES AND OLD PEOPLE

The 8 million men and women over the minimum retirement age in June 1965 fell into three main groups. By far the largest of these groups consisted of the 80% (see Table 3.1) who were receiving Retirement Pensions or other National Insurance benefits. In the second group were those who had a prospective title to a Retirement Pension and who would receive one when they or their husbands retired. Finally, there was the small group of 480,000 people who either depended on National Assistance or else received no social security benefits at all.

Most of the information used in this section is derived from the 1965 enquiry of the Ministry of Pensions and National Insurance,[1] and for this reason relates only to the first of these three groups. In view of the size of this group, and the fact that those in the second group are less likely to fall below the poverty line, this may not be a serious drawback. However, it is important to bear in mind that although the third group of old people is small, it probably contains some of the old people with the lowest incomes. For this reason, I have discussed at the end of this section the information that is available about the incomes of *all* old people rather than just Retirement Pensioners.

Retirement Pensioners

The basic Retirement Pension in June 1969 is £4 10s. for a single person and £7 6s. for a married couple. As we have seen, this is below the corresponding Supplementary Benefit scale — even before allowing for any housing expenditure. If we assume that they pay an average rent, then a married couple receiving nothing but the Retirement Pension would fall below the Supplementary Benefit scale by £2 8s. and a single person by £2 1s.

It may be the case that the total state pension received by an old person is above the basic rate: either because he has earned increments by remaining at work after the minimum retirement age, or through the graduated pension scheme. However, these sources provide only a small addition to the basic pension. In the year ending 30th June 1967, only 29% of those retiring had taken advantage of the provision to earn increments by staying on at work, and the average increment earned in these cases was 9s. 1d. a week.[2] The effect of the graduated pension scheme was also small: in 1966 (when the scheme had been in operation for 5 years) the average graduated pension earned by those retiring was 2s. 7d. a week and the maximum was 7s. 6d.[3] As a result, the total pension including these additions is for most people little higher than the basic rate. According to the

---

1   Ministry of Pensions and National Insurance, *Financial and other circumstances of Retirement Pensioners* (H.M.S.O., 1966). I have throughout this chapter referred to this enquiry as 'the Ministry enquiry', except where there is any possibility of confusion.

2   Ministry of Social Security, *Annual Report for 1967* (H.M.S.O., 1968), Table 11.

3   Ministry of Social Security, *Annual Report for 1966* (H.M.S.O., 1967), p. 27.

Table 3.1.   Population over the Minimum Retirement Age [a] — June 1965

	Total Number ('000's)	Percentage %
Retirement Pensioners	6 190	
Receiving other National Insurance Benefits or war pensions[b]	220	} 80
Prospective title to pension[c]	1 110	14
Others with National Assistance[d]	200	
Others not receiving National Assistance	280	} 6
TOTAL	8 000	100

Source: *Financial and other circumstances of Retirement Pensioners, Table I.1*

Notes: [a] Minimum retirement age is 65 for men, 60 for women.

[b] National Insurance widow beneficiaries, war widow pensioners, industrial injuries widow pensioners, and war disablement pensioners receiving unemployability supplement.

[c] Retirement deferred or wives of men not yet retired.

[d] Including non-contributory old age pensions (now combined with Supplementary Benefits).

Ministry enquiry in 1965, 61% of married couples, 76% of single men and 88% of single women had total Retirement Pensions which were no more than 5s. above the basic rate.[1]

It appears then that a Retirement Pensioner will fall below the Supplementary Benefit scale (I.A.R.) unless he has some other source of income besides the state pension, and for this reason we must examine the alternative sources. In fact, a substantial minority of Retirement Pensioners do not have any such additional income (apart from National Assistance) — see Table 3.2. One in five Retirement Pensioners in the Ministry enquiry had no other income besides the Retirement Pension, and for single women the proportion was as high as one in three. Moreover, there was a pronounced tendency for the proportion with no other income to rise with age — nearly half those over 85 had no other income.

For those Retirement Pensioners who did receive income apart from their pension, the Ministry enquiry provides information about the most important sources.

---

[1] *Financial and other circumstances of Retirement Pensioners,* op. cit., Table III.15. There are a number of Retirement Pensioners who receive less than the basic rate (on account, for example, of a low contribution record).

Table 3.2. Retirement Pensioners with No Income apart from the Retirement Pension (and National Assistance) — June 1965

| Age: | Percentage with No other Income[a] | | | |
	Couples %	Single Men %	Single Women %	All Retirement Pensioners[b] %
60–64	–	–	20	20
65–69	9	22	27	16
70–74	11	24	31	20
75–79	15	22	41	27
80–84	21	31	42	34
85 and over	24	35	50	44
All ages	12	25	32	20

Source: *Financial and other circumstances of Retirement Pensioners*, Table II.4.

Notes: [a]   Apart from National Assistance.

[b]   The figure for all Retirement Pensioners is calculated with an adjustment for non-response.

Table 3.3 shows the proportion receiving income from different sources and the average amount received by those with income from a particular source. For married couples and single men, pensions from previous employment were the most important: about a half received occupational pensions and the average amount was of the order of £2 10s. to £3 a week (it should be noted, however, that these averages concealed wide dispersion and for a third of those receiving these pensions the amount was less than £1 10s.). In the case of single women, on the other hand, only 14% were receiving occupational pensions. This low figure can be attributed to two factors: [1] the fact that occupational schemes have in the past granted relatively few pensions to the widows of deceased employees, and secondly that the proportion of women employees covered by occupational schemes is very much lower than that of men.

Savings were a common source of income for all types of pensioner household, but the average amount received was relatively low, and it does not appear that independent savings are a major source of income in retirement. Finally, there are earnings. Where a pensioner had earnings, these represented on average a substantial addition to income (between £3 10s. and £4 10s.). However, only a quarter of married couples and about 1 in 10 of single pensioners were in fact still earning.

Although most Retirement Pensioners had some source of income apart from the

---

[1] This aspect is discussed in the memorandum by the Government Actuary's Department included in *Financial and other circumstances of Retirement Pensioners*, op. cit., Appendix V.

Table 3.3. Sources of Income apart from Retirement Pension – June 1965[a]

	Proportion with Income from that Source			Average Income from that Source [b]					
	Married Couples %	Single Men %	Single Women %	Married Couples £ s.		Single Men £ s.		Single Women £ s.	
Pension from Previous Employment or Forces Pension	51	40	14	3	1	2	16	2	15
War or industrial disability benefits	9	7	3	3	5	3	0	3	17
Income from savings:									
(a) stocks, shares, property, etc.	14	12	14	1	17	1	15	1	13
(b) interest	56	46	46		8		9		7
Earnings[c]	24	11	13	4	8	4	0	3	11

Source: *Financial and other circumstances of Retirement Pensioners*, Table II.4.

Notes: [a] These figures relate only to those pensioners with incomes of less than £20 a week (95% of the respondents).

[b] For those pensioners receiving income from that source.

[c] Earnings exclude profit from boarders.

state pension, in a substantial number of cases this was not sufficient to raise them to the National Assistance level. The Ministry enquiry showed that in June 1965 34% of married couples, 40% of single men and 62% of single women had incomes (before National Assistance) which were below the National Assistance scale then in force.[1] In other words, nearly half of all Retirement Pensioners (47%) were in a position where they would fall below the national minimum unless they applied for National Assistance. It can hardly be claimed that this achieves the Beveridge objective of ensuring 'that every citizen, fulfilling during his working life the obligation of service according to his powers, can claim as of right when he is past work an income adequate to maintain him'.[2]

From the results of the Ministry enquiry, we can see that certain groups were

1   These figures include those who would be disqualified from receiving National Assistance because they had £600 or more 'unprotected capital'. ('Unprotected capital' is that (apart from an owner-occupied house) which does not qualify for treatment as 'war savings'). See *Financial and other circumstances of Retirement Pensioners*, op. cit., page 88.

2   *Social Insurance and Allied Services*, op. cit. paragraph 239.

very much more likely to have incomes below the National Assistance scale. The figures just given show that single women were particularly badly placed and not only did nearly two thirds fall below but over a quarter had incomes more than £1 below their needs. There was also a marked tendency for the proportion with incomes below the National Assistance scale to rise with age — see Figure 3.1. This is particularly true of married couples, for whom the proportion falling below was over twice as high among those aged 85 plus as for those in the age group 65—69, but was also noticeable in the case of single men and women. This increase with age may in part reflect the greater importance of special needs (for heating, laundry, domestic assistance, etc.) and hence the higher allowances for discretionary additions in assessing need according to the National Assistance scale. However, it seems likely that it also reflects the falling importance with age of occupational pensions and earnings as sources of income. For example, 60% of married couples aged 65—69 received occupational pensions compared with 39% of those aged 85 and over, and for single men the corresponding percentages were 53% and 32%.[1] The average amount received from occupational pensions also fell with age; for a married man aged 65—69 the average amount was £4 6s. but for one aged 85 and over it was £2 10s. This reflects both the rise over time in the amounts awarded to occupational pensioners and the fact that in many cases pensions in payment are not adjusted for rising prices. The high proportion of single women falling below the National Assistance scale can also be explained to a considerable extent by the fact that only a small number received any occupational pension — we have seen that only 14% of single women had any income from this source.

The results of the Ministry enquiry show in fact that whether or not a Retirement Pensioner household was receiving an occupational pension made a great deal of difference to its chances of falling below the National Assistance scale. According to Table 3.4, the proportion of those without occupational pensions who fell below the National Assistance scale was nearly three times the corresponding proportion for those with occupational pensions. These figures illustrate very clearly Professor Titmuss' picture of 'two nations in old age' — the privileged with occupational pensions and those without who depend on Supplementary Benefits to bring them to the national minimum.

It is commonly argued that, with the increased coverage of occupational pension schemes and the growing benefits from the graduated pension for those not covered by occupational schemes, the problem of 'two nations in old age' will soon disappear. This argument, if correct, would obviously have important implications for social policy towards old people, and for this reason I discuss briefly whether such an optimistic conclusion is justified. (No account is taken in this discussion of the proposed National Superannuation scheme which is examined in detail in Chapter 7).

---

[1] The proportion receiving occupational pensions may have been inflated in the case of the age group 65—9 by the tendency for those with occupational pensions to retire earlier than those without.

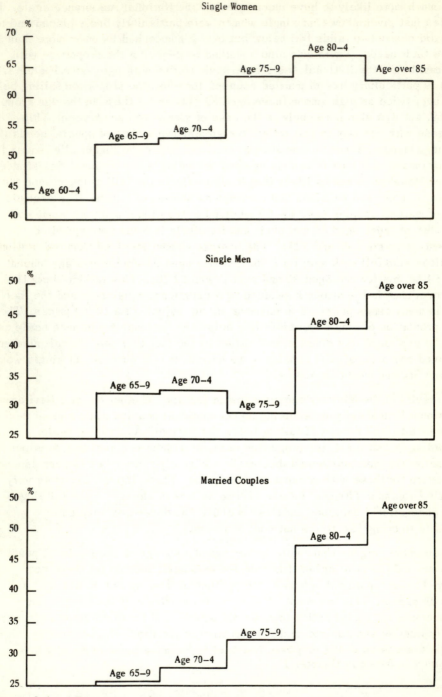

Figure 3.1.   Proportion of Retirement Pensioners in Different Age Groups with
Incomes below the National Assistance Scale – June 1965

Source: Derived from *Financial and other circumstances of Retirement Pensioners*
Tables III.4 and BR.1.

Table 3.4. Retirement Pensioners below the National Assistance Scale –
Those with Occupational Pensions and Those Without – June 1965

	Percentage of those receiving occupational pensions who had incomes[a] below National Assistance Scale	Percentage of those not receiving occupational pensions who had incomes[a] below National Assistance Scale
	%	%
Married Couples	20	49
Single Men	17	56
Single Women	30	67
All Retirement Pensioners	22	60

Source: *Financial and other circumstances of Retirement Pensioners*, Table BR. 9

Note: [a] Income before National Assistance.

Occupational Pensions

We have seen that the proportion of Retirement Pensioners receiving occupational pensions falls with age. Moreover, the most recent survey by the Government Actuary shows that two thirds of all male employees are now covered by occupational pension schemes,[1] which again suggests that occupational pension will provide a growing source of income in old age. However, in its White Paper on National Superannuation the Government predicts that even by the end of the century only two thirds of pensioner households will be receiving occupational pensions. This is partly attributable to the natural lags in the process, but also reflects the following factors:

(a) Even when occupational schemes had reached their full development, it seems unlikely that all workers will be covered. Firstly, there are the self-employed. Secondly, operation of an occupational scheme is not in general feasible for small employers.

(b) Most existing schemes include only limited provisions for the payment of pensions to the widows of employees. In 1967 only 10% of schemes had unconditional widows' pensions (although more included an option which allowed the employee to 'buy' a widow's pension by foregoing part of his own pension).

(c) Although two thirds of all male employees are now covered by occupational schemes, only a quarter of women employees are covered.

Even if the Government's prediction about the increase in coverage of

---

1 *Occupational Pension Schemes – Third Survey by Government Actuary* (H.M.S.O., 1968).

occupational schemes may be over-pessimistic, there remains the problem of maintaining the value of pensions in payment. Although the practice of augmenting pensions in payment is growing, it is still far from universal and in very few cases is it automatic (so that the pensioner does not have the security of knowing that it will be augmented). Where augmentation is given it is on average sufficient only to compensate for rising prices [1] so that the pensioner will almost certainly find his income slipping behind that of the rest of the population as real earnings levels rise.

Graduated Pension Scheme

One of the principal aims of the graduated pension scheme was to 'institute provision for employed persons who cannot be covered by an appropriate occupational scheme to obtain some measure of pension related to their earnings' (although this came second to that of placing 'the National Insurance scheme on a sound financial basis').[2] So far the graduated pension has not made any substantial difference to the incomes of old people, but we cannot of course judge the scheme on the results of only 5 years of operation. The original White Paper of 1958 showed that under the proposed scheme a man entering at 18 who paid contributions all his life on earnings of £13 a week [3] would qualify at the age of 65 for a graduated pension of £1 7s. With a flat-rate pension of £2 10s. in 1958 (single person), this would raise him comfortably above the National Assistance scale (I.A.R.) which was then £3. However, this calculation totally ignored changing prices and levels of earnings.

Under the scheme, contributions earn a certain *cash* pension at retirement and £1 contributed now earns the same amount of extra pension as £1 contributed in 1980. As a result, the Government's calculation undoubtedly gives a far too optimistic picture of the impact of the scheme. If prices rise, there is no adjustment to the pension earned by earlier contributions and its real value falls. Moreover the scheme takes no account of the fact that with rising real earnings levels £1 7s. will represent a very much smaller proportion of average earnings when the person retires than when he was contributing earlier in his life: even if there is no inflation, the scheme makes no allowance for rising standards of living.

In Table 3.5 I have tried to estimate the impact of the graduated pension on the basis of more realistic assumptions about the annual rate of increase of earnings (5½%) and prices (3%). The table shows the graduated pension received by a man retiring at different dates before the end of this century (assuming that the scheme continues in operation). The pension shown is that earned by a man whose

---

[1] *Occupational Pension Schemes*, op. cit., pp. 24–6.

[2] Ministry of Pensions and National Insurance, *Provision for Old Age* (H.M.S.O., 1958), paragraph 45.

[3] The average weekly earnings of an adult male manual worker in manufacturing were then about £13.

Table 3.5. Estimated Future Value of Graduated Pension for Man with
Average Earnings

	Year of Retirement			
	1975	1980	1990	2000
	£ s.	£ s.	£ s.	£ s.
1. Cash graduated pension at retirement	1 3	1 18	3 19	7 10
2. Real value in terms of 1969 prices	1 0	1 7	2 2	2 19
3. Graduated pension as % of national average earnings in year of retirement	3.5%	4.2%	5.1%	5.6%

Notes: The pension is that based on contributions paid by a man with earnings
equal to the average for adult male manual workers in manufacturing and
certain other industries (as published by the Department of Employment
and Productivity) in October of each year. It is assumed that after 1968
average earnings will rise at a rate of 5½% per annum.

It is assumed that the contributions payable on average earnings after
1968 remain the same proportion of earnings. (If we compare 1961 and
1968, then in the former year they were 1.7% and in the latter 2% for a
man with average earnings).

It is assumed that prices rise at the rate of 3% per annum.

earnings in each year are equal to the national average for adult manual workers.
In order to calculate the amount of the pension, some assumption is needed about
the contribution rates, which have changed several times since the scheme began.
The precise assumption made is described in the notes to the table.

The results of this calculation show that the cash pension to be expected under
the scheme will rise substantially over the rest of the century. The real value
(in terms of 1969 prices) will also rise and by the year 2000 will be nearly 3 times
that in 1975. In terms of the level of earnings however the increase is less
marked. In the year 2000 the graduated pension awarded to someone just retiring
is less than 6% of the average level of earnings. Comparing this with the
flat-rate Retirement Pension, which at present represents nearly 20% of average
earnings for a single person, the graduated pension will not represent a very
substantial addition. Moreover, these figures relate only to pensions awarded,
and since the pension is fixed in cash terms the pensioner will find its real value
falling steadily over his retirement — there is not even the limited augmentation
available under some private schemes.

It seems fair to conclude that these results support the statement of the
Government in its recent White Paper on National Superannuation that 'The
pensions provided in return for graduated contributions, combined with the

flat-rate pensions, still offer no prospect of achieving the original objectives of the Beveridge plan. The graduated pension scheme fails in two respects: its pensions are left unprotected against inflation and it cannot be adjusted for economic growth'.[1]

All Old People

The chief sources of information about the incomes of all old people are the two surveys carried out by Cole and Utting in 1959–60 and by Townsend and Wedderburn in 1962.[2] Since the latter is more recent and is based on a larger sample, it is the one on which I shall concentrate. This survey covered all old people over 65 (except for women married to men under 65) and thus included all the three groups referred to at the beginning of this section (although not women aged 60–64 unless their husbands were included). The composition of the total of 6½ million old people represented by the sample was very similar to that shown in Table 3.1 for 1965: 80% of the households were receiving Retirement Pensions, 5% were deferring retirement and 10% were retired but ineligible for a Retirement Pension. Of this last group, a half were receiving National Assistance but a half were living on occupational pensions or income from their savings.

The first interesting point to emerge from the survey is the degree of dependence of the households on state benefits (pension and National Assistance). As many as 37% were solely dependent on state benefits for their income – which is very much higher than in the case of Retirement Pensioners alone. Since the inclusion of those still working would tend to lower this proportion, the position of retired people not receiving the Retirement Pension must have been considerably worse.

As far as the sources of non-state income were concerned, the Townsend–Wedderburn survey showed similar results to those from the Ministry enquiry, although earnings were rather more important (as would be expected). In the case of occupational pensions, the survey supports the earlier finding that the proportion of single women receiving them was very small – only 11%. There was also a tendency for the proportion receiving occupational pensions to fall with age.

The nature of the survey data did not allow any precise statement about the number with incomes below the National Assistance scale. However, 27% of the households were receiving National Assistance and it was estimated that a further 11% would have been entitled if they had applied. This is very similar to to the figure of 41% obtained for Retirement Pensioners alone.[3] Single women

---

[1] Department of Health and Social Security, *National Superannuation and Social Insurance* (H.M.S.O., 1969), paragraph 20.

[2] D. Cole with J. Utting, *The Economic Circumstances of Old People*, Occasional Papers on Social Administration, Number 4 (Codicote Press, 1962.).
P. Townsend and D. Wedderburn, *The Aged in the Welfare State*. Occasional Papers on Social Administration, Number 14, (Bell and Sons, 1965).

[3] The figure of 41% is obtained from that given earlier (page 48) by subtracting the 6% who would have been disqualified on account of unprotected capital.

were again worse off than other groups — 36% alone were receiving National Assistance.

It seems fair to conclude that the evidence from the Townsend—Wedderburn survey provides broad support for the earlier analysis. Moreover, their survey includes a group who are probably rather better off (those still in regular work), which suggests that the small group of retired people who do not qualify for a Retirement Pension may have considerably lower incomes than the Retirement Pensioners. Without more detailed information, however, we cannot be more definite.

2. OLD PEOPLE AND NATIONAL ASSISTANCE

From the evidence discussed in the previous section, it appeared that in 1965 nearly half of all Retirement Pensioners had incomes (apart from National Assistance) which were below the National Assistance scale. On the face of it, these pensioners were entitled therefore to receive National Assistance, but in fact a substantial proportion were not doing so. Table 3.6 shows that although nearly 3 million Retirement Pensioners had incomes below the assistance scale, only just over a half of them were receiving National Assistance at the time of the Ministry enquiry in 1965. In this section I examine this further and explore some of the reasons why people do not claim the National Assistance to which they are entitled.

It is possible that some of the pensioners with incomes below the National Assistance scale were in fact disqualified from receiving National Assistance because they had savings in excess of the permitted maximum.[1] Line 3 of Table 3.6 shows, however, that this was only true of a small proportion of those with incomes below the National Assistance scale: only 1 in 8 had savings which would have disqualified him from receiving assistance. This still leaves a large proportion of those apparently eligible for National Assistance who were not claiming it.

A second explanation is that some of the households may have under-stated their income or that the investigator may have over-estimated their needs, so that they did not in fact fall below the scale and if they had tried to apply for National Assistance their application would not have succeeded. In order to check this, the Ministry paid a second visit to the households in their sample who had incomes apparently below the National Assistance scale and suggested that they applied for National Assistance. About half of them did so, and for these households it was possible to check the accuracy of the information. This test revealed that about 15% of those apparently eligible had in fact incomes above the National Assistance scale. However, the check also revealed errors in the opposite direction. Allowing for these, the Ministry estimated that the total of Retirement Pensioner households which would have received National Assistance

---

1   See footnote 1 on page 48.

Table 3.6.   Retirement Pensioners Eligible for and Receiving National
Assistance – June 1965

	Married Couples ('000's) %		Single Men ('000's) %		Single Women ('000's) %		All Retirement Pensioners ('000's) %	
1. Income (before National Assistance) below National Assistance Scale	490	34	240	40	1720	62	2940	47
2. Receiving National Assistance	250	18	130	22	930	34	1560	25
3. Not Entitled to National Assistance on account of savings	70	5	30	5	190	7	360	6
4. Entitled to National Assistance but not receiving it	160	11	80	13	590	21	990	16
		%		%		%		%
5. Proportion of those entitled to National Assistance not receiving it[a]		39		38		39		39

Source: *Financial and other circumstances of Retirement Pensioners*, Tables III.2
and III.4 (2).

Notes: Figures are adjusted for non-response.

Figures are rounded and for this reason totals may not balance exactly.

[a] Ratio of column 4 to (column 1 – column 3).

had they applied for it was rather more than 700,000. These households contained
about 850,000 people – or some 14% of all Retirement Pensioners.

This conclusion of the Ministry enquiry confirmed the results of earlier
investigations. As we have seen, Abel-Smith and Townsend's analysis of the
1960 Family Expenditure Survey data suggested that a substantial minority of
the population were not receiving National Assistance although they appeared to
qualify for it and that this problem was particularly acute among old people.
Earlier, Cole and Utting had estimated on the basis of their 1959–60 survey of
pensioner households that 9% of these households were apparently eligible for
National Assistance but not receiving it, and as we have seen, the 1962 enquiry
by Townsend and Wedderburn gave the very similar figure of 11%. Finally, a
special survey carried out for the (Allen) Committee of Inquiry into the Impact of
Rates on Households led them to estimate that 'about half a million retired

households are apparently eligible for assistance but not getting it'.[1]

Why did pensioners not claim the National Assistance to which they were entitled? In her discussion of this, Mrs. Wedderburn suggests that:

'Partly this is due to the regulations which govern what amounts and kinds of resources can be ignored in calculating entitlement to National Assistance. More important, it is due to a deep-rooted and widespread aversion to anything which smacks of a means test. It is probably true that some of the group which the survey (the 1959—60 Cole and Utting survey) identified as entitled to but not receiving National Assistance were ignorant of their entitlement. More important, however, are those who are too proud. They are determined to "manage while they can", without going to ask for "charity".[2]

Certainly the interviews with old people reported by her and by Townsend[3] support this interpretation, and suggest that, despite the formal abolition of the Poor Law in the Act of 1948, National Assistance retained sufficient stigma for people still to prefer to live below the National Assistance scale rather than apply.

In its enquiry the Ministry explored the reasons why people did not claim the National Assistance to which they were entitled. In the second interview with the group who appeared to be eligible for assistance but were not claiming it, they asked them why they had not done so. The answers are set out in Table 3.7. One of the principal reasons was that people were ignorant or misinformed about the provisions and were not aware that they were entitled. For example, some thought that a few hundred pounds in the bank or a small pension from a previous employer would disqualify them. A further substantial proportion said that they were 'managing all right' without the assistance supplement. However, while this may have meant that help from relatives or friends (disregarded by the National Assistance Board) was sufficient to bring them up to the N.A. scale, it does not explain why they did not claim the assistance to which they were entitled rather than become a burden on relatives or friends. (In other words, there must have been something stopping them claiming the addition to their income that would have been given by the National Assistance Board.) Finally, there were a significant number (between a quarter and a third) who said that they did not apply because they disliked charity or the National Assistance Board, or because their pride would not let them ask for help. It is also interesting that only just over half of those interviewed for a second time accepted application forms for National Assistance and not all of these sent them in.[4] This may give a truer

---

1 *Report of the Committee of Inquiry into the Impact of Rates on Households* (H.M.S.O., 1965).

2 D. Wedderburn, 'Financial Resources Available to Older People: Lessons for Social Policy', in P. From Hansen (ed.), *Age with a Future* (Munksgaard, 1964).

3 P. Townsend, *The Family Life of Old People* (Routledge and Kegan Paul, 1957) and Townsend and Wedderburn, op. cit.

4 *Financial and other circumstances of Retirement Pensioners*, op. cit., page 46.

indication of the reasons why people did not claim assistance, and suggests
that something like half would not claim it even when they were aware that they
were entitled.

Table 3.7.   Reasons for not Applying for National Assistance – June 1965[a]

Proportion giving the following reasons:[b]	Married Couples %	Single Men %	Single Women %
Lack of knowledge or misconception	37	34	35
'Managing all right'	20	30	38
Pride, dislike of charity, dislike of going to National Assistance Board	33	27	23

Source: *Financial and other circumstances of Retirement Pensioners*, Table III.21

Notes: [a] The question was only put to those Retirement Pensioners apparently
entitled to National Assistance.

[b] Some pensioners gave more than one reason and are counted twice.

This analysis suggests two main reasons why people do not claim the National
Assistance to which they are entitled – lack of knowledge and dislike of
receiving assistance. The first of these points to a need for more extensive
advertising of the available provisions and for simplification of the regulations,
both of which the Government undertook when it introduced Supplementary
Benefits in 1966. (The impact of the Supplementary Benefit scheme is discussed
in detail in the next chapter.) As far as the dislike of receiving assistance is
concerned, it might be expected that the reluctance to apply for assistance would
be found principally among the oldest pensioners, who have memories of the bad
old days, and that it will therefore die a natural death. This view is not, however,
supported by the evidence from the Ministry enquiry – see Table 3.8.

Table 3.8 shows first of all the proportion of those eligible who claimed
National Assistance. There is no noticeable tendency for this to be higher in the
younger age groups. In fact for married couples the proportion not claiming is
rather higher for the youngest age group. Secondly, the table shows the
proportion of those apparently eligible for National Assistance but not claiming
who gave as a reason for not doing so dislike of charity or of the National
Assistance Board or that their pride would not let them apply. Again there is no
noticeable tendency for the proportion to vary with age, and the proportion for the
youngest age group differs very little from the overall average (except possibly
for single men). On the basis of this evidence there are no strong grounds for
expecting that the problem will disappear with time.

Table 3.8.   Retirement Pensioners not Claiming National Assistance to which
Entitled and Reasons for not Doing so by Age — June 1965

	Percentage of those eligible not claiming			Percentage of those not claiming attributing it to pride, or to dislike of charity or National Assistance Board		
	Married Couples	Single Men	Single Women	Married Couples	Single Men	Single Women
	%	%	%	%	%	%
Age:						
60–64	–	–	38	–	–	20
65–69	45	35	40	31	14	25
70–74	33	36	36	32	36	24
75–79	40	40	37	45	35	22
80–84	36	39	35	30	21	23
Over 85	37	42	39			
All Ages	39	38	39	33	27	23

Source: *Financial and other circumstances of Retirement Pensioners,*
Tables III.4 (2) and III.21.

SUMMARY OF CHAPTER 3

This chapter has concentrated on the problem of poverty among old people.

The first section dealt with the incomes of old people before allowing for any
National Assistance they received. This showed that 1 in 5 Retirement
Pensioners in 1965 had no income apart from the Retirement Pension, which was
considerably below the National Assistance scale (allowing for average rent).
The remaining 4 out of 5 had some additional income in the form of occupational
pensions, savings or earnings, but for a substantial minority this was not
sufficient to being their total income up to the National Assistance level. As a
result, nearly half of all Retirement Pensioners were in a position where they
would fall below the national minimum if they did not claim National Assistance.

The two groups most likely to fall below the National Assistance scale were
single women and the very old. This can be explained in part by the fact that
these groups received very little income from occupational pensions. Whether or
not a person had an occupational pension was in fact an important factor in
determining whether he fell below the National Assistance scale. It was the aim
of the graduated pension scheme to fill this gap, but it seems unlikely that it
will do this even when in full operation. In view of this, and the fact that
occupational pension schemes (in their present form) cannot be expected to
provide for all old people, there are no strong grounds for expecting the problem
to disappear in the near future.

The second section examined the impact of National Assistance on the incomes of old people and the finding that many of them did not apply for the assistance to which they were entitled. Some 850,000 Retirement Pensioners in 1965 did not apply for National Assistance even though they were eligible to receive it. There appeared to be two principal reasons for this:

(a) people were not aware that they were entitled for assistance,

(b) people disliked receiving National Assistance because of the stigma attached to it.

Although one might expect the stigma associated with assistance to be a relic of pre-war days, there is no evidence that younger pensioners are more willing to apply for National Assistance.

4 The Effect of Introducing Supplementary Benefits

The evidence discussed in the previous chapters suggested that in the early 1960s a substantial minority of people were not claiming the National Assistance to which they were entitled. In the case of Retirement Pensioners, this was confirmed by the Ministry of Pensions and National Insurance enquiry in 1965, which showed that over 700,000 pensioner households could have received assistance if they had applied for it.

In response to this evidence, the Government decided in 1966 to replace National Assistance by the Supplementary Benefit scheme, which was to be administered as part of the new Ministry of Social Security by the Supplementary Benefits Commission. The aim of this change was 'to eliminate those features of the existing scheme which are misunderstood or disliked, while preserving the humanity and efficiency of its administration'. This, it was hoped, would 'ensure that the elderly will have no hesitation in claiming the new benefit to which they are entitled and which will be awarded with dignity'.[1]

According to Government spokesmen, the Supplementary Benefits scheme has been very successful in achieving this aim. Mr. Houghton, for example, has claimed that 'the abolition of the National Assistance Board, and the deletion of the word "assistance" from the dictionary of Social Security, has had remarkable success. Some half a million more people applied within a few weeks'.[2] The White Paper on National Superannuation put forward a similar view.[3]

In this chapter, I examine these claims for the success of Supplementary Benefits and try to assess whether it has in fact led to a major reduction in the number of those eligible for assistance who do not apply for it. I begin in Section 1 with a description of the changes which took place in 1966 and a discussion of the method to be adopted in measuring their effect.

(This chapter is more technical than the others and can be omitted by those willing to take my conclusions on trust. The conclusions are summarised on page 76).

---

1 Ministry of Pensions and National Insurance, *Ministry of Social Security Bill 1966* (H.M.S.O., 1966), paragraph 1.

2 D. Houghton, *Paying for the Social Services*, Occasional Paper 16 (Institute of Economic Affairs, 1967), p. 12.

3 *National Superannuation and Social Insurance*, op. cit., p. 7.

1. THE SUPPLEMENTARY BENEFITS SCHEME

Under the Ministry of Social Security Act 1966, the Supplementary Benefits scheme replaced National Assistance with effect from November 1966. The basic principles of the new scheme were identical with those of National Assistance: it provided non-contributory benefits subject to a means test and certain other conditions. There were, however, a number of changes (apart from the re-christening), the most important of which were the following. [1]

(a) The provision of a specific *entitlement* to benefit for people satisfying the conditions laid down in the Act and its regulations.

(b) The introduction of a new long-term addition for those over pension age and for certain people below pension age.

(c) Simplification of the procedure for claiming benefits.

At the same time there was a substantial increase in the assistance scale, and the provisions for disregarding income and savings were made more generous than they had been under National Assistance. Finally, the Ministry of Social Security embarked on an extensive advertising campaign, boosting Supplementary Benefits as 'Social Security's Best Buy'.

If we look at the change in the number of households receiving assistance payments, Mr. Houghton's claim is certainly borne out. Figure 4.1 shows that there was a dramatic increase between September and December 1966, with the total receiving assistance rising by 440,000 – or over 20%. This level has been maintained since then, and in March 1969 the figure was 30% above that in September 1966. However, this increase clearly cannot be attributed solely to the introduction of Supplementary Benefits, because at the same time there was a large increase in the assistance scale. This increase in the assistance scale would have led to a rise in the number receiving assistance *even if National Assistance had remained in force*, so that it cannot be counted as part of the improvement. (The more generous provisions for disregarding income and savings would also have the same effect).

The problem is therefore to separate the effect of the increase in the assistance scale from that of the changes in the assistance system introduced with Supplementary Benefits. In other words, we have to estimate what would have happened if the National Assistance scheme had remained in force but the assistance scale (and the disregards) had been increased to their post-November 1966 levels. In an attempt to do this, I have adopted two independent approaches. The first is based on a statistical analysis of the effects on the number receiving assistance of earlier changes in the National Assistance scale (over the period 1951–65). The second uses the information provided about the incomes of pensioners by the enquiry of the Ministry of Pensions and National Insurance

---

[1] The changes are described in detail in the explanatory memorandum *Ministry of Social Security Bill 1966*, op. cit. and in the *Report of the Ministry of Social Security for the year 1966*, Chapter VI.

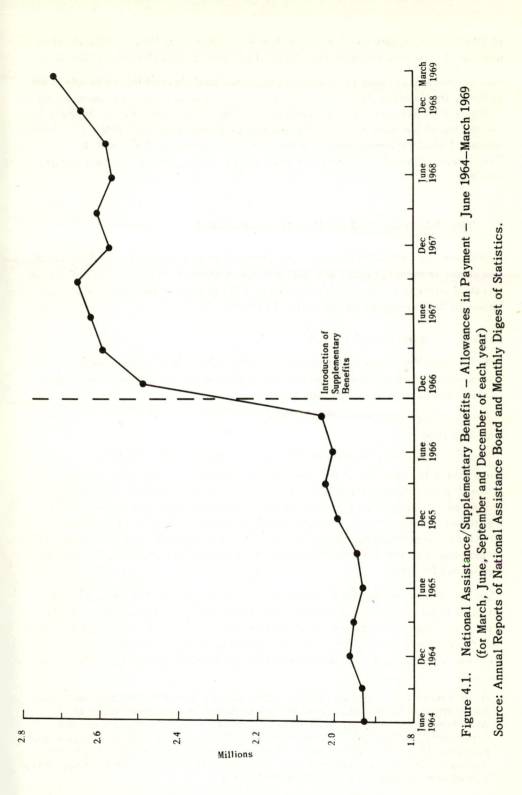

Figure 4.1. National Assistance/Supplementary Benefits – Allowances in Payment – June 1964–March 1969 (for March, June, September and December of each year)

Source: Annual Reports of National Assistance Board and Monthly Digest of Statistics.

in 1965. These approaches are described in Section 2, and the results are then used in Section 3 to estimate the effect of introducing Supplementary Benefits.

The evidence discussed in Chapter 2 suggested that the problem of people's not applying for National Assistance was most acute among those over pension age. Retirement Pensioners also account for the largest part (80%) of the increase in the number of households receiving assistance since September 1966. For these reasons I shall concentrate in this chapter on the position of Retirement Pensioners, although extending the analysis to other groups gives very similar results.

2. THE 'DEMAND' FOR NATIONAL ASSISTANCE

In this section I examine the principal determinants of the number of Retirement Pensioner households receiving National Assistance in an attempt to isolate the effect of changes in the assistance scale. I begin by discussing the approach based on the experience of the period 1951—65.

Evidence from the Period 1951—65

A Retirement Pensioner household would have been eligible for National Assistance if its income fell short of its requirements as calculated according to the National Assistance scale: i.e. if[1]

Retirement Pension + 'Other income'

was less than

National Assistance fixed scale + Housing Expenditure

From this it is clear that if we take housing expenditure and 'other income' as given, then the number eligible for assistance would have risen when the fixed component of the National Assistance scale was increased and fallen when the Retirement Pension was increased. In other words, the number of Retirement Pensioner households receiving National Assistance could have been expected to increase with the difference between the National Assistance scale and the Retirement Pension.

This hypothesis can be tested with reference to the period 1951—65. The top panel of Figure 4.2 shows the proportion of Retirement Pensioner households receiving National Assistance in December of each year. The lower panel shows how the National Assistance scale (not including rent) and the Retirement Pension have changed over the same period for a single person (the rates for a

---

[1] At this point I am ignoring complications arising from discretionary additions, disregarded income, etc. It should also be borne in mind that National Assistance (and Supplementary Benefit) payments cover a person and his dependants, so that a pensioner couple would receive *one* National Assistance payment. I have throughout this chapter referred to the National Assistance unit as a 'household', although this is not strictly accurate (for example, where a pensioner is living with a son or daughter.)

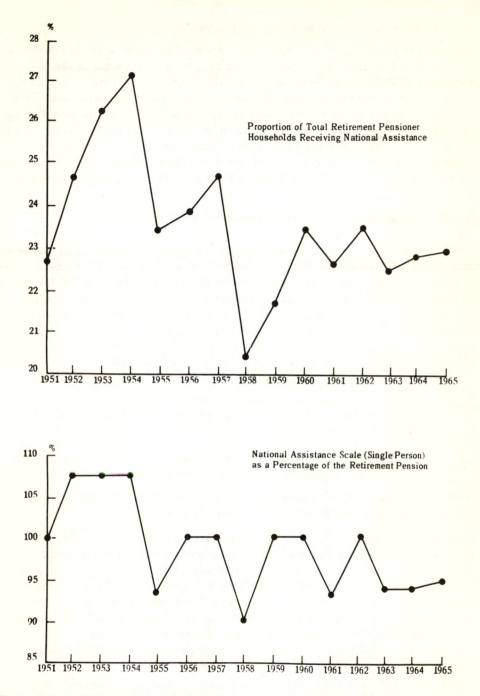

Figure 4.2. Proportion of Total Retirement Pensioner Households Receiving National Assistance in Relation to the National Assistance Scale and Retirement Pension – 1951–65 (December of each year)

Source: Annual Reports of the National Assistance Board.

Note: The National Assistance scale does not include any allowance for rent.

married couple have moved in a very similar way).[1]

According to our hypothesis, a rise in the National Assistance scale relative to the Retirement Pension would be expected to lead to an increase in the proportion of Retirement Pensioner households receiving National Assistance. The evidence presented in Figure 4.2 tends to bear out this expectation. When in 1962, for example, the National Assistance scale for a single person went up 4s., while the Retirement Pension remained unchanged, the proportion receiving National Assistance increased noticeably. When seven years earlier the Retirement Pension went up by 7s. 6d. and the National Assistance scale by only 2s. 6d., the proportion fell from 27.1% in December 1954 to 23.4% in December 1955.

In order to explore this relationship further, I have estimated a number of regression equations. The most important of these equations are discussed briefly below, but fuller details are provided in Appendix D. The chief variable used to explain changes in the proportion receiving assistance is the ratio of the National Assistance scale to the Retirement Pension (as shown in the lower part of Figure 4.2). A simple equation using this variable and a constant term to explain the variation in the percentage of Retirement Pensioner households receiving National Assistance gives the following result:

(1)
$$ Y = \underset{(\ 4.6)}{24.4} \left(\frac{NA}{RP} \right) - \underset{(4.5)}{0.6} \qquad \bar{R}^2 = 0.64 $$

where

Y is the percentage of Retirement Pensioner households receiving National Assistance

$\left(\dfrac{NA}{RP} \right)$ is the ratio of the National Assistance scale (not including housing expenditure) to the Retirement Pension (both for a single person)

Both these figures relate to December of each year (1951–65). The figures in brackets below the coefficients are their standard errors.

This equation suggests that there is a significant positive relationship between the proportion receiving National Assistance and the ratio of the National Assistance scale to the Retirement Pension – confirming the impression given by Figure 4.2. The coefficient of (NA/RP) is significant at the 1% level and the overall level of explanation is quite high (the constant term is not, however, significant). The coefficient of (NA/RP) may be interpreted in the following way. In December 1965, when the National Assistance scale was £3 16s. and the Retirement Pension £4, (NA/RP) = 0.95. Suppose that the National Assistance

---

[1] For most of the analysis I have taken the rates for a single person – for the reason that single persons account for the majority of Retirement Pensioners. Appendix D does, however, consider the effect of using the rates for a married couple. It should be noted that in Figure 4.2, I have shown the ratio of the National Assistance scale to the Retirement Pension rather than the absolute difference – in view of the general rise in money incomes over the period this seems a more reasonable procedure.

scale had been increased by 8*s.*, the pension being unchanged, so that (NA/RP) = 1.05. Then according to equation (1), the proportion of Retirement Pensioner households receiving National Assistance would have gone up 2.4%, which would have meant an absolute increase of some 120,000 households.

One important factor which is not taken into account in equation (1) is the sudden jump in the total number of Retirement Pensioners in July 1958 when about 400,000 'late-age entrants' qualified for Retirement Pensions.[1] There are good reasons to expect that the proportion of these late-age entrants claiming assistance was smaller than for other pensioners. They were on average younger than other pensioners (the oldest being 75), and since they were not compulsorily insurable under the pre-war contributory scheme it seems likely that they were receiving an above-average income when at work and that many received an occupational pension on retirement.[2] We should, therefore, expect the proportion receiving National Assistance to fall after July 1958. If we make an adjustment for this (for details see Appendix D), the regression equation becomes:

$$(2) \qquad Y = 20.1 \left(\frac{NA}{RP}\right) + 4.0 - 1.7D + 0.3T \qquad \bar{R}^2 = 0.74$$

$$ (4.9) \phantom{\left(\frac{NA}{RP}\right) +} (5.1) \quad (0.7) \quad (0.1)$$

where D is a dummy variable for the period 1958–65 (i.e. 0 for 1951–7 and 1 for 1958–65)

 T is the number of years since 1958. (The other variables are as defined for equation (1)).

The fit (as measured by $\bar{R}^2$) is improved by this adjustment, while the coefficient of (NA/RP) is similar to that in equation (1). In Figure 4.3 I have shown the actual number of Retirement Pensioner households receiving National Assistance over the period 1951–65 (the solid line) and the number predicted using equation (2) (the dashed line). This suggests that the equation provides quite a good explanation of changes over the period.

These equations can be refined in a number of ways, some of which are explored in Appendix D. These include the effect of allowing for housing expenditure and

---

1 Under the provisions of the National Insurance Act of 1946, people then aged between 55 and 65 who had not previously been insured did not qualify for pensions until ten years after the start of the scheme in July 1948. This meant that in 1958 there was an increase of 8.5% in the number of Retirement Pensioners in addition to the normal annual growth.

2 For details of the pre-war contributory pension scheme, see *Social Insurance and Allied Services*, op. cit., Appendix B. The most important exclusion as far as employees were concerned was for non-manual workers earning over £420 a year. According to the *Report of the Ministry of Pensions and National Insurance for the year 1958*, 60,000 of the late-age entrants were earning sufficient to have their pensions extinguished by the earnings rule. For these reasons, it is to be expected that they were less likely to need National Assistance — one of them who certainly did not was Lord Montgomery, who is shown claiming his pension in the Ministry's 1958 report.

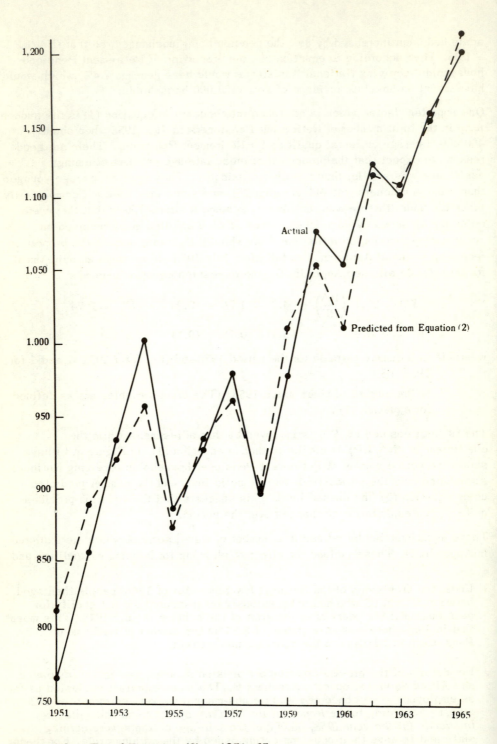

Figure 4.3. Fit of Equation (2) – 1951–65
(in terms of total Retirement Pensioner households receiving National Assistance in December of each year)

variation in employment opportunities for old people, neither of which turn out to contribute very much to the explanation of the proportion receiving assistance. More interesting is the finding that there appears to be some delay before pensioners adjust to increases in the National Assistance scale; in the first year after an increase the effect may be only half the ultimate effect. This no doubt reflects the fact that it takes some time after an increase in the assistance scale for people to become aware that they are entitled to assistance. We should not, however, expect any delay in the opposite direction: the National Assistance Board would adjust at once for any increase in the Retirement Pension.

Evidence from the Ministry Enquiry in 1965

The enquiry of the Ministry of Pensions and National Insurance in 1965 into the circumstances of Retirement Pensioners provides an independent source for estimating the effect of increases in the assistance scale, which allows us to check the results obtained above.

The report gave the distribution of income for pensioner households in relation to the National Assistance scale. From this we can estimate what would have been the effect of an increase in the assistance scale on the number *eligible* for National Assistance. Suppose, for example, that the scale for a single person had gone up by 8s., with the same percentage increase for a married couple (13s. 3d.). This would then have had the effect of increasing the number of Retirement Pensioner households eligible for National Assistance by 580,000.[1] Not all of these of course would have claimed. If we assume that the proportion claiming is the same as that of people who were in fact just below the National Assistance scale in 1965 (less than 10s. below), then the overall increase in the number expected to be *receiving* assistance would be around 170,000. This figure is rather higher than that of 120,000 obtained earlier using the regression equation (1), suggesting that if anything the estimates based on the first approach tend to under-state the effect of a rise in the assistance scale.

3.   THE EFFECT OF INTRODUCING SUPPLEMENTARY BENEFITS

Using the results of the previous section, I now try to estimate how much of the increase in the number of Retirement Pensioner households receiving assistance since November 1966 can be attributed to the more generous assistance scale and how much represents a genuine change in attitude on the part of old people.

Before examining the effect of the higher assistance scale, it should be pointed out that part of the increase must be accounted for simply by the growth in the total number of Retirement Pensioners. As has been stressed by the Government

---

[1] This calculation is based on *Financial and other circumstances of Retirement Pensioners*, op. cit., Table III.4, with an adjustment for non-response.

in recent statements,[1] the number of Retirement Pensioners has grown very rapidly in the past couple of years. Between December 1965 and December 1968, there was an increase of 10%, and this must have led to some increase in the number receiving assistance. In Figure 4.4, I have shown (by the lower of the dashed lines) the increase that would have been expected if the proportion of households receiving assistance had remained at the same level as in December 1965.

The Effect of the Increase in the Assistance Scale

The extent of the increase in the assistance scale in November 1966 is shown in Table 4.1, together with the subsequent changes in the Retirement Pension and Supplementary Benefits. In November 1966 the assistance scale for a single pensioner rose by 14s. (or 18%). (This includes the 9s. long-term addition).[2] Meanwhile the Retirement Pension for a single person remained unchanged at a level of £4 from March 1965 to October 1967, when it went up to £4 10s. At that time, the Supplementary Benefit scale was increased by only 5s. (for a single person), but in October 1968 it was raised again by 6s. It is clear from Table 4.1, however, that despite this leap-frogging the Supplementary Benefit scale has been consistently higher relative to the Retirement Pension since November 1966.

On the basis of our earlier analysis, we should expect this large increase in the assistance scale in November 1966 to have led to an increase in the proportion of Retirement Pensioner households receiving assistance. Using the regression equation (1) to estimate what the effect of this increase would have been, we obtain the results set out in Table 4.2 and illustrated in Figure 4.4. (In both cases the estimates are expressed for convenience in terms of the absolute numbers receiving assistance).

In the case of the increase in the scale in November 1966, the prediction obtained from equation (1) shows a rise of 260,000 in the number of households receiving assistance − or two-thirds of the rise that actually occured. When the Retirement Pension went up by more than the assistance scale in 1967 equation (1) predicted a somewhat larger fall than actually took place, but for the whole period 1965−68 the predicted figure represents over 80% of the actual increase. If we were to use equation (2), then the predicted increase between December 1965 and December 1966 amounts to 57% of the actual increase, and between December 1965 and November 1968 it amounts to 74%.[3] These estimates are lower than those from equation (1) but the difference is relatively small.

These results suggest that around two-thirds of the increase in the number receiving assistance could have been expected as a result of the increase in the

---

[1] See Department of Health and Social Security, *Memorandum on the National Insurance (No. 2) Bill 1969* (H.M.S.O., 1969), p. 4.

[2] This is discussed further below, page 73.

[3] See Appendix D, page 214.

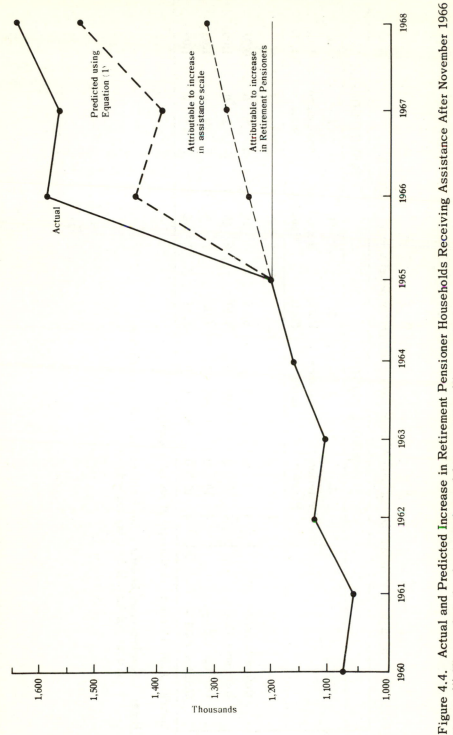

Figure 4.4. Actual and Predicted Increase in Retirement Pensioner Households Receiving Assistance After November 1966
Notes: (1) The predicted values are derived from equation (1) — see text.
(2) The figures for 1967 and 1968 relate to November, the other figures relate to December of each year.

Table 4.1. Retirement Pension and National Assistance/Supplementary Benefit Scale – 1966–8

	SINGLE PERSON			MARRIED COUPLE		
	1. Retirement Pension	2. Assistance Scale	3. Ratio (2/1)	1. Retirement Pension	2. Assistance Scale	3. Ratio (2/1)
	£ s. d.	£ s. d.		£ s. d.	£ s. d.	
Before November 1966	4 0 0	3 16 0	0.95	6 10 0	6 5 6	0.97
November 1966 –	4 0 0	4 10 0	1.13	6 10 0	7 2 0	1.09
October 1967 –	4 10 0	4 15 0	1.06	7 6 0	7 10 0	1.03
October 1968 –	4 10 0	5 1 0	1.12	7 6 0	7 19 0	1.09

Source: Annual Reports of Ministry of Social Security.

Note: Supplementary Benefit scale includes the long-term addition.
It does not include housing expenditure.

Table 4.2. Actual and Predicted Numbers of Retirement Pensioner Households
Receiving Supplementary Benefits — Equation (1)

	Retirement Pensioner households receiving assistance ('000's)			
	Dec. 1965	Dec. 1966	Nov. 1967	Nov. 1968
Total:				
Actual	1 196	1 577	1 557	1 620
Predicted (equation (1))	1 173	1 433	1 389	1 523
Increase over December 1965:				
Actual	—	381	361	424
Predicted (equation (1))	—	260	216	350
Predicted increase as % of actual increase	—	68%	60%	83%

Notes: From 1967, statistics classifying Supplementary Benefits recipients by type have been collected for November rather than December of each year. In making the predictions shown, I have used equation (1) without any adjustment.

In making the predictions, the assistance rates used were those shown in Table 4.1 (i.e. including the long-term addition).

assistance scale. There are, however, three qualifications that must be taken into account:

(a) *Discretionary Additions* As we have seen, part of the increase in the assistance scale in November 1966 took the form of the new long-term addition, which was intended to replace in many cases the discretionary additions given under National Assistance. The Supplementary Benefits Commission can still increase the allowance to cover exceptional needs, but only where these exceed the amount paid automatically in form of the long-term addition. This means that the effective increase in the assistance scale for a household receiving discretionary additions under National Assistance was less than that shown in Table 4.1. For example, a single person with no special needs received an increase of 14s., but someone who had previously received a discretionary addition of 5s. would only have gained to the extent of 9s. As a result, the estimates just given will tend to over-state the effect of the increase in the assistance scale. To correct for this, I have made an alternative estimate based on the average discretionary addition received by Retirement Pensioners in December 1965 (for details, see Appendix D). This estimate is shown in line 3 of Table 4.3. The proportion of the increase between 1965 and 1968 which is explained by the higher assistance scale is reduced, but is still nearly two-thirds.

(b) *Delayed Response* In Section 2, I suggested that the reaction to increases in in the assistance scale might well be delayed (it taking time for old people to become aware that they were eligible). If this is so, then it will affect the

Table 4.3.　Actual and Predicted Increases in the Number of Retirement
Pensioner Households Receiving Assistance — Alternative Estimates

| | Increase in Retirement Pensioner Households Receiving Assistance | | | |
| | Dec. 1965–Dec. 1966 | | Dec. 1965–Nov. 1968 | |
	('000's)	Predicted increase as % of actual increase	('000's)	Predicted increase as % of actual increase
1. Actual	381	—	424	—
2. Equation (1)	260	68	350	83
3. Equation (1) with adjustment for discretionary additions	178	47	273	64
4. Equation (5) (allowing for delayed response)	134	35	303	72
5. Equation (5) with adjustment for discretionary additions	98	26	230	54

Notes: See notes to Table D.2, Appendix D.

estimates presented earlier — particularly since in 1966 the increases came into effect less than a month before the date to which the figure refers. From the results of equation (5)[1] it appears that the effect in the first year of an increase may be only half its ultimate effect. If we use this equation to predict the increase in the number receiving assistance over the period 1965–8, we obtain the results shown in line 4 of Table 4.3. The increase from December 1965 to December 1966 is reduced to a third of the actual increase, although over the whole period 1965–8 the proportion of the increase explained by the higher benefit scales remains around three-quarters. (Line 5 of Table 4.3 shows the combined effect of adjusting for discretionary additions and allowing for the delayed response).

(c) *More Generous Disregards for Income and Savings* The estimates made above have taken no account of the more generous provisions for disregarding income and saving introduced in November 1966. These changes would have led to an increase in the number of households eligible for assistance, and to this extent the estimates given will tend to under-state the increase that could have been expected had National Assistance remained in force. No adjustment is made for this factor, but it should be borne in mind when interpreting the estimates.

(These qualifications are discussed further in Appendix D, where the estimates obtained from different equations are compared in more detail).

---

1 See Appendix D, Table D.1.

The evidence from the Ministry enquiry in 1965 can be used to provide an independent check on these results. As described in Section 2, we can estimate from this the effect in June 1965 of increases in the assistance scale on the number of Retirement Pensioner households eligible for and claiming National Assistance. Table 4.4 shows what would have happened if the assistance scale had in fact been raised in June 1965 to the post-November 1966 level — both with and without adjustments for discretionary additions.

Table 4.4. Estimates of the Effect of Increases in the Assistance Scale Obtained from the Ministry Enquiry

| | Increase in Retirement Pensioner Households — June 1965 | |
	Eligible for Assistance ('000's)	Claiming Assistance ('000's)
With no adjustment for discretionary additions	850	250
With adjustment for discretionary additions	550	160

Source: estimated from *Financial and other circumstances of Retirement Pensioners*, Table III.4(2)

Note: The figures are adjusted for non-response.

The estimate for the number *claiming* assistance is based on the assumption that the proportion of those becoming eligible as a result of the increase who did in fact claim is the same as that for people previously just below the scale (as in Section 2). The resulting figures are close to those obtained using the first approach: for example, the increase of 250,000 (not allowing for discretionary additions) is very similar to that obtained for December 1965–December 1966 using equation (1).

The Effect of Supplementary Benefits

From the evidence discussed above it appears that between a half and two-thirds of the increase between December 1965 and November 1968 in the number of Retirement Pensioner households receiving assistance can be attributed to the more generous assistance scale. Although the total receiving assistance rose by 424,000 between December 1965 and November 1968, a substantial increase would have taken place in any case if National Assistance had remained in force.

On this basis, the introduction of Supplementary Benefits as such (the entitlement to benefit, the simplified procedure for claiming, the advertising campaign, etc.) does not appear to have had a very large effect. The increase between December 1965 and November 1968 not explained by the higher assistance scale amounts only to some 100,000–200,000 and no allowance has been made in these figures for the more generous provisions for disregarding income and savings. Although the Ministry of Social Security's Annual Report for 1966 claimed 300,000 'new' beneficiaries (in the sense that there was no record of their having received National Assistance in recent years), many of them must have been people who had just become eligible for assistance rather than people who were claiming for the first time the assistance to which they had been entitled all along.

The introduction of Supplementary Benefits may, however, have led to people applying more quickly for the benefits to which they became entitled as a result of an increase in the assistance scale. The proportion of the increase that can be explained by the higher assistance scale is lower for December 1965– December 1966 than for the longer period. In this respect the advertising campaign may have been very effective.

These results should naturally be treated with caution, since predicting what would have happened if National Assistance had remained in operation is a risky business and the estimates are undoubtedly subject to considerable error. Nonetheless, the fact that the results based on two different approaches lead to broadly similar answers suggests that the overall picture is probably not far wrong. If this is the case, then it indicates that the introduction of Supplementary Benefits has not had a major impact on the problem of people not applying for the assistance to which they are entitled. Even if we assume that it reduced the number not applying for assistance by 200,000, this still represents only about a quarter of the number who were found by the Ministry enquiry to be not claiming in 1965. Moreover, the higher assistance scales themselves have increased the number eligible, so that the *proportion* of those eligible who claim may actually have fallen since 1966.

CHAPTER 4 – CONCLUSIONS

In this chapter I have examined how far the introduction of Supplementary Benefits in November 1966 has fulfilled its objective of ensuring that people do in fact claim the assistance to which they are entitled.

Since November 1966 there has been a large increase in the number of people receiving assistance – particularly in the case of Retirement Pensioners. However, a large part of this increase can be explained by the rise in the assistance scale which accompanied the introduction of Supplementary Benefits. Using two independent approaches, I have estimated that for Retirement Pensioners between a half and two-thirds of the increase can be accounted for by the more generous assistance scale. As a result, the increase attributable to the introduction of Supplementary Benefits is considerably smaller than appears at first sight. On an optimistic view, the reduction in the number not claiming the assistance to which they were entitled was only a quarter of those found to be not claiming by the Ministry enquiry in 1965.

My conclusion is that while the new scheme may have led to some reduction in the number of old people not applying for the assistance to which they are entitled, a problem of considerable size still remains. If people are better informed about their entitlement to assistance, there are still a good many who are reluctant to apply.

5 Low Incomes and Those Below Pension Age

In this chapter, I examine in more detail the position of people below pension age who are living in poverty, giving particular attention to the problems of those who are in full-time work.

One of the most striking findings of Abel-Smith and Townsend's study *The Poor and the Poorest* was the extent of poverty among households with at least one wage-earner. Earnings were the primary source of income in households containing nearly one fifth of all those below the poverty line and in very few cases was there any important additional source. This was subsequently confirmed by the Ministry of Social Security enquiry in 1966 into the circumstances of families receiving Family Allowances,[1] which showed that out of the 3 million families where the father was in full-time work, more than 2% fell below the National Assistance scale then in force — or 70 000 families containing more than a quarter of a million children. These findings are obviously very important, and Sections 1 and 2 of this chapter are devoted to further examination of the problems of low income families where the father is in full-time work.

In the case of families where the father is out of work (or else there is no male bread-winner), we have seen in Chapter 2 that there were two main reasons why they fell below the poverty line: failure to claim the National Assistance to which they were entitled, and the wage stop. The first of these problems has already been discussed at length in the case of Retirement Pensioners and I shall not go into it again here. As shown in the previous chapter, the introduction of Supplementary Benefits in 1966 has not provided a complete solution to the problem for Retirement Pensioners and there is no evidence that it has been any more successful in the case of those below pension age.[2] The second factor — the wage stop — will be discussed further in Section 3.

---

1 *Circumstances of Families*, op. cit. This survey is referred to below as the 'Ministry of Social Security enquiry' where there is no risk of confusion.

2 The number of households below pension age receiving assistance increased from 588,000 in September 1966 to 790,000 in November 1968. A regression analysis similar to that for Retirement Pensioners described in Chapter 4 suggested that a large part of this increase could be explained by the more generous assistance scale (and by the rise in unemployment).

1. LOW INCOMES, THOSE IN WORK AND FAMILY ALLOWANCES

For Beveridge, the cause of poverty among families supported by a man in full-time work was quite clear:

> 'The social surveys of Britain between the two wars show that in the first thirty years of this century real wages rose by about one-third without reducing want to insignificance, and that want which remained was almost wholly due to two causes – interruption or loss of earning power and large families'.[1]

Since he felt that the problem was basically one of 'large families', the solution he recommended was Family Allowances. These were to be paid to all families with two or more children (as they are at present) and would thus raise the net income of families where the father was working. The exclusion of families with one child was justified on the grounds that 'very few men's wages are insufficient to cover at least two adults and one child'.[2] However, after more than 20 years of Family Allowances, the problem of poverty among families with children still remains. In this section, I examine the reasons why this is so, and try to assess the contribution made by Family Allowances to helping these families.

As we have seen in Chapter 2, one of the major periods of want in the 'life of a labourer' distinguished by Rowntree in 1899 was the time when he had dependent children. The evidence discussed there suggested that it was equally true today that households with dependent children are a 'high risk' group; and there are obviously good reasons for expecting this to be so – not only are the needs of the household greater, but also the wife may be prevented from going out to work. Rowntree, however, went further than this and tried to distinguish between two chief causes of poverty among families with children (although he recognised that very often more than one cause was operating at the same time):

(i) 'Largeness of family, i.e. cases in which the family is in poverty because there are more than four children, though it would not have been in poverty had the number of children not exceeded four.'

(ii) 'Lowness of wage', where the wage is 'insufficient to maintain a moderate family (i.e. not more than four children) in a state of physical efficiency.'[3]

(It was presumably to this distinction between 'low wages' and 'large families' that Beveridge was referring in the quotation given above, since Rowntree's 1936 survey had shown that the importance of the former had fallen very markedly since 1899.)

It may be useful to see whether Rowntree's distinction between 'large families' and 'low wages' can throw any light on the problems of families with low incomes

---

1 *Social Insurance and Allied Services*, op. cit., p. 154.

2 ibid, p. 155.

3 *Poverty*, op. cit., pp. 119–20.

today. The information available to us is, however, less satisfactory for this purpose than that used by Rowntree seventy years ago, and we have to rely on piecing together information from two very different sources: the Ministry of Social Security enquiry in 1966, which covered families with two or more dependent children, and the recent enquiry into earnings by the Department of Employment and Productivity, covering all people in employment.[1]

From the information provided by the earnings enquiry, we can examine the relationship between the earnings of adult men in full-time employment and the Supplementary Benefit scale (I.A.R.) for households of different sizes — see Table 5.1. If we take Rowntree's definition of a 'moderate' family as one with four children, then 8% of all adult men working full-time earned less than the amount required to reach this level (after allowing for National Insurance contributions, income tax and the Family Allowances). However, four children would probably be considered more than 'moderate' in 1968, and a figure of two children may be more appropriate. From Table 5.1 we can see that 3% of adult men working full-time (nearly half a million in all) earned less than the amount required to reach the Supplementary Benefit scale (I.A.R.) for a family with two children. Of course, these figures do not mean that all (or indeed any) of these men necessarily fell below the poverty line — that would depend on whether they did in fact have dependent children, which is something we cannot establish from the earnings enquiry.

There is one further conclusion of considerable importance that can be derived from Table 5.1. According to the estimates given there, 2% of adult men working full-time (or some 200 000 in all) had earnings below the level required to bring *a family with only one child* to the Supplementary Benefit level (I.A.R.). This shows that the assumption of Beveridge that very few men had wages which were insufficient to cover at least two adults and one child is no longer necessarily valid. A small but significant minority earn less than the amount required to reach the national minimum even for a family of this size. Indeed, nearly 1% earned less than the amount required to support a married couple with no children at this level. These results have important policy implications, to which I return later.

The second source of information about families where the father is in full-time work — the Ministry of Social Security enquiry — provides evidence relating specifically to those families that actually fell below the National Assistance scale in 1966 — or 70 000 families in all.

In Table 5.2, I have classified these families according to the number of children. The first point that emerges from this classification is that a very much higher proportion of large families fell below the poverty line than was the case with families of two or three children — see column 3. Among the largest families, 14% of those with six or more children fell below the National Assistance scale compared with only 1% of families with two children. Not surprisingly, large

---

1 Department of Employment and Productivity, 'Results of a new survey of earnings in September 1968', *Employment and Productivity Gazette, 1969*.

Table 5.1.   Earnings of Adult Men in Relation to Supplementary Benefit Scale
(I.A.R.) for Different Household Types — 1968

Household Type:	Gross weekly earnings required to reach Supplementary Benefit scale (I.A.R.)			Men (over 21) working full-time with earnings below this level	
	£	s.	d.	%	('000's)
Married Couple and:					
no children	10	7	0	0.7	100
1 child	12	8	0	2.0	200
2 children	13	5	0	3.4	400
3 children	14	1	0	5.1	600
4 children	14	17	0	7.5	900

Source: Earnings figures derived from 'Results of a new survey of earnings in
September 1968', op. cit., Tables 1 and 2.

Notes: The Supplementary Benefit scale is that introduced in October 1968. It
is assumed that each household pays average rent (as defined in
Appendix B). The allowances for children are taken as the average of
those for children aged 5—10 and 11—12.

Gross earnings are calculated allowing for Family Allowances, National
Insurance contributions (flat-rate and graduated) and for income tax. The
Family Allowances were those introduced in October 1968. The figures
are rounded to the nearest 1s.

families were at much greater risk than those with two or three children (and
presumably than those with one or no children).

It does not appear to be true, however, that large families accounted for anything
like all those that fell below. Families with two children made up over a third
of all those below the National Assistance scale, and if we add in those with
three children, then together they accounted for over half. Even in terms of the
total number of *children* in families below the National Assistance scale,
families with two or three children accounted for nearly 40%. Finally, among
those families where poverty was most acute (those falling more than £2 below
the National Assistance scale), over two-thirds had three or fewer children.

This evidence about the size of low income families where the father is in full-
time work can be supplemented by that from the Abel-Smith and Townsend analysis
of the 1960 Family Expenditure Survey. Table 5.3 shows the size distribution of
low income households with one wage-earner. Over 40% had two children or
fewer, and only 14% had five or more children.

This evidence suggests that a substantial minority of the low income families
where the father is in full-time work fall below the poverty line even though they
have three or fewer children. This must therefore reflect low earnings (or high
rents). Using the Ministry of Social Security enquiry, we can further assess the

Table 5.2. Distribution of Low Income Families by Size — Ministry of Social Security Enquiry 1966

Column	1. Total number of families of this size	2. Families with incomes below N.A. scale.	3. Proportion of families of this size with incomes below N.A. scale.	4. Proportion of total low income families which were of this size.	5. Proportion of total children in low income families which were in families of this size.	6. Proportion of total families with incomes more than £2 below N.A. scale which were of this size.
	('000's)	('000's)	%	%	%	%
Families with:						
2 children	1535	21	1	33	18	60
3 children	690	15	2	24	20	8
4 children	280	11	4	17	19	10
5 children	91	7	7	11	15	6
6 children or more	68	10	14	16	28	16
All families.	2664	63	2	100%	100%	100%

Source: *Circumstances of Families*, Tables III.4, A.3, A.4 and A.8.

Note: These figures are not adjusted for non-response (which accounts for the discrepancy between the total in column 2 of 63 000 and the figure of 70 000 quoted in the text). Because of rounding, the columns do not always add up to the totals shown.

N.A. = National Assistance (including housing expenditure of each family).

These figures relate to families with a father in full-time work.

Table 5.3.   Size of Low Income Households with one Wage-earner — 1960

	Proportion of total low income households with one wage-earner %
No children	12
One or two children	29
Three or four children	45
Five or more children	14
TOTAL	100

Source: *The Poor and the Poorest*, Table 19.

Note: A low income household is defined as one with an income below the National Assistance scale + 40%.

importance of low earnings by classifying the low income families according to their net income in relation to the National Assistance scale (I.A.R.) for a family with three children — see Table 5.4. (N.B. Net income includes Family Allowances).

Table 5.4 shows that 34% of the low income families in the Ministry's sample would not have fallen below the National Assistance scale (I.A.R.) if they had had only three children. On the other hand, 42% of the families had only two or three children and had net incomes below the level required to bring a family with three children to the National Assistance scale (I.A.R.). In fact some 5 000 families had a net weekly income of less than £10 — or little more than the National Assistance scale (I.A.R.) for a family with only one child.

From this analysis it appears that Beveridge's diagnosis of the problem is only partially correct. Poverty among large families is clearly a serious problem, and families with four or more children are very much more likely to fall below the poverty line than other families. However, poverty among households supported by a male breadwinner cannot be attributed *solely* to large families. There are a substantial number of families with three or fewer children where the father does not earn enough to support them at the Supplementary Benefit level. Indeed, some 2% of adult men working full-time earn less than the amount required to reach the Supplementary Benefit scale (I.A.R.) for a family with only one child. Poverty among these households should be seen therefore as the result of a *combination* of factors — including not only large families but also low earnings and other problems such as high rents. This in turn suggests that the solution of this problem will require a combination of policy measures rather than a single panacea. Before developing the implications for Government policy, however, we must examine the contribution at present made by Family Allowances.

The Effect of Family Allowances

From the Ministry of Social Security enquiry we can estimate how many families would have fallen below the assistance scale in 1966 if it had not been for the Family Allowances (then 8s. for the second child and 10s. for subsequent children). This table is based on the assumption that the families received the full benefit. Since Family Allowances are taxable, this assumption will tend to overstate their effect (although it is unlikely that families only slightly above the National Assistance scale will pay a great deal of tax). The estimate given in Table 5.5 (column 2) suggests that without the Family Allowances twice as many families would have fallen below the assistance scale — 5% instead of 2½%. It also suggests, rather surprisingly, that if there were no Family Allowances, families with four or more children would still only account for only half of the low income families.

Table 5.4.   Low Income Families Classified by Net Income and Size — Ministry of Social Security Enquiry 1966

Net income[c] in relation to National Assistance scale (I.A.R.) for family with 3 children:	Proportion of Total Families[a] with Incomes Below National Assistance Scale[b] — %	
	With 2 or 3 children	With 4 or more children
Above	15%[d]	34%
Below	42%	9%

Source: *Circumstances of Families,* Table A.7.

Notes: a   These figures relate to families with a father in full-time work.

   b   The National Assistance scale is calculated by taking the average of the allowances for children aged 5—10 and 11—15, and assuming average rent (as defined in Appendix B).

   c   Net income includes Family Allowances.

   d   The 15% with only 2 or 3 children and net income *above* the National Assistance scale (I.A.R.) must have had above average rents.

In considering these results, it is important to bear in mind that the Family Allowances in 1966 were very much below the level envisaged by Beveridge. In fact the 8s. rate for the second child was the same as that proposed by Beveridge in 1942 — though prices have more than doubled since then! Beveridge proposed that the allowances should be sufficient to cover the subsistence costs of children of different ages. Accordingly, they were to be set at the same rate (apart from for the first child) as the allowances for children under the National Insurance scheme, which in turn was to be at least equal to the subsistence rate embodied in the National Assistance scale. However, the Family Allowances introduced in 1946 were only at the rate of 5s., which was in real terms

Table 5.5. Effect of Family Allowances and of 1968 Increase on Families with Low Incomes where Father in Full-Time Work

Column	1.	2.	3.	
	With incomes below National Assistance scale in 1966	Below National Assistance level in 1966 if no Family Allowances paid	Raised above National Assistance scale in 1966 by 10s. increase in Family Allowances	
Families with:	('000's)	('000's)	('000's)	%
2 children	21	40	4	20
3 children	15	27	10	67
4 children	11	26	7	68
5 children	7	14	6	84
6 or more children	10	23	8	82
All families	63	129	35	56

Source: calculated from *Circumstances of Families*, Table A.8.

Notes: These figures are not adjusted for non-response (see note to Table 5.2).

It is assumed that all the families have incomes below the level at which they would begin to pay income tax.

It is assumed that families with 6 or more children have an average of 6¼.

considerably below the level proposed by Beveridge, and they were not graded according to the age of the child. Moreover, they were considerably lower than the National Assistance scale for children introduced in 1948, which ranged from 7s. 6d. for a child under 5 to 10s. 6d. for a child aged between 11 and 15. In the twenty years after Family Allowances were introduced, they were increased only twice and in 1966 they amounted to less than half the National Assistance allowance for a child aged under 5 and less than a third of that for children between 11 and 15.

In response to the findings of the Ministry of Social Security enquiry, the Government decided to raise Family Allowances and they were increased by 7s. per child in April 1968 and a further 3s. per child in October 1968 — so that they are now effectively double their level in 1966. (This measure was accompanied by a reduction in the child tax relief, which is discussed in Chapter 8.)

Using the information provided by the Ministry enquiry, we can estimate what would have been the effect in 1966 of an increase of this size, which the Government itself had claimed would 'deal with family poverty' — see Column 3, Table 5.5. It is clear from this that they would have made a great deal of difference: of the 70000 families below the National Assistance scale in 1966 where the father was in full-time work, 56% would have been raised above by a 10s. increase. Since the increase did more to help larger families, the proportion of children raised above would have been even higher (64%). For those still below, the shortfall would have been smaller, a family with five children receiving an increase of £2 in its total income. In addition, those families below the poverty line without a father in full-time work would also have benefitted from the increase.[1]

Nonetheless, it cannot be maintained that the problem of family poverty has been 'dealt with' if 44% of the low income families (containing nearly 150 000 people) still remain below the poverty line. Moreover, there are two reasons why the estimates given in Table 5.5 may be expected to over-state the effectiveness of the increase in Family Allowances. With rising prices, a 10s. increase in 1968 means less to these families than a 10s. increase in 1966. Secondly, for those families who pay income tax, the effective increase is smaller than 10s. − both because the Family Allowances are taxable and because the child tax allowances were reduced at the same time. Finally, we must bear in mind that the increase in Family Allowances would have done nothing for low income households where the father is in full-time work but where there is only one child or no children at all.

Conclusions

These estimates suggest that the 1968 increase in Family Allowances provided a substantial addition to the incomes of families with two or more children and would have raised above the National Assistance scale over half of those who fell below in 1966. Even so, the present Family Allowances have only gone part of the way towards solving the problem of family poverty. There are two principal reasons for this:

(a) Even with the 1968 increase, Family Allowances are still considerably below the level which the Government considers to represent the subsistence needs of a child. The present Family Allowance (for the third and subsequent children) is only 74% of the Supplementary Benefit scale for a child under 5 and is under half that for a child aged between 11 and 13. In this way the present provisions fall a long way short of the Beveridge objective of providing allowances at a subsistence level for all children (except the first).

(b) Raising the Family Allowances to the level proposed by Beveridge would still, however, not be enough, since, as we have seen, his assumption that earnings are enough to support a family with only one child is no longer necessarily valid. There are people whose earnings are so low that they could not support a wife and one child at the Supplementary Benefit scale (I.A.R.).

---

[1] They would, however, have gained rather less, since there was at the same time a reduction in the allowances payable for children under the National Insurance benefits.

These problems will be taken up in Chapter 8, where I discuss measures both to increase the benefits given to families with children and to help those with low earnings.

2.   LOW EARNINGS

The analysis of the previous section suggested that low earnings are a more important problem than is commonly believed. In this section I examine the incidence of low earnings in more detail in preparation for the discussion in Chapter 8 of measures to help the low paid.

The questions with which I shall be primarily concerned are:

(a) To what extent are low earnings a temporary phenomenon for a particular worker? Do they simply reflect a short working week?

(b) How far can low earnings be attributed to ill-health or other disabilities?

(c) Are low earnings concentrated in particular industries or regions? Are they associated with workers of a particular age?

(a)   Temporarily Low Earnings and Short Hours

Firstly, it may be the case that low earnings are essentially a temporary phenomenon for any particular worker — representing a bad week when, for example, bonuses fell below normal. If this is so, the evidence discussed in section 1 is less disturbing than at first sight, since it is with a person's normal earnings that we are really concerned.

In the case of their 1966 enquiry, the Ministry of Social Security estimated that about 1 in 5 of the low income families where the father was in full-time work had normal earnings which were higher than those in the week of the enquiry. It does not follow, however, that they would have been sufficiently higher to raise them above the National Assistance scale, and there were undoubtedly some families above the poverty line in the week of the enquiry who would normally have fallen below. In the case of the Department of Employment and Productivity 1968 earnings survey, the figures quoted were adjusted to include average amounts of bonuses etc. over a representative period (where these differed from the actual amount received) and people paid for less than their normal hours were excluded. Much of the temporary fluctuation in earnings had therefore already been eliminated from these figures. On this basis, it appears that people with temporarily low earnings account for only a small proportion of the total low paid. This is supported by the results of the 1966 Family Expenditure Survey, which collected information about both 'last week' earnings and 'usual' earnings. [1] This showed relatively little difference between the two; for example, 9.2% had last week earnings below £13, compared with 8.0% who had usual earnings below this level.

---

1   Ministry of Labour, *Family Expenditure Survey, 1966* (H.M.S.O., 1967).

It might be argued that rather than just averaging over a period of a few months, we should take account of cyclical fluctuations in the level of activity in the economy, and consider whether it is possible that low earnings can be explained as a cyclical phenomenon. As far as the Ministry of Social Security enquiry is concerned, however, this explanation is not very plausible, since the enquiry was carried out in mid—1966, when unemployment was 1.1% and average weekly earnings had risen by some 8% in the previous year.

It is of course possible that low weekly earnings reflect short working hours rather than a low hourly rate of earnings. In the case of the Ministry of Social Security enquiry, the fathers of the families with incomes below the assistance scale worked an average of 42 hours a week, and although this is less than the average for fathers above the scale (47 hours), it does not indicate widespread short-time as a cause of low earnings. The 1968 earnings enquiry provided details of the distribution of hourly as well as weekly earnings. If we take a weekly level of £15 as our criterion for low earnings and assume that this applies to a standard week of 40 hours, then a person can be said to have low hourly earnings if they fall below 7s. 6d. From the results of the enquiry, we can estimate that 14.4% of adult men working full-time had hourly earnings below this level (compared with 7.9% with weekly earnings below £15). An estimated 3.3% had hourly earnings below 6s. 3d. (which would give £12 10s. for a 40 hour week). On this basis, there appear to be a substantial number of people with low hourly earnings, and the problem cannot simply be put down to short hours.

(b) Ill-Health as a Cause of Low Earnings

In recent years there has been increasing interest in the extent to which low earnings are a reflection of ill-health or some degree of mental or physical disability. There is, however, at present only very limited information about this aspect.

In the Ministry of Social Security enquiry in 1966, each father in work was asked whether his health was normally good. Where the answer was no, he was then asked whether he felt that his earning power was limited by ill-health. In the case of families with incomes below the National Assistance scale, 14% said that their earnings were in fact limited by ill-health, compared with only 4% in the whole sample. Not too much weight can, however, be attached to these answers since, as the report emphasises, people vary considerably in their awareness of ill-health and in their willingness to reveal it (particularly in the case of mental illness). It may be noted, however, that 51% of the fathers of low income households had been absent from work during the preceding year as a result of sickness or injury, compared with 32% for the whole sample. Moreover, of the wage-stopped families visited by the Supplementary Benefit Commission when it reviewed the operation of the wage-stop in 1967, only a third said that they were in good health and it was clear that in a good many cases ill-health was an important cause of their low earning capacity.

In the course of the 1968 earnings enquiry by the Department of Employment and

Productivity, employers were asked whether the employee concerned suffered from a mental or physical handicap, and when the results from this are available, they should throw further light on the extent to which low earnings can be attributed to disabilities of this kind.

(c) The Industrial and Regional Distribution of Low Earnings

As a basis for examining the industrial and regional distribution, I have adopted two definitions of 'low earnings'. The first is based on the level of gross weekly earnings required to bring a family with one child to the Supplementary Benefit scale (I.A.R.). This gives a figure for September 1968 of around £12 10s.[1] (The reasons why this level is of interest should be apparent from the discussion of the previous section.) As a basis for the second definition of low earnings I take the rather higher figure of £15 a week which has been put forward by a number of the proponents of a national minimum wage.

From the recent Department of Employment and Productivity survey, we can find the proportion of workers in different industries whose earnings were below these two levels in September 1968. The results are set out in Table 5.6, which relates to all adult employees (both manual and non-manual) working full-time. In interpreting these figures, it should be borne in mind that:

(i) earnings include a 'normal' level of shift-payments, commission and bonuses,

(ii) any income in kind and in gratuities is excluded (which may be important in the case of such industries as agriculture and catering).

As we should expect, the overall figures conceal wide variation between industries. The first striking difference is that between manufacturing and non-manufacturing industries: whichever of the two definitions of low earnings that we adopt, the proportion falling below was over twice as high in non-manufacturing as in manufacturing. There are, however, wide variations within non-manufacturing itself, and we can distinguish certain industries where low earnings are particularly widespread: agriculture, distribution, professional and scientific services, miscellaneous services (including catering and garages) and government service. Others (such as transport and construction) do not differ very much from manufacturing. Also, of course, there are industries within manufacturing that have a high proportion of low paid workers, although this does not show up very clearly with the rather broad industrial groupings at present available.

These results suggest, as we should expect, that there are certain industries where low pay is prevalent. However, it should not be assumed that these industries necessarily account for most of the low paid workers in the country. The five non-manufacturing industries singled out above account for only slightly over half of those earning less than £15 a week, and in fact nearly a quarter of those below this level are in manufacturing. It does in fact appear that low paid

---

1 This figure is based on the Supplementary Benefit scales that came into force in October 1968.

workers are spread quite widely over a range of industries and that there are not just a few 'sweated trades'.

Table 5.6.   Industrial Distribution of Low Earnings — 1968

	Proportion of men (21 and over) working full-time earning less than	
	£12 10s. a week %	£15 a week %
All industries	2.1	7.9
All manufacturing industries	1.3	4.1
All non-manufacturing industries	3.5	10.7
Agriculture	14.5	36.6
Mining and quarrying	1.5	9.7
Construction	1.3	4.6
Gas, electricity and water	0.8	3.7
Transport and communication	1.4	4.7
Distributive trades	4.2	13.9
Insurance, banking and finance	3.4	9.3
Professional and scientific services	4.4	13.6
Miscellaneous services	9.2	18.2
Public administration	3.2	14.3

Source: derived from 'Results of a new survey of earnings in September 1968' op. cit., Tables 15 and 16.

Note: The figures for earnings below £12 10s. are obtained by linear interpolation, and for this reason may not be so accurate as those for the £15 level.

The results so far available from the 1968 earnings survey are based on rather broad industrial groupings, and in order to obtain information at a finer level of detail we have to go back to the enquiry into earnings carried out in 1960.[1] This is rather unsatisfactory, not only because it is now out of date but also because the coverage of the enquiry was incomplete. It covered only manual workers and excluded a number of major industries outside manufacturing. Using the results of this enquiry, Mrs. Judith Marquand has, however, made a number of interesting points about the characteristics of low paid industries.[2] She defines as 'low paid industries' those that fall in the bottom quarter when industries are ranked according to the earnings received by the worker at the lowest decile (industries

---

[1]   Ministry of Labour, 'Distribution of earnings of manual workers, October 1960', *Ministry of Labour Gazette*, 1961.

[2]   J. Marquand, 'Which are the lower paid workers?', *British Journal of Industrial Relations*, 1967.

are defined in terms of minimum list headings, which are very much narrower than those shown in Table 5.6). On this basis she concluded that:

(i) the industries right at the bottom were mostly ones where Wages Councils were in operation,

(ii) there was stong tendency for the manufacturing industries with widespread low pay to be ones which were contracting or expanding less rapidly than the average.

The results of the 1960 enquiry also support the earlier conclusion that low earnings are not concentrated in a few low paying industries. If we take all the industries which Marquand considered to be low paid, then they accounted for under half of all the workers whose earnings in 1960 were less than £10 a week (which was roughly the same proportion of national average earnings as £15 a week in 1968). The Wages Councils industries just referred to accounted for less than 5%.

Turning to the question of the regional distribution of those with low earnings, I have shown in Table 5.7 the proportions in different regions earning less than £12 10s. and £15 as derived from the 1968 earnings enquiry. As might be expected, a number of regions had a much higher than average proportion of low paid workers. These included East Anglia, the South West, Wales and Scotland, which had around twice the proportion in the South East and the Midlands (although the South East still accounted for nearly a quarter of all those earning less than £15). The enquiry did not cover Northern Ireland; the results of the 1967 Family Expenditure, however, showed that 31% of full-time adult male employees earned less than £15 in Northern Ireland, compared with 14% for the United Kingdom as a whole.

It seems reasonable to expect that those with low earnings would be more heavily concentrated in the youngest and oldest age groups – reflecting the tendency for earnings to rise with age in the twenties and to decline after reaching a peak in the late forties. This expectation is borne out by the evidence from the earnings survey as shown in Table 5.8. Low earnings were more common for those in the youngest age group (21–4) and for those aged over 50. In fact about half (47%) of all workers earning less than £15 a week were over 50.

Summary

It may be helpful to summarise the conclusions of this section:

(a) Low pay cannot be explained as purely a temporary phenomenon for a particular worker or purely as a result of short hours.

(b) It is difficult to assess the effect of ill-health until further information is available, although it is undoubtedly important in a number of cases.

(c) There are a number of industries with above average proportions of low paid workers, but low paid workers are spread fairly widely over the range of industries.

Table 5.7.　Regional Distribution of Low Earnings – 1968

Region	Proportion of men (over 21) working full-time with weekly earnings below	
	£12 10s. %	£15 %
South East	2.0	5.6
East Anglia	4.0	12.0
South Western	3.5	10.9
West Midlands	2.1	6.3
East Midlands	2.0	7.2
Yorkshire and Humberside	2.8	9.6
North Western	2.4	7.8
Northern	2.6	9.4
Wales	3.2	11.1
Scotland	3.4	11.0
GREAT BRITAIN	2.1	7.9

Source:　'Results of a new survey of earnings in September 1968', op. cit.,
Table 10.

See note to Table 5.6.

Table 5.8.　Distribution of Low Earnings by Age – 1968

Age:	Proportion of men working full-time with weekly earnings below	
	£12 10s. %	£15 %
21–4	5.2	14.9
25–9	1.9	5.6
30–9	1.3	3.9
40–9	1.4	5.1
50–9	2.3	8.6
60–4	4.3	15.2

Source:　'Results of a new survey of earnings in September 1968', op. cit.,
Table 8.

See note to Table 5.6.

(d) There is a tendency for the industries with low pay to be ones where Wages Councils operate, and where employment is contracting.

(e) There are definite regional differences in the importance of low earnings.

(f) Nearly half of the workers with low earnings are over 50.

Finally, it should be stressed that this section has been concerned only with those in employment and not with the self-employed. From the Ministry of Social Security enquiry, it can be seen that the self-employed account for about 1 in 5 of the 70 000 families which fell below the National Assistance scale even though the father was in full-time work. However, as the report emphasises, information obtained about income from self-employment may not be very accurate.

3.   THE WAGE STOP

In this section, I consider the problems of families where the father is out of work and the Supplementary Benefit received by the family is restricted as a result of the *wage stop*. In Chapter 2, I described the main features of the wage stop and showed how it meant that a person who normally earned less than the Supplementary Benefit scale would not receive the full Supplementary Benefits when he was unemployed or temporarily sick.

The Ministry of Social Security enquiry into families receiving Family Allowances in 1966 showed that out of 55 000 families where the father was sick or unemployed and receiving National Assistance, 15 000 — or 26% — were subject to the wage stop. It was also estimated that if the Supplementary Benefit scale introduced in November 1966 had been in operation when the enquiry took place, then this figure would have risen to 20 000.

The Annual Report of the Ministry of Social Security for 1966 shows that at the end of 1966 25 000 households in all were subject to the wage stop — 22 000 where the father was unemployed and 3 000 where he was 'temporarily out of the employment field, mainly because of sickness'. By November 1967, this figure had increased to 32 360 households (containing 95 000 children). It should be borne in mind that these figures do not include families whose eligibility for Supplementary Benefits is lost completely as a result of the wage stop (in other words, where the deduction wipes out the assistance payment altogether). The amount deducted from the Supplementary Benefit payment ranges from a few shillings to several pounds. In 1965, the average deduction was £1 17s. 6d. and for nearly 20% it was £3 or more.[1]

In the past few years, the wage stop has attracted a great deal of criticism, and in 1967 the Supplementary Benefits Commission decided to review its operation. In the course of this review, they visited 52 families to see 'what living on the wage stop meant in everyday terms', and the results of this enquiry are described

---

[1] *Report of the National Assistance Board for the year ended 31st December 1965* (H.M.S.O., 1966), p. 30.

in the Commission's report.[1] The majority of the fathers were unskilled labourers, although most of them had not worked for over a year. Their potential net earnings were in most cases estimated at £9 10s. − £11 10s. (after allowing for National Insurance contributions, tax and working expenses). Only a third of the men said that they were in good health (19 out of 52 were registered as disabled) and in a number of cases it was evident that their earning capacity was impaired by ill-health. Most of the families contained 3 or more children. The amount of the wage stop deduction ranged from under 10s. to £6 or over, though for the majority it was £2 10s. or less. This left a total household income in most cases of between £10 and £13. Two thirds of the families said that they could only just manage or could not manage at all (half of the families had rent arrears and about 2 in 5 had other debts). The Supplementary Benefit Commission concluded that 'the general impression derived from the visits was not so much one of grinding poverty in any absolute sense as one of unrelieved dreariness with, in some cases, little hope of improvement in the future'.

As a result of this investigation, the Supplementary Benefit Commission decided to make a number of important changes in the administration of the wage stop. The most significant of these concerned the wage rates used to assess the normal earnings of labourers. These had previously been based on local average earnings; under the new regulations, they are now based instead on the rates fixed for manual workers by the National Joint Council for Local Authorities. This has benefitted many of those subject to the wage stop by raising the assessment of their normal earnings. Other changes included the abolition of a 7s. 6d. flat-rate deduction from earnings for working expenses, and more generous treatment of earnings by the wife. The period for which sickness is to be regarded as 'temporary' has also been reduced from 6 months to 3 months (which will reduce the period for which the wage stop is applied). Finally, the Supplementary Benefit Commission undertook to review all wage-stopped cases where there was an element of disability to see whether the requirement to register for employment could be lifted (and with it the wage stop).

The implementation of these changes began early in 1968, although the Minister of Social Security warned that the detailed changes would take some time to introduce and that the third stage (the review of disabled cases) would not take place until the Autumn. It is clear that when operative the changes will help a large proportion of the households subject to the wage stop. For example, the adoption of local authority wage rates as a basis for assessing normal earnings and the removal of the 7s. 6d. deduction for working expenses benefitted some 14 000 households − over half of those wage-stopped.[2] Nonetheless, there will undoubtedly remain a considerable number of families who are still subject to the wage stop. In May 1969 there were in fact still 24 700 households who were

---

1 Ministry of Social Security, *Administration of the Wage Stop* (H.M.S.O., 1967).

2 Minister of Social Security, House of Commons, April 8, 1968 (oral answer).

wage-stopped — which is not a great deal lower than the figure for November 1967.[1]

The rationale of the wage stop is clear. If a person could receive more on Supplementary Benefits than he could earn by working, then there would be little financial incentive for him to re-enter the labour force and he would be treated more generously than his counterpart in full-time work.

In this context two points should be made. Firstly, and very importantly, the wage stop is only necessary because a man's earnings are below the level required to bring his family to the Supplementary Benefit level. As the Supplementary Benefits Commission points out in its report, the wage-stop is not by itself a cause of poverty: 'it is a harsh reflection of the fact that there are many men in work living on incomes below the Supplementary Benefit standard'. The source of the problem is that people do not have sufficient incomes when working full-time to bring their family to the national minimum — the problem discussed in the first sections of this chapter. This applies not only to earnings but also to Family Allowances: the 1968 increase would have reduced the number of households subject to the wage stop — because their normal incomes when at work would have been increased.

The second point is that if the objective of the wage stop is to reduce the disincentive effect, it is only necessary to apply the wage stop to those who are in a position to make the choice between working and not working. This is important as far as the sick and disabled are concerned: if they are effectively unable to enter the labour force then there is no reason for them to be wage-stopped at all. In its report on the administration of the wage stop, the Supplementary Benefit Commission argued that exempting the disabled would be difficult because those disabled persons who were working at low wages would then be treated inequitably. This, however, is surely an argument for more generous treatment of disabled workers rather than a case for retaining the wage stop.

The number subject to the wage stop can, of course, be expected to vary cyclically, but if we express this figure as a percentage of the total unemployed receiving Supplementary Benefits (11%), then it is not much lower than in November 1967 (14%). Part of the reduction in the number subject to the wage stop must also be attributed to the increase in Family Allowances.

PART II   REFORMING SOCIAL
SECURITY

6   Introduction

In this chapter I discuss the general approach to be followed in examining the impact of possible reforms of the social security system. In the first section, I summarise the findings of Part I and describe the ground to be covered in Part II. In Section 2, I then discuss the framework to be adopted in evaluating the different proposals for reform, and finally in Section 3, I provide a brief treatment of some of the considerations underlying the possible effect of the proposals on work incentives.

1.   OVERVIEW

The evidence discussed in Chapter 2 showed that a significant minority of the population (between 4% and 9%) have incomes which are below the poverty line adopted in this study — the 'national minimum' defined by the Government through the Supplementary Benefit scale. A large proportion of these people are receiving pensions or other social security benefits, but a considerable number are people living in households which fall below the poverty line even though supported by a man in full-time work.

Old People

In Chapters 3 and 4, I examined the position of old people in more detail. Since the total state pension (flat-rate and graduated) is not by itself sufficient to bring a pensioner household to the Supplementary Benefit level, old people who have no occupational pension and cannot work are forced to rely on Supplementary Benefits. The situation is in fact well summarised by the Government in its White Paper on National Superannuation of January 1969:[1]

> 'Neither the flat-rate scheme by itself, nor the present combination of flat-rate and graduated schemes, has succeeded in providing adequate pensions by right of contribution. For those without occupational pensions or private means, it is not the national insurance scheme which provides security in old age, but the supplementary benefits scheme. The latter is not, as was intended, just a "safety net" for the exceptional case. Instead it is a vast platform which now helps support some two million people over pension age.'

The role of National Assistance/Supplementary Benefits has not therefore been the minimal one envisaged by Beveridge; instead the number receiving assistance

---

[1] *National Superannuation and Social Insurance* op. cit., p. 11.

has increased substantially over the post-war period. Even this, however, has failed to provide complete security in old age. We have seen that in 1965 there were 700 000 Retirement Pensioner households entitled to National Assistance which did not claim it — either because they were ignorant or misinformed about the provisions or because they were deterred by the stigma associated with receiving assistance. Faced with this evidence of the failure of National Assistance, the Government decided in 1966 to replace it by the Supplementary Benefits Scheme and made a number of important changes in its administration. In Chapter 4, I examined the effect of these changes and argued that they had not led to a substantial improvement in the situation. Although the number receiving assistance has risen considerably since 1966, at least half of this increase can be attributed to the higher assistance scales rather than to a change in the attitude of those unwilling to claim. On an optimistic view, the reduction in the number not claiming the assistance to which they were entitled was only a quarter of those found to be not claiming in 1965.

As far as old people are concerned, there are therefore two principal problems. Firstly, the present state pension provisions are not sufficient to bring an old person to the Government's own minimum standard of living without the aid of Supplementary Benefits. Secondly, the Supplementary Benefit system has not proved wholly successful in providing such a safety net. Many old people still slip through, and as a result are living on incomes below the poverty level.

The results of the Ministry of Social Security Act 1966 suggest that the second of these problems has no straightforward solution, and for this reason the discussion in Chapter 7 concentrates on schemes designed to reduce the dependence of old people on Supplementary Benefits. The most obvious way in which this could be achieved is through a return to the policy recommended by Beveridge of setting the Retirement Pension at the level of the assistance scale. This 'Back to Beveridge' strategy is therefore the first to be discussed in Chapter 7.

A quite different approach to helping old people with low incomes is that adopted by the Government in its proposal for National Superannuation which would replace the present Retirement and graduated pensions by a wholly earnings-related scheme. This proposal has a number of objectives, but in Chapter 7 I am concerned with only one aspect of the scheme — the effect on old people with low incomes. In particular, I examine how far it would guarantee a pension at the Supplementary Benefit level (I.A.R.) — both when it reached full operation and in the more immediate future. To the extent that it is successful in doing this, the dependence of old people on Supplementary Benefits would be substantially reduced and only those with above average rent or exceptional needs would need to apply for assistance.

People Below Pension Age

One of the most disturbing findings of the recent surveys of households with low incomes is the incidence of poverty among those supported by a man in full-time work. The Ministry of Social Security enquiry in 1966 of families receiving

Family Allowances showed that 2% of those where the father was in full-time work had incomes below the National Assistance scale. These families received no social security benefits apart from the Family Allowances, and if the father were to become sick or unemployed, the Supplementary Benefit paid would be reduced through the operation of the wage stop. The problems of households which fell below the poverty line even though supported by a man in full-time work were discussed in more detail in Chapter 5, where particular attention was given to the effect of Family Allowances (including the 1968 increase). This analysis suggested that the present allowances have failed to provide a fully satisfactory solution to the problems of family poverty.

There are two principal reasons why Family Allowances have not fulfilled the hopes of Beveridge and others who championed them in the inter-war period. The first is that the Family Allowances have not been set at the subsistence level recommended by Beveridge. Even with the substantial increase in 1968, they are still much lower than the allowances for children provided under Supplementary Benefits. Secondly, the assumption of Beveridge that earnings would be sufficient to meet the needs of a family with 1 child is no longer satisfied. A significant minority of men over 21 working full-time earn less than the amount required to support a family with 1 child at the Supplementary Benefit level (I.A.R.).

The measures discussed in Part II may similarly be divided into 2 groups: those which would raise the level of child benefits for low income families, and those directed at the problem of low earnings.

The most straightforward way of helping families with children is through raising Family Allowances — a policy which, as we have seen, gave considerable benefit to low income families in 1968. The first possibility considered in Chapter 8, therefore, is a 'Back to Beveridge' increase in Family Allowances, under which they would be raised to the 'subsistence' level embodied in the Supplementary Benefit scale. From there I go on to discuss two recent proposals for reforming the present system of child benefits which have been made by the Child Poverty Action Group and Sir John Walley. These schemes would not only increase the benefit given to low income families at present receiving Family Allowances, but would also help the low income family with only 1 child. A rather different approach to the same problem through a scheme of 'negative income taxation' is discussed in the first section of Chapter 9.

The second group of measures — those to help low paid workers — are discussed in Sections 2 and 3 of Chapter 8. There I consider the possible benefit from minimum wage legislation, and the scope for helping those with low earnings by reducing the burden of social security contributions. In the latter context, I examine the effect of the new contribution schedule proposed for National Superannuation and the suggestion recently made by Sir Paul Chambers that the contributions should be abolished altogether and the benefits financed from income taxation.

The Comprehensive Approach

The measures considered so far are all directed at helping particular groups of low income households — those over pension age, those with children, those with low earnings. Even if all these measures were adopted, however, there might still be people who slip through the net. For example, a person receiving unemployment or sickness benefit who was deterred by the stigma from claiming Supplementary Benefits might still fall below the poverty line.

For this reason, there have been a number of proposals for a comprehensive reform to provide a guaranteed minimum income to everyone, rather than being directed at particular categories. In the second part of Chapter 9, I discuss one of these proposals, which is commonly referred to as a 'social dividend' scheme, although it has considerable affinity to proposals for a negative income tax.

2. A FRAMEWORK FOR THE ANALYSIS

The aim of Part II is to examine the benefits and costs of each of the reforms mentioned above. In order to provide some framework to the analysis, it may be helpful to discuss a number of the general problems that arise in evaluating these costs and benefits. This will, in particular, give me an opportunity to emphasise some of the limitations of the approach adopted here.

Benefits

In examining the benefit from a particular reform, I shall be primarily concerned with its effect on people with incomes below the poverty line adopted in this study. The principal indicator that I have used therefore in assessing the effectiveness of a scheme is the proportion of people at present below the Supplementary Benefit scale who would be raised above it if the scheme were introduced. It is important to emphasise, however, that this is no more than an indicator, and that it may give very misleading results if not used with care. We may, for example, have a scheme which would give considerable benefit to those with low incomes without actually raising any of them above the poverty line. It must be borne in mind that the 'depth' of poverty is at least as important as its 'breadth'. It should also be stressed that many of those who are above the Supplementary Benefit scale are still far from well off, and any benefit given to them should clearly be taken into account.

To assess the effect of a reform we need a great deal of detailed information about the circumstances of the people it is designed to help. At the very least we need to know a person's income and the number of his dependants; but in many cases this is not sufficient and we also need to know the ages of any children, the extent to which the income is made up of earnings, the level of housing expenditure, and so on. This information is not however generally available in the form required: as we saw in Chapter 2, our knowledge of the circumstances of those with low incomes is only very limited. This means that it is often difficult to judge the effectiveness of a scheme with any accuracy.

As a result, many of the estimates given here of the effectiveness of different schemes are based on a number of strong assumptions and must be regarded as subject to considerable error. They are presented in the belief that an approximate estimate is better than no estimate at all, and will, I hope, be interpreted in this spirit.

Costs

A number of the reforms discussed in Part II would involve an increase in government expenditure, and in these cases I have calculated the budgetary cost that they would impose. This cost can then be expressed, for example, in terms of the increase in the standard rate of income tax required to raise this revenue. It is on this aspect of the cost that attention is usually focussed, but this does of course represent only part of the picture — particularly in the case of schemes which are partially or completely self-financing.

First of all, this calculation is a purely budgetary one and does not necessarily reflect the cost in terms of claims on current resources. A redistribution of child benefits may, for example, have no budgetary cost, but might well redistribute purchasing power from those with a low marginal propensity to consume to those whose marginal propensity is higher, and hence add to the level of demand. To offset this effect on the level of demand, taxation might have to be increased even though there was no extra cost to the Exchequer. This qualification should be borne in mind in the analysis, although I have not made any estimate of the allowance that would have to be made.

Secondly, we are interested in the *distribution* of the cost as well as in its *total*. In so far as the cost is to be raised through general taxation, the distribution of the burden is of course in the hands of the Government; but a number of the schemes involve in themselves an element of redistribution. Child benefits again can be used to illustrate this point. It would be possible to help families with low incomes by redistributing the amount now spent on Family Allowances so as to give more to those at the bottom and less to the rich. As a result the budgetary cost might be small or non-existent. However, it would mean that the burden of helping low income families fell on the rich with children and not on the rich without children, and this might not be regarded as wholly equitable.

Thirdly, the new scheme may impose *indirect* as well as *direct* costs on the community through its effect on work incentives or on saving. It may be argued that the method by which the transfer to those with low incomes is made, or the method by which the necessary revenue is raised, would lead people to work less (or to save less) with consequent additional costs for the community. Since this argument is one which is used frequently, I have discussed in each case the possible effect of the reform on work incentives or (in the case of pensions) on savings. In preparation for this discussion, I have outlined in the next section some of the most relevant considerations for decisions about work effort.

Finally, the new scheme may involve an increase in the costs of administration — for the Government, for employers, for the individual recipient or tax payer. The extent of the additional cost is, however, very difficult to estimate, and although this is an important subject, it is not one that I discuss at any length.

A Broad Approach

From this discussion, it should be clear that the evaluation of proposals for reform is not a simple matter of adding up costs and benefits — even if the information required to do that accurately were available. Both benefits and costs have many dimensions. This is particularly true of the costs of a scheme, since we have to take account not only of the revenue required, but also of clashes with other objectives of Government policy — such as securing an equitable distribution of income above the poverty line or raising the level of savings. In assessing the benefits, account must be taken of the effect on people in different circumstances — to say nothing of the fact that the 'benefit' given by an extra £1 of income will depend on whether it is given 'of right' or through a means test.

In what follows, I have tried to consider both costs and benefits in the broadest terms, although the limitations of space and time mean that I have not explored them as fully as I should like.

3. WORK INCENTIVES

In 1771 Arthur Young remarked that everyone but an idiot knew that the poor must be kept poor, or they would not work.[1] Although views nowadays are less extreme, one objection that is frequently raised to proposals to reform the social security system is that they would reduce the incentive to work. In this section, I review some of the considerations underlying decisions about work effort as a basis for discussing the possible disincentive effect of different schemes.

The disincentive effect of a scheme might take one of two forms: it might lead a person to work shorter hours (or if he is on piece-rate to work less intensively), or it might lead him to stop work altogether. In discussing the effect on work effort, it may be useful therefore to distinguish two separate decisions: whether or not to enter the labour force, and how many hours to work.

The Decision Whether to Work

It is of course arguable how far this decision is relevant at all to people without private incomes — apart from the obvious cases of married women and those over retirement age. The social security regulations include provisions designed to prevent people remaining 'voluntarily' unemployed while receiving benefits. Able-bodied men can be disqualified from National Insurance benefit for refusing fresh work without just cause, and sanctions are also employed under

---

[1] See J.R. Poynter, *Society and Pauperism — English Ideas on Poor Relief, 1795–1834* (Routledge & Kegan Paul, 1969), p. xvi.

Supplementary Benefits (including of course the wage stop).

However, the picture of the 'workshy' man living on social security benefits is one that many people appear to believe to be true. The Government itself seems to be in two minds about the importance of this phenomenon. The Minister of Social Security recently argued that:[1]

'High social security benefits relative to wages presents a new moral dilemma to the individual worker. If he is unemployed for a considerable period, our laws say that he cannot receive as much in social security benefits as he would if he were in work. But he may be working hard for very little more than he would have if he were not in work. What is remarkable is that only a fractional proportion of low earners in this situation do seek to evade their responsibilities.'

On the other hand, the Government felt sufficiently concerned about the problem to introduce recently new sanctions against unemployed single men under 45 who had been drawing Supplementary Benefit for 4 or more weeks.[2]

As far as the disincentive effect of social security benefits is concerned, the Minister's analysis is theoretically correct: the incentive to return to work will depend (other things being equal) on the gap between a man's earnings when at work and his income when out of work. A reform of the social security system which had the effect of narrowing this gap might, therefore, lead to an increase in 'voluntary' unemployment; similarly one which widened this gap, as for example by paying higher child allowances to those in work, might reduce the problem of the 'workshy'.

The significance of this effect depends critically on the magnitude of the problem of the 'workshy'. The evidence from official surveys of the long-term unemployed does in fact suggest that the Minister was correct in saying that they were only a 'fractional proportion'. A survey by the Ministry of Labour in 1964 of the reasons for the difficulty in placing unemployed men showed that in only 24 000 out of 237 000 cases was the man's attitude to work regarded as a difficulty, and lack of financial incentive was mentioned in only 3 600 cases.[3] A more detailed enquiry was carried out by the National Assistance Board in 1956, covering unemployed men receiving assistance who were under 60 and who had been unemployed for two months or more.[4] Only 7% of these men were regarded by the Board's interviewing officers as 'workshy', and even of these three-fifths had some

---

1   *The Times*, 10 September 1968, p. 1.

2   See *Annual Report of Department of Health and Social Security for 1968*, op. cit., p. 251–2.

3   Ministry of Labour, 'Characteristics of the Unemployed: Survey Results', *Ministry of Labour Gazette*, 1966.

4   *Report of the National Assistance Board for the Year Ended 31st December 1956* (H.M.S.O., 1957).

physical or mental disability. The Board concluded that 'Wilful idleness as distinct from an understandable lack of keenness arising from physical or mental disability or other causes would seem to account for the lengthy unemployment in very few cases indeed'.[1]

This evidence suggests that the problem of the 'workshy' is at present very largely a figment of the public imagination, and my own feeling would be that an increase in the social security benefits paid to those out of work would not be very likely to lead to any radical change in this situation.

The Decision How Many Hours to Work

This second aspect of decisions about work effort is the one that normally receives most attention, and since there is already an extensive literature on the subject, I shall discuss it only briefly.[2]

The usual treatment is based on the assumption that a person has some degree of freedom in choosing his working hours (or work intensity) and that this choice reflects his preferences between income and leisure. On this basis we can distinguish between the *income* and *substitution* effects of a particular scheme. The income effect relates to the change in his total net income (after taxes and social security benefits). If we assume that leisure is a 'normal' good (a person consumes more of it as his net income rises), then he will tend to work less if he is better off. The substitution effect relates to the net earnings from an additional hour's work — if this is reduced by the introduction of a new scheme, then it too will tend to lead him to reduce his hours of work.

There is unfortunately very little empirical evidence on which we can draw in assessing the effect on work effort. There have been a number of studies of the effect of income taxation, but these have failed to produce any very definite conclusions and even if they had shown a definite disincentive (or incentive) effect, this would not have allowed us to distinguish between the income and substitution effects.

---

1 The discussion of this paragraph draws heavily on an article 'Where are the "workshy"?' in *Poverty — Journal of the Child Poverty Action Group*, Winter 1968. *The Annual Report of the Department of Health and Social Security for 1968* (op. cit.) describes a special enquiry carried out in January 1968 into the problem of the 'workshy', which concluded that there was 'some reason to think that in a wide range of occupations some people might be too ready to rely on the supplementary benefit scheme'. However, not only is this conclusion highly qualified (clearly *some* people are bound to abuse the scheme, the important question is how many), but the enquiry on which it was based was much less detailed than those carried out earlier by the National Assistance Board.

2 For a recent review of the empirical evidence, see C.V. Brown and D.A. Dawson, *Personal Taxation, Incentives and Tax Reform* (P.E.P., 1969). For a good discussion of the theoretical issues in the context of negative income taxation, see P.A. Diamond, 'Negative Taxes and the Poverty Problem — A Review Article', *National Tax Journal*, September 1968.

It can be questioned, however, whether the analysis given above is really adequate. Firstly, the assumption that a person is free to adjust his hours of work may be unrealistic for a large proportion of the labour force. Not only are standard working hours fixed in many occupations, but also there are institutional constraints on the possibilities for overtime (including compulsory overtime) and moonlighting. Of course, standard working hours are probably (in the long-run) responsive to the number of hours people want to work, but this will be a collective decision. This means that a reform which affects only part of the labour force (such as families with children) may have no impact on the standard working week — even though the families affected would like to work less, they would be outnumbered by those unaffected by the change. It should also be noted that standard working hours are likely to be more important at the lower end of the income scale, and for this reason we may expect any possible disincentive effect to be smaller if it is those with low incomes that are primarily affected.

More fundamentally, it has been argued that the emphasis on money incentives is misplaced. To quote Professor Townsend,[1]

> 'the controls over work are in fact much more social than economic. The structure of society exerts powerful constraints on men both to work and to adjust to different types and earning-levels of work. A man works to preserve the respect of his wife, children, friends and neighbours, to fulfill the psychological needs induced by the customs and expectations of a life-time and to occupy time fruitfully and replenish the stock of information, cautionary tales and anecdotes which he requires to maintain his participation in the web of social relations.'

While this view is more appealing than that of purely pecuniary incentives put forward by Arthur Young, again we do not have the empirical evidence required to draw any definite conclusion.

Finally, I would stress that many of those concerned with the question of incentives appear to consider that any reduction in work effort must be undesirable and to attach no value to leisure. The indirect cost of any effect on incentives is however that it reduces work effort below the *socially optimal level*, and relates only to the difference between the social value of labour time and that of leisure.

---

[1] P. Townsend, 'The difficulties of negative income tax', in *Social Services for All?* Part Four, Fabian Tract 385.

7　New Pensions and the Old

This chapter is concerned with the reform of the social security system to help old people with low incomes and with the new pension schemes that have been proposed.

1.　'BACK TO BEVERIDGE' PENSIONS

In Chapter 1, I have emphasised that it was an essential aspect of the Beveridge Plan that the National Insurance Retirement Pension would provide a guaranteed income at the national minimum level and people would not be forced to rely on National Assistance because the insurance benefits were insufficient. In this section I examine the implications of the Government's adopting (rather belatedly) this recommendation of Beveridge and raising the Retirement Pension to the level of the assistance scale. This discussion will serve as useful reference standard in the subsequent discussion of the National Superannuation scheme and other reforms, and is also of interest in its own right, since a 'Back to Beveridge' policy of this type has recently been advocated by Sir Paul Chambers.[1]

Since the Supplementary Benefit Scale includes housing expenditure, payment of Retirement Pensions to every pensioner at that level would only be possible if details of each individual household's rent were available. I shall concentrate therefore on the objective of raising pensions to the assistance scale *including average rent*.[2] The level of the Retirement Pension and of the Supplementary Benefit scale (I.A.R.) in June 1969 were:

	Retirement Pension			Supplementary Benefit (I.A.R.)		
	£	*s.*	*d.*	£	*s.*	*d.*
Single person	4	10	0	6	11	0
Married couple	7	6	0	9	14	0

1　*The Beveridge Memorial Lecture, 1969*, to be published by the Institute of Statisticians. Also, 'An opportunity to simplify the pension system', *The Times*, June 9, 1969.

2　Sir Paul Chambers appears to favour the payment of an allowance for actual housing expenditure in conjunction with the Retirement Pension. This is intended as an interim measure until 'there is a freer market for housing'. However, he gives no indication as to how even in this interim period the necessary information about rents is to be collected.

(From November 1969, the Retirement Pension is to be increased by 10s. for a single person and 16s. for a married couple. At the same time, the Supplementary Benefit scale is due to rise by 5s. and 8s. respectively.) To raise the Retirement Pension to the Supplementary Benefit scale (I.A.R.) would mean, therefore, an increase of 46% for a single person and 33% for a married couple. Even at the post-November 1969 levels, it would still mean increases of 36% and 25% respectively.

A 'Back to Beveridge' Increase and Those with Low Incomes

Raising the Retirement Pension to the assistance level including average rent would not, of course, eliminate the need for Supplementary Benefits. Those pensioners with above average rent, or with exceptional needs (such as for special diet, extra heating or domestic assistance), would still fall below the poverty line unless they claimed Supplementary Benefits. It would, however, do a great deal to help pensioners with low incomes and would substantially reduce their dependance on Supplementary Benefits. From the information provided by the Ministry of Pensions and National Insurance enquiry into the financial circumstances of Retirement Pensioners in 1965, it can be estimated what would then have been the effect of a 'Back to Beveridge' increase in pensions. Table 7.1 shows two such estimates. From the first estimate (line 2), it can be seen that increasing the pension to the National Assistance level (I.A.R.) would have reduced the proportion of pensioners falling below the National Assistance scale

Table 7.1.   Effect of a 'Back to Beveridge' Increase in Retirement Pensions – June 1965

	Retirement Pensioners with incomes[a] below National Assistance scale			
	Married Couples ('000s) %	Single Men ('000s) %	Single Women ('000s) %	All Retirement Pensioners ('000s) %
1. Retirement Pension as in June 1965	410 29	210 35	1 520 55	2 560 41
2. Retirement Pension raised to National Assistance scale (IAR)	175 12	95 16	680 25	1 125 18
3. Retirement Pension raised by 36% single 25% couple	110 8	60 10	425 15	700 11

Source : *Financial and other circumstances of Retirement Pensioners*, Table III.4

Notes : a Before allowing for any National Assistance in payment. The figures are adjusted for non-response and exclude those with incomes below the assistance scale whose savings disqualify them from receiving National Assistance.

by over a half: from 41% to 18%. The number of Retirement Pensioners falling below the poverty line would be reduced from 2½ million to just over 1 million. The second estimate given in Table 7.1 (line 3) shows the effect of raising the Retirement Pension by the same percentage as would be required to reach the Supplementary Benefit scale (I.A.R.) in 1969 (after the November increases). The proportion with incomes below the assistance scale in this case is only 11%.

Such a policy would, though, do nothing to help those who do not qualify for a Retirement Pension. As we saw in Chapter 3, in June 1965 there were some 480 000 people in this position (apart from those who were receiving other National Insurance benefits or not yet retired). These people are likely to have low incomes (a high proportion are at present receiving assistance), and they are mostly old and therefore likely to have greater needs. There is a strong case for including in a 'Back to Beveridge' policy the extension of Retirement Pensions to this group, as has in fact been suggested several times in Parliament.[1]

The Cost of a 'Back to Beveridge' Policy

The principal objection to the policy of raising the Retirement Pension to the Supplementary Benefit level is that it would be extremely costly. In June 1969 there were around 7 million Retirement Pensioners, of whom some two thirds were single persons. If the pension were to have been increased to the Supplementary Benefit level (I.A.R.), the annual gross cost would then have been of the order of £650 million, which would represent an increase of about a quarter in total government expenditure on social security. Moreover, we have not allowed for the cost of extending Retirement Pensions to those who are too old to qualify.

Against this gross cost should be set the saving from the increased income tax that would be paid by better-off pensioners and from the Supplementary Benefits that would no longer be necessary. It seems likely that the first of these would be moderately small, since a large proportion of pensioners do not at present pay any tax. For example, a single pensioner whose only income was the Retirement Pension would still be £85 per year below the income at which he would have to begin paying tax — even after the pension had been increased to the assistance level. In Appendix E, I have made a detailed estimate of the saving from tax and from Supplementary Benefits, and the resulting 'net' cost is given below:

		£ million (1969–70)
	Gross cost of higher pensions	650
Less	Saving on Supplementary Benefits	−205
Less	Increase in income tax yield	−75
Plus	Gross cost of extending Retirement Pensions to those not covered	+125
	NET COST	495

---

[1] See *The Economist*, 17 April 1965.

Even after allowing for the savings on tax and Supplementary Benefits, the budgetary cost of the 'Back to Beveridge' scheme is still considerable. In revenue terms alone this would mean an increase of 1s. 9d.–2s. in the standard rate of income tax; or if the revenue were to be provided out of National Insurance contributions, shared equally between employer and employee, then the employee's flat-rate contribution would have to rise by around 5s. If we consider the effect on the level of demand, then the required increase in contributions (or income tax) will almost certainly be larger, since the pensioners' marginal propensity to consume is undoubtedly higher than that of the contributors.[1]

'Back to Beveridge' — Conclusions

The effects of this policy can be summarised very briefly. It would do a great deal to help Retirement Pensioners with low incomes but would not eliminate the need for Supplementary Benefits and the budgetary and real cost would be high.

2. NATIONAL SUPERANNUATION

The approach adopted by the Government to the reform of our pension system is quite different from the 'Back to Beveridge' policy discussed in Section 1. Under the proposal for National Superannuation which was announced in January 1969, the present Retirement and graduated pensions would be replaced by a pension which was wholly earnings-related.[2] These proposals were heralded as 'the most fundamental changes' since National Insurance, and they undoubtedly have far-reaching implications for the development of the social security system. However, it is not my intention here to try and evaluate the plan as a whole, and I shall concentrate solely on its impact on old people with low incomes. I shall not, therefore, discuss such issues as whether the state should provide earnings-related pensions rather than their being left to (improved) occupational schemes.[3]

Description of the National Superannuation Scheme

When the proposed National Superannuation scheme reached full operation, the pension received by a man retiring in a given year would depend on the relationship between his lifetime average earnings and the national average level

---

1 For a discussion of the effect of increases in National Insurance benefits and contributions on the level of demand, see W.A.B. Hopkin and W.A.H. Godley, 'An Analysis of Tax Changes', *National Institute Economic Review*, May 1965.

2 *National Superannuation and Social Insurance*, op. cit.

3 For a good discussion of the plan as a whole, see R.M. Titmuss, 'Superannuation for all', *New Society*, 27 February 1969. For a rather different view, see Sir Paul Chambers, *The Beveridge Memorial Lecture, 1969*, op. cit.

of earnings at that date.[1] Suppose that a man retiring in April 1968 had lifetime average earnings of £18, whereas the national average was then £22. His pension would be 60% of his lifetime average earnings up to half the national average (£11) plus 25% of the remainder: i.e.

$$60\% \times £11 + 25\% \times £7 = £8 \; 7s. \; 0d.$$

(The basic formula is 60% of lifetime average earnings up to half the national average and then 25% on the remaining earnings up to the scheme's ceiling of one and a half times national average earnings). For the purpose of calculating each person's lifetime average earnings, his earnings in each year would be revalued to take account of changes in the national average level of earnings — see below.

The pension of a single woman is calculated in the same way as for a single man. For a married woman, the pension may be calculated in whichever of two ways is the more favourable to her: (i) on the basis of her own lifetime earnings (as for men and single women), or (ii) a flat-rate pension as at present plus an earnings-related addition of 25% of her own lifetime average earnings. The pension of a widow over 60 would be based on her own earnings-related pension or on the personal rate of pension which her husband was receiving when he died — again whichever is the more favourable to her.[2]

As with the graduated pension scheme, there would be provisions for employers with occupational pension schemes to contract out of the National Superannuation. The full details of these provisions have not yet been decided. However, the Government is apparently envisaging a system of *partial* contracting-out under which both contributions and pensions could be reduced by a percentage, providing the occupational scheme guaranteed a pension which was comparable with the amount deducted from the state pension.

The White Paper makes a great deal of the fact that National Superannuation would be 'dynamic' and the pensions 'inflation-proofed', and in these respects the scheme does represent a radical departure from the existing state pensions and from nearly all occupational pension schemes. It is, however, important to make clear exactly what these claims mean, and to distinguish two quite separate aspects of the scheme:

(a) the treatment of a person's contributions when determining the pension to be awarded when he retires,

(b) the extent to which his pension is adjusted *after retirement* for changes in prices and in the general level of earnings.

---

[1] For the purposes of the National Superannuation scheme, the term 'national average earnings' is taken to mean the average earnings of adult male manual workers in manufacturing and certain other industries, as obtained from the Department of Employment and Productivity's half-yearly enquiry into earnings.

[2] This is only a brief description of the provisions of the scheme; fuller details are provided in the White Paper, Chapter 3 and Appendix 1.

In calculating the pensions to be awarded under the National Superannuation scheme, a man's contributions would be revalued to take account of the change in national average earnings since they were paid. For example, if earnings doubled between 1955 and 1968, £1 contributed in 1955 would count for twice as much as £1 contributed in 1968. This means that a person earning exactly the national average earnings in each year of his life would receive a pension based on national average earnings in the year he retires. In this respect the scheme does represent a radical departure from the present graduated pension, where contributions earn a certain cash pension and £1 contributed when the scheme started in 1961 counts for exactly the same as £1 contributed in 1968.[1]

In determining the pension to be awarded at retirement, the scheme would, therefore, take full account of rising standards of living. However, after a person retires the pension would not necessarily be adjusted for changes in the national average level of earnings. All that the Government commits itself to in the White Paper is a biannual review of pensions in payment which would compensate for increased prices. Above that 'the actual amount of improvement ... must be left for decision by the Government of the day'.[2] The inflation-proofing itself is of course a major improvement. Nonetheless, if the Government did no more than compensate for rising prices, a pensioner would find himself getting worse and worse off relative to the rest of the population as he grew older. A person who retired 20 years ago with lifetime earnings equal to the national average would be considerably worse off than a person retiring today with lifetime earnings equal to the national average. Moreover, it should be emphasised that limiting the increases to inflation-proofing, would be considerably less generous than the actual increases which have taken place in the Retirement Pension: in 1948 the Retirement Pension was 18% of average earnings in manufacturing but by 1968 it had risen slightly to 20%.[3]

It is clear that National Superannuation is fully earnings-related as far as (a) is concerned − the up-dating of contributions − but not in the case of (b) − the treatment of pensions in payment. This has important implications for those with low incomes, to which I return later.

---

[1] In other words, the rate of interest used in compounding the contributions is zero under the graduated scheme, but equal to the rate of growth of national average earnings under National Superannuation.

[2] *National Superannuation and Social Insurance*, op. cit., p. 31.

[3] Incidentally, it is interesting to note that this performance cannot be matched by the private scheme quoted by Sir Paul Chambers as an example of the generous treatment of pensions in payment under occupational schemes (*Beveridge Memorial Lecture*, 1969, op. cit.). Between 1950 and 1969 the occupational pension rose by 150% whereas national average earnings rose by over 200%.

The Full Effect of National Superannuation: (a) Pensions Awarded

The Government plans to introduce National Superannuation in April 1972, but it would not reach full operation at once. Rights to the new pensions would be built up gradually over a 20 year transition period and it would not be until 1992 that the first pensions were awarded at the full rate. I begin by examining the implications of the scheme for old people with low incomes *when it is fully operational*, and then turn to the problems of the more immediate future.

In order to illustrate the full effect of the scheme, the White Paper shows what pensions would have been awarded in 1968 if the scheme had then been in full operation. In Figure 7.1, I have shown the National Superannuation pension that would have been received by people with different lifetime earnings levels and compared this with the flat-rate Retirement Pension and the Supplementary Benefit scale (I.A.R.) in force in April 1968.[1] With the National Superannuation scheme there is no minimum pension, but a single person would in fact have received more than the current flat-rate pension if his earnings over his lifetime had averaged more than the equivalent of £7 10s. in 1968. His National Superannuation pension would have been above the Supplementary Benefit scale (I.A.R.) had his average lifetime earnings exceeded £10 5s. The position of married couples depends on the extent to which the wife has acquired her own rights to a pension. Figure 7.1 is drawn on the assumption that she receives only the flat-rate pension. On this *minimum* assumption, the couple will receive a pension above the Supplementary Benefit scale (I.A.R.) providing that the man has average lifetime earnings of more than £10 12s.

From the recent enquiry by the Department of Employment and Productivity into earnings in September 1968, we can estimate the proportion of old people whose pension on retirement under the National Superannuation scheme would be at least equal to the Supplementary Benefit level (I.A.R.). If we take the figure of £10 10s. as that required by both single and married men, then from the results of the enquiry we can estimate that only 0.8% of all adult men working full-time would have had earnings below this level in April 1968.[2] On this basis, very few of the men would receive a National Superannuation pension below the assistance scale. Moreover, there are two reasons for expecting this to be an *over*-estimate of the proportion falling below:

(a) the earnings reported in the enquiry relate to one week and it seems likely that this leads to an over-statement of the proportion with low *lifetime* earnings. For example, a man nearing retirement may be earning very much less than he was a few years ago (particularly in the case of manual workers).

---

1 In this calculation (and those following) no allowance is made for any addition to the basic pension such as that earned by remaining at work after the minimum retirement age.

2 This is estimated from the enquiry by adjusting for the increase in average earnings between April and September 1968. The position of the self-employed is not considered here.

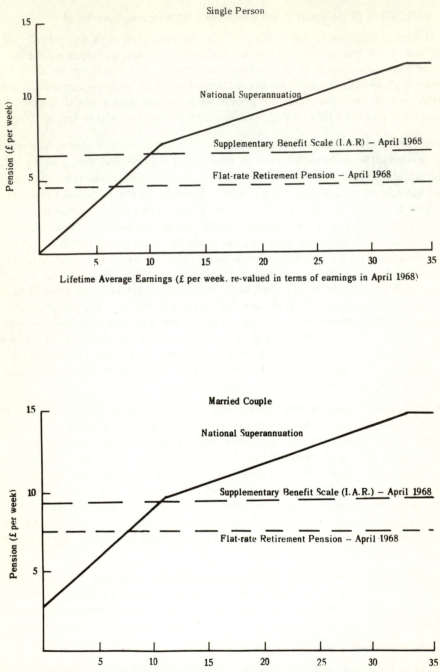

Figure 7.1.   National Superannuation Pensions when the Scheme is in Full
Operation

Note: For married couples the pension is shown on the assumption that the wife
receives only the flat-rate £2 16s. 0d.; if she has contributed in her own
right, then the pension will be higher.

(b) as already noted, the assumption that the wife has earned no pension in her own right means that the pension received by married couples is probably under-stated.

In the case of single women pensioners, we must distinguish widows from those who have never been married.[1] Since the former would receive a pension at least as high as that received by their husband before he died, we can assume that the proportion with a pension below the assistance scale would be no higher than the 0.8% suggested earlier. However, those women who have never been married would receive a pension based solely on their own earnings record. From the earnings survey it is clear that a very much higher proportion of women earn less than £10 5s. − in April 1968 there were an estimated 30% of adult (18 and over) women working full-time who earned less than this amount. Indeed some 6% earned less than the £7 10s. required to give a pension at the present flat-rate level. While the lifetime average earnings for unmarried women are probably higher than these figures for *all* women, it seems quite possible that the National Superannuation scheme would be much less generous to women who rely on their own earnings record to provide their pensions.[2] One of the consequences of an earnings-related pension is that it preserves in old age the inequality between men's and women's pay before retirement, and as far as unmarried women are concerned the new scheme hardly justifies its claim that it is a 'new deal for women'.

These calculations show what the effect of the National Superannuation scheme would have been if it had been in full operation in 1968. In order to project these results forward to 1992, when the scheme would in fact reach maturity, we have to make some assumptions about the future course of the Supplementary Benefit scale. In the past the assistance scale has tended to rise approximately in line with the national average level of earnings and if anything has tended to rise faster (as shown in Figure 1.2). For this reason, I assume when discussing the future impact of the National Superannuation scheme that the Supplementary Benefit scale (I.A.R.) will bear the same relationship to national average earnings as it did in April 1968. If we make this assumption, then we can deduce from the earlier analysis that less than 1% of couples, single men and widows would be awarded pensions below the assistance scale (I.A.R.) although the proportion of unmarried women falling below might be considerably higher.

The Full Effect of National Superannuation : (b) Pensions in Payment

So far we have only discussed the pensions that would be *awarded* under the National Superannuation scheme; we must also examine what would happen to *pensions in payment*. The White Paper only commits the Government to maintaining the real value of pensions in payment, although it would of course be open to it

---

1 The position for divorced women and separated wives is not discussed here.

2 Although it should be noted that the scheme is more generous than the graduated scheme, which gives lower benefits per £ of contributions for women.

to do more. In what follows I examine the implications of two alternative policies :

(i) pensions in payment are increased at the rate of increase of national average earnings.

(ii) the Government goes no further than its minimum commitment of maintaining the real value of pensions in payment.

The implications of the first policy are straightforward to analyse. A person's pension would remain the same percentage of current national average earnings, and if it is above the assistance scale when awarded, then it would remain so throughout the person's retirement (under our assumption about the future Supplementary Benefit scale). This means that fewer than 1% of *all* pensioners (apart from unmarried women) would receive pensions below the assistance scale. On this basis, the need for Supplementary Benefits would be reduced very considerably, although it would still be required for those with above average rent or exceptional needs (as in the case of the 'Back to Beveridge' policy).

If, however, the Government followed the less generous policy of only increasing the pensions in payment so as to maintain their real value, then the National Superannuation scheme would be very much less effective in helping old people. Suppose for the sake of argument that the scheme had been fully operative in 1948. A person then retiring with lifetime average earnings equal to half the national average would have received a pension on the National Superannuation formula of some £2 2s. – or substantially higher than the Retirement Pension which he in fact got under the National Insurance scheme (£1 6s.). If this National Superannuation pension had then been increased in line with the retail price index, in April 1968 it would have been £4 6s. – or 4s. *less* than the flat-rate Retirement Pension. In other words, while he would have been better off with National Superannuation at the outset, if he lived to be over 80 then his pension would have dropped below the Retirement Pension. Moreover, he would receive only 65% of the pension awarded to someone retiring in 1968 whose lifetime average earnings were also equal to half the national average.

The adoption of this less generous policy means that even though a person's pension would be above the assistance scale when he retired, it may fall below as he gets older and the assistance standard rises in real terms. Since a person's needs are likely to increase with age rather than to fall, this would be an extremely unsatisfactory outcome.

Using the information from the 1968 earnings survey, I have estimated the overall proportion of pensioners falling below the assistance scale (I.A.R.) if the Government only maintains the real value of pensions in payment – see Table 7.2. These estimates are based on our assumption that the Supplementary Benefit scale (I.A.R.) rises in line with earnings (the other assumptions are described in the notes to the table). Overall, nearly a third of the pensioners would receive pensions below the Supplementary Benefit scale (I.A.R.) – even with the scheme in full operation. The proportion receiving less than the assistance scale rises sharply with age – from 12% in the case of those aged 65–9 to nearly 90% of those aged over 85. The difference between single women and the other groups is also striking; this reflects the lower earnings of women and the fact that they both retire earlier and live longer.

Table 7.2.   Effect of Government's Limiting Increases in Pensions in Payment to Maintaining their Real Value (When National Superannuation Scheme is in Full Operation)

Age Group	Proportion receiving National Superannuation pension below Supplementary Benefit level (I.A.R.)			
	Married Couples	Single Men	Single Women	All Pensioners
	%	%	%	%
60–64	–	–	18	18
65–69	1	1	34	12
70–74	8	5	52	24
75–79	26	21	68	44
80–84	46	44	82	64
85 and over	72	67	100	89
ALL AGES	12	20	51	30

Notes :   The distribution of earnings is taken from the Department of Employment and Productivity survey in September 1968, op. cit., Table 1, which relates to all adults in full-time employment. It is assumed that real earnings rise at the annual rate of 2½%.

In the case of married couples it is assumed that the wife receives the flat-rate pension (and that this is increased in line with earnings).

The distribution of pensioners by age and type (couples, single men, etc.) is based on *Financial and other circumstances of Retirement Pensioners*, op. cit., Table BR. 1.

It is assumed that those in the age group $65 + x$ to $69 + x$ retired $x + 2$ years ago in the case of couples and single men, and $x + 7$ years ago in the case of single women. For married couples the age shown is that of the husband.

In the case of single women the breakdown between those dependent on their own contributions and those receiving a pension on their husband's insurance is based on *Financial and other circumstances of Retirement Pensioners*, op. cit., Table III. 15.

No allowance is made for any addition to the basic pension such as that earned by remaining at work after the minimum retirement age.

No allowance is made for people who contract out or are self-employed.

115

I have concentrated so far on the effect of the scheme when it is fully in operation, which would not be until 1992 (as at present planned). I now consider the implications of the proposal for those retiring before 1992 — or for those aged 42 plus in 1969 (or 37 plus if they are women).

Those now retired (or retiring before 1972) would not, of course, receive any benefit from National Superannuation. Those retiring between 1972 and 1992 would receive less than the rates set out above. Under the transition formula, a person retiring x years after the scheme is introduced would receive

$x/20$ of the new benefit $+ [1 - x/20]$ of the benefit to which he is entitled under the present scheme.

So that a person retiring in 1977 would receive a quarter of the National Superannuation pension plus three-quarters of the present pension (flat-rate and graduated). Table 7.3 shows the pension (as a percentage of lifetime average earnings) awarded to people retiring at different dates in the transition period.

Table 7.3.   National Superannuation Pensions Awarded to People Retiring
1976—92

Date of Retirement	Pension as a % of his lifetime average earnings awarded to a single person with lifetime average weekly earnings (in terms of April 1968 levels) of			
	£11 %	£15 %	£20 %	£25 %
1976	45	35	29	24
1980	49	39	32	28
1984	53	43	36	32
1988	56	47	40	36
1992	60	51	44	40

Notes : It is assumed that the flat-rate pension would be increased in line with national average earnings.

The graduated pension is calculated on the following assumptions : (i) the person is not contracted out, (ii) his earnings have risen at the same rate as the national average, and (iii) that the contribution rates remain at their post-November 1969 level until 1972.

No allowance is made for any addition to the basic pension such as that earned by remaining at work after the minimum retirement age.

The last line (1992) shows the pension that would be awarded when the scheme is in full operation. The table also shows the relationship between the pension and the Supplementary Benefit scale (I.A.R.) — on the assumption that the latter rises in line with national average earnings. Above the heavy line, the pension

Table 7.4.   Pensions below the Supplementary Benefit Level (I.A.R.) in 1980, 1990 and 2000 with the National Superannuation Scheme.

| | Proportion with pension below Supplementary Benefit (I.A.R.) | | | |
Year	Married couples %	Single men %	Single women %	All pensioners %
1980	79	86	95	88
1990	23	37	52	38
2000	2	5	26	13

Notes :   See notes to Table 7.2.

It was assumed that the flat-rate pension would be increased in line with national average earnings, as would the Supplementary Benefit scale (I.A.R.).

The graduated pension was calculated on the assumptions described in Note (2) to Table 7.3.

It was assumed that widows receiving pensions on their husbands' insurance were married to men of the same age as themselves.

is less than the Supplementary Benefit scale (I.A.R.), and it is clear that for lower paid workers it would be quite a long time before the pension was above this level. A person earning the equivalent of £15 a week in April 1968 would, for example, not reach this level if he retired before 1982.

Under the transition provisions of the National Superannuation scheme, it would therefore be a number of years before the pensions awarded to those retiring reached the assistance scale. This in turn means that for a much longer period there would still be a substantial proportion of pensioners below this level. In Table 7.4 I have estimated the proportion of pensioners receiving pensions below the Supplementary Benefit level (I.A.R.) in the years 1980, 1990 and 2000. These estimates are based on the assumption that the Government would follow the more generous of the two policies with regard to pensions in payment and would raise both the National Superannuation component and the Retirement Pension in line with increases in national average earnings.[1] The percentage receiving a pension below the assistance scale should, therefore, be compared with a figure of 1% for couples, single men and widows (and rather more for unmarried women) when the scheme is in full operation.

According to the results set out in Table 7.4, over a third of the pensioner population would be receiving a pension below the assistance scale in 1990 and even in the year 2000 one in eight pensioners would still fall below this level. And it should be stressed that these estimates are based on the most favourable

---

1 Although the graduated pension would remain fixed in cash terms.

117

assumption about the Government's treatment of pensions in payment; if it only fulfilled its minimum commitment of maintaining their real value, then the position would look considerably worse.

The Cost of National Superannuation

The National Superannuation scheme would clearly lead to a large increase in expenditure on state pensions. In an Appendix to the White Paper, the Government Actuary has estimated the additional cost (above that of the present pension schemes) in terms of April 1968 earnings levels (on the assumption of no contracting out). By the year 2002–3, this would reach £1 097 million – a figure which makes even the cost of the 'Back to Beveridge' policy seem quite small.

The cost of the National Superannuation scheme would be met (in the early years more than met) by the new contributions, which would replace the present flat-rate and graduated contributions. The employee's contributions would be proportional to earnings (at the rate of 6¾%) up to the scheme's ceiling of 1½ times national average earnings. The employer would pay the same percentage contribution with no ceiling.[1]

The Government clearly feels that the earnings-related nature of the benefits makes it possible for the extra revenue to be raised in this way whereas this would not be the case with flat-rate increases of a 'Back to Beveridge' type.[2] This is in part a question of the effect on incentives and in this the Government may well be right (although it is a far from straightforward matter). However, it is to a large extent a question of political judgement about which I have little useful to say.

National Superannuation – Conclusions

It seems fair to conclude from this analysis that the proposed National Superannuation scheme would eventually do a great deal to help old people with low incomes. When the scheme was in full operation, most old people would qualify at retirement for a pension above the Supplementary Benefit scale (including average rent), and if the Government increased pensions in payment in line with rising national average earnings, then they would remain above the assistance scale throughout their retirement. National Superannuation would play a very important role of helping those old people who are not receiving occupational pensions and who, as we have seen, are more likely to fall below the poverty line. In this it would prove very much more effective than the present graduated pension scheme.

---

1 4¾% of the employee's contribution would be for National Superannuation; the remaining 2% would be for social insurance benefits, industrial injury benefits and a contribution to the National Health Service. In the case of the employer's contribution, 4½% would be for National Superannuation, 2% for social insurance benefits etc., and ¼% for the Redundancy Fund.

2 See, for example, the comments of the Secretary of State for Social Services on the proposals of Sir Paul Chambers (quoted by Chambers in the Times article referred to above).

118

However, this conclusion must be qualified in three major respects :

(a) Although the scheme would provide virtually all men and married women with a pension above the assistance scale, a much larger proportion of unmarried women would fall below.

(b) The effectiveness of National Superannuation would depend critically on the Government's policy with regard to raising pensions in payment. If this was limited to the minimum commitment of maintaining the real value, then even when the scheme was fully matured, over a third of all pensioners would receive less than the assistance scale. Moreover, it is the oldest pensioners who would receive the lowest pensions.

These qualifications are especially important because they relate to groups which we have seen in Chapter 3 to have particularly low incomes − single women and the very old.

The final qualification is that it would take a very long time before the National Superannuation scheme became fully effective. It would be 1990 before half the pensioners were receiving a pension of at least the Supplementary Benefit scale (including average rent) − and this is on the most favourable assumption about the treatment of pensions in payment. Dorothy Wedderburn's comment on earlier pension legislation applies equally to National Superannuation : 'the recent spate of pension legislation, based on commendable principles, has all too often left a gap between the actual living conditions of the aged today and the goals for future pensioners which are written into the statutes'.[1] For this reason, I discuss in the next section measures designed to provide more immediate benefit to old people with low incomes.

3.   HELPING OLD PEOPLE IN THE IMMEDIATE FUTURE

In this section, I examine some of the possible ways of helping old people during the transition period before the National Superannuation scheme would become fully effective. I begin by considering measures within the framework of the present National Insurance system − raising Retirement Pensions either uniformly or 'selectively' − and then discuss the proposal that there should be a new income supplement scheme for old people.

Uniform Increases in the Retirement Pension

It appears from the increases announced in the 1969 Budget that the solution favoured by the Government is to raise the flat-rate Retirement Pension. In November 1969, the pension is to go up by 10s. for a single person and 16s. for a couple.

---

1 D. Wedderburn, 'Economic Aspects of Ageing', *International Social Science Journal*, 1963.

This increase comes nowhere near the 'Back to Beveridge' increase discussed in Section 1, but it will nonetheless reduce the proportion of Retirement Pensioners living below the Supplementary Benefit scale. From the information provided in the Ministry 1965 enquiry, we can estimate what effect this increase would then have had. In doing so, we must bear in mind that in *real* terms the increase is not very large. If we calculate the real value of the Retirement Pension using the special price index for pensioner households that has recently been published by the Department of Employment and Productivity, then we get the following results :[1]

	Real value (in June 1965 prices)			
	Single Person		Married Couple	
	£	s.	£	s.
June 1965	4	0	6	10
After November 1969 increase	4	6	7	0

So that in real terms, the overall increase between June 1965 and November 1969 is only 6s. for a single person and 10s. for a couple.[2] The second line in Table 7.5 shows what the effect of this increase would have been on the proportion with incomes below the National Assistance scale in June 1965. The proportion would in fact have fallen by less than a quarter, and a third of all Retirement Pensioners would still have had to rely on National Assistance to bring them to the national minimum level.

If we consider the effect of larger increases in the Retirement Pension, then they would, of course, be more effective in reducing the number below the National Assistance scale. The third line in Table 7.5 shows that an increase of 12s. for a single person and 18s. for a couple in June 1965 would have reduced the proportion from 41% to 26%. The gross cost of this increase would have been of the order of £170 million in June 1965. The cost of an equivalent increase in 1969 would be considerably higher than this – both because the number of Retirement Pensioners has increased (by some 10–15%) and because of rising prices.

'Selective' Increases in Retirement Pensions

In Chapter 3 we have seen that some groups of old people are more likely to fall below the poverty line than others – particularly single women and the very old.

---

1 These price indices were published in the *Employment and Productivity Gazette*, June 1969. In the calculations shown it was assumed that there would be no increase in prices between the first quarter of 1969 and November 1969. To the extent that prices do rise over this period, the real increase will be smaller than shown. The price indices exclude housing expenditure.

2 As a percentage of national average earnings, the post-November 1969 pension will be no higher than in 1965.

Table 7.5. Effect of Uniform and 'Selective' Increases in the
Flat-Rate Retirement Pension — June 1965

	Retirement Pensioners with Incomes below National Assistance Scale				Gross Cost of the Increase in June 1965
	Married Couples %	Single Men %	Single Women %	All Retire-ment Pensioners % ('000's)	£ million
1. Retirement Pension as in June 1965	29	35	55	41 2 560	—
2. Retirement Pension increased by 6s. single 10s. couple	22	29	46	33 2 080	90
3. Retirement Pension increased by 12s. single 18s. couple	16	23	36	26 1 620	170
4. Retirement Pension increased by £1 single (no change for couple)	29	16	25	26 1 590	175
5. Retirement Pension in increased by 12s. single 18s. couple PLUS Age-Related increases (see text)	13	16	26	19 1 200	245

Source and Notes — see Table 7.1.

For this reason we ought to consider the possibility that making 'selective' increases in the Retirement Pension so as to give more help to these groups would be a more effective policy than the 'uniform' increases just discussed.

The suggestion that higher pensions should be paid to single women has been made on several occasions by Dorothy Wedderburn.[1] She recognises, however, that in political terms it might be very difficult to pay a lower flat-rate pension to single men than to single women. An alternative is to raise the pension for all single pensioners — both men and women. For example, suppose that instead of raising the pension for a couple by 18s. and that for a single person by 12s., the whole of this money (in gross terms) had been devoted to raising the pension for single persons, which would have given an increase of just under £1 for single pensioners. (This extreme form of discrimination between single pensioners and couples would probably have also been politically infeasible, but it serves to illustrate the possibilities of this approach). The effect of this increase on the proportion of Retirement Pensioners falling below the poverty line is shown in the fourth line of Table 7.5. It would certainly correct the 'balance' between couples and single women in that it reduced the percentage of single women falling below the poverty line to more or less the same level as for married couples. However, in terms of the total Retirement Pensioners below the poverty line, there would be virtually no improvement over the uniform increase.

The second possible 'selective' increase in the Retirement Pension is to give more to older pensioners.[2] This idea is at first sight an attractive one. As we have seen, the proportion of pensioners with incomes below the National Assistance scale in 1965 rose quite markedly with age. Old people tend to have both lower incomes and greater needs. As they get older, they are less able to supplement their pension through earnings and their savings become exhausted.[3] At the same time, they have increased needs for such things as fuel, domestic assistance and special diet.

To illustrate the effect of giving age-related increases in the Retirement Pension, we may examine what would have happened in June 1965 if in addition to uniform increase of 12s. for a single person and 18s. for a couple, there had been the following special increases:

> 10s. for a man over 75 and for a single woman over 70
> 15s. for a man over 80 and for a single woman over 75.

The bottom line of Table 7.5 shows what effect this additional increase would have had on the proportion of Retirement Pensioners falling below the National Assistance scale. This proportion would in fact have been reduced from 28% to

---

1 See, for example, *The Economic Circumstances of Old People*, op. cit., page 105.

2 This was suggested in 1953 by B. Abel-Smith, *The Reform of Social Security*, Fabian Research Series 161.

3 For evidence on the level of savings, see *Financial and other circumstances of Retirement Pensioners*, op. cit., Table II.6.

under 20% — at an additional gross cost of some £75 million. As one would expect, it would provide particular benefit to single women and might be a very effective way of 'indirectly' singling them out for extra help.

An Income Supplement Scheme for Old People

While 'selective' increases in the Retirement Pension may have some success in helping old people with low incomes, they can only provide at best a partial solution to the problems of the transition period before National Superannuation reached full operation. As has been pointed out by Dorothy Wedderburn, a policy

'designed to select a group for help not directly on the basis of an investigation of financial resources, but by some indirect device which it is hoped is closely associated with financial resources, is bound to be inefficient in some sense. This is an argument in favour of some income tax administered supplement to a basic pension level. The argument is that a means test administered through the completion of an income tax return which is compulsory for all, is less objectionable than the present system of national assistance. ... an income tax administered pension might bring considerable saving as compared with the cost of a substantial increase in pensions all round'.[1]

She then discussed the possibilities of an income supplement scheme for old people — which is in fact very similar to the negative income tax discussed in Chapter 9.

Under this 'income supplement' scheme, the pension would be paid in two parts : the present flat-rate (and graduated) pension, and the income supplement. If a person had no other income besides the Retirement Pension, then he would receive the full income supplement. If, however, he had other income (such as an occupational pension), then the supplement would be reduced at the rate of 10s. for every £1 of other income. So that a person with £1 10s. of other income would receive the supplement less 15s. If his other income were more than twice the total income supplement, then he would receive only the present pension.

To illustrate the effect of the income supplement, let us take the Supplementary Benefit scale (I.A.R.) in June 1969 — £6 11s. for a single person, £9 14s. for a couple as the guaranteed income to be provided. The effect on a single pensioner is illustrated in Figure 7.2. The scheme would benefit single pensioners with other income up to £4 2s. per week — or with a total annual income including the Retirement Pension of some £450. Married couples would benefit if their other income was less than £4 16s. per week.

Number of Retirement Pensioners Receiving Income Supplement

From the information provided by the Ministry of Pensions and National Insurance enquiry in 1965, we can estimate how many Retirement Pensioners would have benefitted from the supplement if the scheme had then been in force. Again it is assumed that the minimum income would be set at the assistance scale (I.A.R.).

---

1 *The Aged in the Welfare State*, op. cit., p. 129.

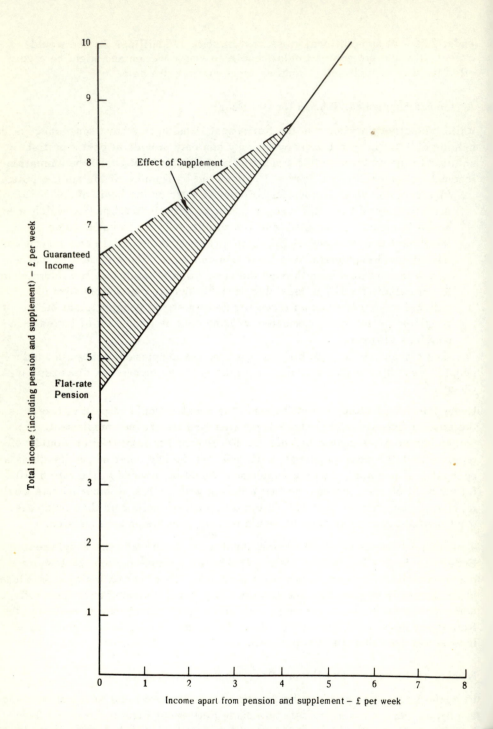

Figure 7.2. Effect of Income Supplement Scheme on Single Pensioner – June 196

Note: No account is taken in this figure of any income tax payable.

Table 7.6.   Retirement Pensioners Eligible for Income Supplement — June 1965

	Eligible for Supplement	
	%	('000's)
Married couples	38	1 080
Single men	57	350
Single women	70	1 940
ALL PENSIONERS	54	3 370

Source : *Financial and Other Circumstances of Retirement Pensioners,*
op. cit., Table BR.1.

Notes : It is assumed that all pensioners receive the flat rate
Retirement Pension plus 5*s.* (to allow for graduated pension,
increments for deferred retirement, etc.).

The figures are adjusted for non-response.

The results set out in Table 7.6 show that approximately a third of married
couples and between a half and three-quarters of single pensioners would have
been eligible for the supplement. We may compare this estimate with that of 75%
of all pensioners given by Mrs. Wedderburn on the basis of her survey of the
incomes of old people in 1962. Since her guaranteed minimum would have been
somewhat more generous than the assistance scale (I.A.R.), and her sample
included old people not receiving Retirement Pensions (whose incomes would
tend to be lower), this figure agrees quite well with our estimate.

Since the income supplement is envisaged as a transitional measure covering the
period before National Superannuation becomes fully effective, it would be
reasonable to include as part of 'other income' the excess of the National
Superannuation pension over the present flat-rate pension. This means that the
proportion of pensioners eligible for the supplement would fall as the National
Superannuation pensions increased. However, the need for supplementation would
still remain even when the National Superannuation scheme reached full operation,
since there would be a small proportion of pensioners whose pensions remain
below the Supplementary Benefit level (I.A.R.) — particularly women whose
pensions depend on their own earnings record.

The Income Supplement and the Present Income Tax Provisions for the Elderly

The income supplement scheme would be administered through the income tax
system. This, of course, raises a number of administrative problems which are
discussed below. First, however, we must consider the income supplement in
relation to the special income tax provisions for old people.

There are at present (1969—70) two special concessions for old people : (a) age
exemption and (b) age relief. Under the former, a single person aged 65 and over
is exempt from tax where his income is less than £425 and a married couple

where their income is less than £680. This means, for example, that a couple under 65 will pay tax of £47 on an earned income of £680 but a couple where one partner is over 65 will pay no tax. This exemption is not a deduction in the usual sense, so that old people with incomes above these levels pay tax in the same way as everybody else. There are, however, provisions for marginal relief to avoid the effective tax rate exceeding 100%, which mean that income in excess of £425 (£680) is effectively taxed at a rate of 9s. in the £ until the tax liability is as high as it would have been without the age exemption. The benefit to a person from the age exemption is shown by the shaded area in Figure 7.3. A single person with earned income benefits from the exemption if it is between £328 and £529, and a married couple if their income is between £482 and £944. The size of the benefit first rises with income and then falls, but at its peak it is fairly small (in the case of a single person it is £23 — or 8s. 9d. a week). The second concession for old people — age relief — applies to investment income where total income is below £1 000, and it allows a person over 65 to claim a 2/9 allowance on unearned as well as earned income up to this level. Since both Retirement and occupational pensions are in general treated as earned income, this provision will not be of great value unless a person has substantial savings.

We must now examine the income supplement scheme in relation to the present age exemption. As we have seen, a single pensioner would benefit from the income supplement up to a total income level of £450. This is higher than the age exemption limit (£425), so that the income supplement will 'over-lap' with the income tax, and over this range a £1 of additional income will be taxed at the effective rate of 95% — since not only will the income supplement be reduced by 10s. but also income tax will be payable. For this reason, it would be better to consolidate the income supplement and the age exemption, so that the point at which the income supplement fell to zero coincided with the age exemption limit. If the rate of 45% at present used to give marginal relief above the age exemption limit were changed to 50% in line with the income supplement, then the age exemption could be completely absorbed into the income supplement. This would have the great advantage of making the scheme considerably less confusing to the pensioner. He receives the supplement and is then 'taxed' at the rate of 50% on all other income (beside the Retirement Pension) until he is as well off as he would be under the ordinary tax system with no supplement. (The effect of this change is shown by the dashed line in Figure 7.3). For a married couple, the same 'overlap' problem does not arise, but it would probably still be desirable on grounds of simplicity to amalgamate the income supplement and the age exemption If this were done, then pensioners with total incomes in the range above £630 would be very slightly worse off.

Advantages of the Income Supplement Scheme

The income supplement scheme would guarantee all pensioners a minimum

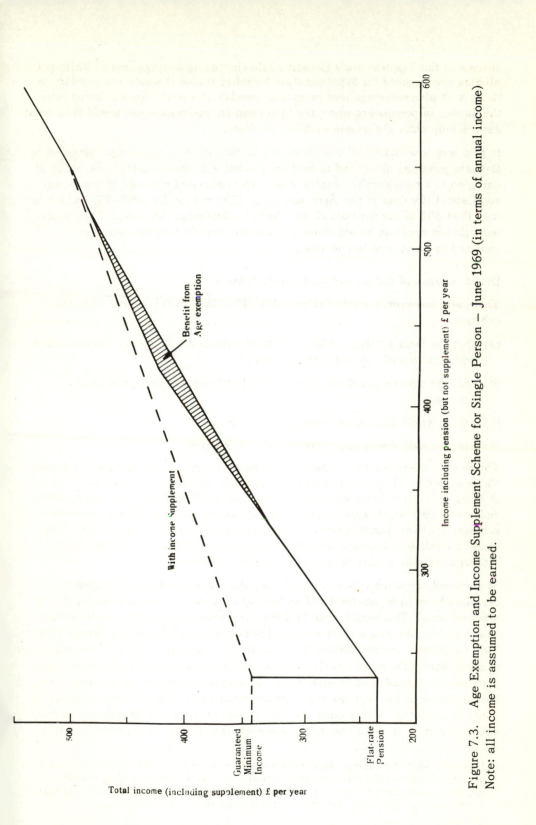

Figure 7.3. Age Exemption and Income Supplement Scheme for Single Person – June 1969 (in terms of annual income)
Note: all income is assumed to be earned.

Income including pension (but not supplement) £ per year

Benefit from Age exemption

With income Supplement

Total income (including supplement) £ per year

Guaranteed Minimum Income

Flat-rate Pension

127

income at the Supplementary Benefit scale (including average rent). [1] While not eliminating the need for Supplementary Benefits (since it would not provide for those with above-average rent or special needs), it would reduce substantially the number of pensioners who have to depend on assistance and would do a great deal to help other old people with low incomes.

In this way it would fulfill the same role as the 'Back to Beveridge' increase in flat-rate pensions discussed in Section 1 — but with the important advantage of doing so at a considerably smaller cost. The estimated net cost of the income supplement (for details see Appendix E) is £295 million for 1969–70 — which is less than 60% of the net cost of the 'Back to Beveridge' increase. This major reduction in cost can be achieved because the benefit from the increase is confined to those with low incomes.

Disadvantages of the Income Supplement Scheme

There are, however, a number of possible objections to the income supplement scheme :

(a) that the large increase in the number of pensioners filing tax returns would add significantly to administrative costs.

(b) that the scheme could not adjust flexibly to changes in a pensioner's income.

(c) that it would discourage saving for retirement.

(d) that it would discourage pensioners from working.

The first of these objections has a great deal of force. From the 1966–7 Inland Revenue survey of personal incomes, it appears that only just over 2 million out of some 5½ million Retirement Pensioner households had incomes above the tax deduction limit which were reviewed for tax purposes. The income supplement scheme, however, would require all pensioners to complete a tax return. This would undoubtedly increase the administrative costs of the Inland Revenue, although the size of this increase is an open question.

The second objection is also a valid one, since the scheme would almost certainly have to be administered on the basis of the tax return filed for the previous year. This would mean that the supplement received by a person was based on his last year's income and not necessarily related to his current income. This could lead to considerable hardship if the financial position of the pensioner changed during the course of the tax year. If, for example, he had been working part-time, but was forced to give it up, his supplement would not increase until the beginning of the next tax year. On the other hand, if his income went up, he could be presented with a large bill for the repayment of the supplement at the end of the year. It should be noted, however, that Canadian experience with a

---

[1] I assume that the income supplement scheme would be extended to those old people not receiving Retirement Pensions (on the basis that they would receive a supplement equal to the total guaranteed income and would be taxed at the rate of 50% until the whole supplement was extinguished).

similar kind of scheme suggests that the worst of these difficulties can be overcome.[1]

As far as saving for retirement is concerned, there would be both an income effect arising from the higher income to be expected in retirement and a substitution effect resulting from the fact that other income would be effectively 'taxed' at 50%. The first of these effects is, however, inherent in any scheme to raise the income of pensioners and it is in the second effect that the income supplement would differ (from, say, the 'Back to Beveridge' policy). Now it can reasonably be argued that the 50% tax rate would lead to some reduction in saving for retirement. In its White Paper on National Superannuation, the Government argued that this kind of scheme would hinder the setting up of occupational pension schemes for lower-paid workers. There are, however, three points that should be borne in mind :

(i) The tax rate of 50% should be compared with the tax rate at present implicit in the treatment of savings under Supplementary Benefits. If a pensioner applies for Supplementary Benefits, then he is taxed at the rate of 100% on any income from an occupational pension or annuity above £1 a week. In the case of other forms of saving, the implicit tax rate may be even higher.[2] It is not clear, therefore, that the income supplement would involve an increased tax rate for a person who would otherwise depend on Supplementary Benefits.

(ii) The income supplement scheme is not envisaged here as a permanent solution to poverty in old age but as a transitional measure to cover the period before National Superannuation would become fully effective. This means that those most affected would either have retired already or else would be due to retire in the next 15 or so years. Those retiring after then would not be affected by the supplement unless their earnings were very low.

(iii) A comparison of asset-holding among old people in Britain with that in Denmark, where they have had since 1891 a pension subject to a means test which discriminates heavily against property income, shows that the proportion with no assets is in fact lower in Denmark than in Britain.[3]

---

1 For a description of the Canadian scheme, see J. Cutt, 'A Guaranteed Income – Next Step in the Evolution of Welfare Policy', *Social Service Review*, 1968, pages 227–8. The scheme includes special provisions for those just retired so as to avoid any hardship that might be caused if the supplement were assessed on pre-retirement income.

2 Capital assets in excess of £300 (apart from an owner-occupied house) are assumed for the purposes of Supplementary Benefits to yield an income of 1s. a week for each complete £25 between £300 and £800 and 2s. 6d. a week for each £25 thereafter. This is equivalent to assuming an annual return of 10.4% and 26% respectively.

3 I am very grateful to Dorothy Wedderburn for suggesting this point.

For these reasons, the effect on saving can be expected to be fairly small.

Finally, it could be argued that the income supplement would act as a disincentive for old people to take up part-time work. Again, however, we must compare the 50% rate of tax with a rate of 100% applied to earnings over £2 under Supplementary Benefits. In addition, we must bear in mind that the present 'earnings rule' for Retirement Pensioners involves a tax rate of 100% on earnings above £8 10s. If the Government was seriously concerned about encouraging pensioners to enter the labour force, then it should reduce the high marginal tax rate involved in the earnings rule.[1]

CHAPTER 7 – CONCLUSIONS

My primary concern in this chapter has been with reforms that would guarantee all old people a pension at least equal to the Supplementary Benefit level (including average rent), and thus reduce substantially the number dependent on Supplementary Benefits.

The first way in which this object could be achieved is by raising the flat-rate Retirement Pension to the level of the Supplementary Benefit scale (including average rent) – a 'Back to Beveridge' policy. This would, however, have a high cost – of the order of £500 million.

Instead the Government has decided to introduce the National Superannuation scheme for earnings-related pensions. When fully in operation, this scheme would be at least as effective in helping those with low incomes as the 'Back to Beveridge' policy for all except unmarried women, although this depends crucially on the assumption that pensions in payment would be raised in line with average earnings. Moreover, the Government feels that it is possible to raise the revenue required to cover the cost of the additional pensions with National Superannuation but that it would not be so with a 'Back to Beveridge' increase.

It would, however, be a long time before National Superannuation reached maturity, and even in 1990 over a third of the pensioners would be receiving a pension below the Supplementary Benefit scale (including average rent). The scheme would in fact do very little to help the pensioners of this century. For this reason, it is important that the National Superannuation scheme be accompanied on the statute book by legislation designed to help old people during the transition period. Increases in the Retirement Pension such as that in November 1969 are not enough, and there is need for a scheme such as the income supplement discussed in Section 3. This scheme would fulfill the same object as the 'Back to Beveridge' increase at a considerably smaller cost, although it would mean increased work for the Inland Revenue and would lack flexibility.

---

1 For a description of the present earnings rule see Appendix A. The relationship between the earnings rule and the income supplement scheme is a problem that would require further consideration.

8 Helping Those in Employment

This chapter is concerned with reforms designed to help people below pension age and particularly those who fall below the poverty line even though they are in full-time work. The problems of this group have been discussed in detail in Chapter 5, where it was argued that the 1968 increases in Family Allowances had not provided a fully satisfactory solution and that many people still remained below the Supplementary Benefit scale. There are two principal reasons for this: the present Family Allowances are not enough to provide for the subsistence needs of a child as assessed under the Supplementary Benefit scale; and a significant minority earn less than the amount required to support a family with only one child at the Supplementary Benefit standard.

The measures designed to deal with this problem can similarly be classified into two groups: those providing more generous child benefits, and those aimed at helping low paid workers. The first group — new child benefits — is discussed in Section 1. The second group forms the subject of Sections 2 (minimum wage legislation) and 3 (reducing the burden of social security contributions on the low paid worker). At the end of each of these sections there is a short summary, and the principal conclusions will be brought together in Chapter 10.

1. NEW CHILD BENEFITS

The Present Benefits

Before examining the proposals that have been made for new child benefits, it may be helpful to discuss the financial aid given at present to families with children. In Chapter 5, I discussed the present Family Allowances, but they are only part of the total financial benefit given to families with children and must be considered in conjunction with the income tax allowances for children. These allowances have a longer history than Family Allowances (the original income tax introduced by Pitt in 1799 included allowances for children) and represent an important source of financial aid to families with children. At present (1969–70) they allow deductions from income for tax purposes at the rate of £115 for a child under 11, £140 for a child between 11 and 16, and £165 for a child over 16 (although these allowances are reduced if the child is eligible for Family Allowances — for further details see Appendix A).

The combined value to a family of Family Allowances and child tax allowances will depend on the level of its income. Since Family Allowances are taxable,

Table 8.1. Value of Present Child Benefits — Family Allowances and Child Tax Allowances — 1969–70

| Income[a] (£ a year) | Value of the benefits (£ a year) to family of that size and income | | | |
| | 1 child (aged 4) | 2 children (aged 9 & 12) | 4 children (aged 4, 8, 12 & 14) | 6 children (aged 4, 6, 9, 11, 13 & 15) |
	£	£	£	£
450	0	47	151	255
500	4	51	155	259
600	28	74	178	282
700	35	98	202	306
800	35	100	225	329
900	42	107	238	360
1 000	47	116	247	378
1 200	47	120	261	387
1 500	47	120	261	395
2 000	47	120	261	402

Notes : It is assumed that none of the children had incomes in excess of the limit allowed for child tax relief.

It is assumed that the only tax allowances which apply are the personal and child allowances.

[a] Income before allowing for Family Allowances. All income is assumed to be earned by the father.

their value will fall as the family's income rises. Child tax allowances, on the other hand, become more valuable as income goes up : an allowance of £115 is worth nothing to a person with low income, but is worth £47 9s. to a person paying the standard rate of income tax and considerably more to a surtax-payer. Table 8.1 shows the combined value of the two benefits for families of different sizes at different levels of income. The top line (£450 a year) shows the value of the Family Allowances alone, since at this level none of the families would pay any tax even if the child tax allowances were abolished (so that they gain nothing from the tax allowances). At higher income levels, the families begin to benefit from the tax allowances and this is more than sufficient to compensate for the tax payable on the Family Allowances. As a result the combined value of the benefits rises with income, so that, for example, a family with two children with an income of £1 500 a year receives over twice the total benefits received by a family of the same size with an income of only £450 a year.

For the standard rate tax payer, the present child benefits taken together fulfil the Beveridge objective of providing for the subsistence needs of all children apart from the first. In the case of the family with 4 children, for example, the Supplementary Benefit allowances for the 3 younger children in June 1969 would have been at an annual rate of £255, compared with a total benefit of £261 from Family Allowances and child tax allowances for a man earning £1 200 or more.

The same is not, however, true for the families lower down the income scale, who receive little or no benefit from the child tax relief and rely on Family Allowances. As we have seen in Chapter 5, Family Allowances have been consistently below the level proposed by Beveridge. Even with the large increase in 1968, they fall a long way short of the Supplementary Benefit allowances for children – see Table 8.2. For a child under 5 the Family Allowance is three-quarters of the Supplementary Benefit scale, and for a child over 11 it is only half. (This also reflects the failure of the Government to adopt Beveridge's recommendation that the Family Allowances be graded according to age, although this principle is followed in the Supplementary Benefit scale.)

New Child Benefits

The most obvious way of helping low income families with children is through a 'Back to Beveridge' policy of raising Family Allowances to a level (graded with age) at which they would cover the subsistence needs of all children apart from the first. If this were done, then all families would be above the poverty line provided that the father earned enough to support a wife and one child at the Supplementary Benefit level. The problem of 'large families' would disappear and only that of 'low earnings' would remain.

The principal objection to such a policy is the expense. To help the 2% of families falling below the poverty line, the same increase (or the same increase less income tax) would have to be given to the other 98%. One solution to this problem would be to adopt the 'claw-back' mechanism used by the Government when it raised Family Allowances in 1968, and to reduce the child tax allowances at the same time so that the person paying the standard rate of income tax would be no better off. Through an extension of this device, the cost of a 'Back to Beveridge' policy could be kept as low as £50 million.[1]

There have recently been a number of proposals to carry the 'claw-back' policy to its logical extreme and abolish the child tax allowances altogether. The present benefits would be replaced by one single scheme for providing financial aid to families with children. This scheme would then provide more generous benefits to families with low incomes, and particularly to the one child families who are not helped by Family Allowances. In the remainder of this section, I shall examine the implications of two of the best known of these proposals – those of the Child Poverty Action Group and of Sir John Walley.

---

1 Estimated for the tax-year 1968–9 by extrapolating from the Inland Revenue survey of personal incomes for 1965–6 (see Appendix F), with the Family Allowances being raised to the level of the post-October 1968 Supplementary Benefit allowances for children.

Table 8.2. Family Allowances in Relation to the Supplementary Benefit Scale for Children — June 1969

	1. Family Allowance for third and subsequent children			2. Supplementary Benefit allowance per child			3. Ratio (1/2)
Age of child :	£	s.	d.	£	s.	d.	%
under 5	1	0	0	1	7	0	74
5–10	1	0	0	1	12	0	63
11–12	1	0	0	1	19	0	51
13–15	1	0	0	2	1	0	49

The Child Poverty Action Group Scheme

The Child Poverty Action Group has proposed that the present Family Allowances and child tax allowances should be replaced by a single tax-free child benefit.[1] This would mean that the value of the benefits given for a child would no longer increase with income as it does at present. The level of benefit rates proposed by the Child Poverty Action Group (see Table 8.3) is designed to ensure that those now paying less than the standard rate of income tax would be better off than at present and that standard rate tax-payers would be approximately as well off. (Surtax-payers would be worse off as a result of the scheme.)

Table 8.3. Proposed Rates for New Child Benefits and Supplementary Benefit Scale for Children

Age of child	Child Poverty Action Group First child			Subsequent children			Walley All children			Supplementary Benefit Scale for children — June 1969 Age of child			
	£	s.	d.	£	s.	d.	£	s.	d.		£	s.	d.
under 11		18	0	1	4	6	1	8	0	under 5	1	7	0
										5–10	1	12	0
11–15	1	2	0	1	8	6	1	10	0	11–12	1	19	0
										13–15	2	1	0
over 16	1	6	0	1	12	6	1	15	0	16–17	2	13	0

Table 8.3 shows for comparison the Supplementary Benefit allowances for children of different ages. It can be seen from this that the rates proposed by the Child Poverty Action Group would still fall below the Supplementary Benefit level, and for children over 11 they would be less than three-quarters of that level. In this

---

[1] Child Poverty Action Group, 'Memorandum to the Chancellor of the Exchequer', Supplement to *Poverty — Journal of Child Poverty Action Group*, Spring 1967.

Table 8.4. Comparison of the Benefits from the Child Poverty Action Group (C.P.A.G.) and Walley Proposals with those from the Present Family Allowances and Child Tax Allowances (1969–70)

Value of benefits (£ a year) to family of that size and income

Income (£ a year)	1 child (aged 4)			2 children (aged 9 and 12)			4 children (aged 4, 8, 12 and 14)			6 children (aged 4, 6, 9, 11, 13 and 15)		
	Present Benefits	C.P.A.G. Scheme	Walley Scheme	Present Benefits	C.P.A.G. Scheme	Walley Scheme	Present Benefits	C.P.A.G. Scheme	Walley Scheme	Present Benefits	C.P.A.G. Scheme	Walley Scheme
450	0	47	73	47	121	151	151	259	302	255	396	453
600	28	47	73	74	121	151	178	259	302	282	396	453
800	35	47	73	100	121	151	225	259	302	329	396	453
1 000	47	47	73	116	121	151	247	259	302	378	396	453
1 200	47	47	73	120	121	151	261	259	302	387	396	453
1 500	47	47	73	120	121	151	261	259	302	395	396	453
2 000	47	47	73	120	121	151	261	259	302	402	396	453
Supplementary Benefit Allowances for children eligible for Family Allowances [a]	0			83			255			445		

Notes: See notes to Table 8.1.

[a] i.e. the total Supplementary Benefit allowances covering all except the first child (£ a year) – as at June 1969.

135

respect the proposal falls short of a 'Back to Beveridge' policy. However, the scheme *would* provide allowances for the first child (unlike Family Allowances), and as a result the total benefit to many families would exceed the amount payable with 'Back to Beveridge' Family Allowances. This is brought out clearly by Table 8.4. The family with 4 children and an income of £600 a year would, for example, receive a total benefit of £259 a year, which is slightly above the Supplementary Benefit allowances payable for the 3 children eligible for Family Allowances, as well as considerably more than it receives at present. Although it does not stretch quite so far in the case of the family with 6 children, the Child Poverty Action Group proposal would obviously go a long way towards fulfilling the Beveridge objective.

The Walley Scheme

The proposal for a 'child endowment' scheme put forward by Sir John Walley is very similar to that of the Child Poverty Action Group in that it involves the replacement of Family Allowances and child tax relief by a single tax-free benefit.[1] The only differences are: (a) The benefits would be independent of a child's position in the family (so that the eldest child would get the same as the others). (b) The child endowment scheme would also replace the present allowances paid for children under the National Insurance benefits.

The rates of child benefit proposed by Walley are rather more generous than those under the Child Poverty Action Group scheme, particularly in that the first child in a family would receive the same as allowance as the other children. Table 8.4 illustrates the greater generosity of the Walley scheme as far as families where the father is in work are concerned. The family with 6 children and an income of £600 a year would be richer than at present to the extent of £3 6s. a week; and even families now paying the standard rate of income tax would gain quite noticeably.

The position of families receiving National Insurance benefits, on the other hand, would be little, if at all, better than at present. A sick or unemployed man with 4 children now receives an addition to his National Insurance benefit of £5 12s.; under the Walley scheme he would receive the same amount if they were under 11 and 8s. a week more if they were all aged between 11 and 15.

Implications of New Child Benefit Schemes

In what follows, I examine three important aspects of these proposals for new child benefits:

(a) their effectiveness in helping low income families,

(b) their probable cost,

(c) their implications for work incentives.

---

1 Sir John Walley, 'New approach to abolishing child poverty', *The Times*, 11 December 1967. See also, Sir John Walley, 'A new deal for the family', *Poverty — Journal of Child Poverty Action Group*, Spring 1969.

(a) Effect on Low Income Families

In estimating the effect of the 1968 increase in Family Allowances in Chapter 5, I used the information from the enquiry by the Ministry of Social Security in 1966 into the circumstances of families receiving Family Allowances.[1] In Table 8.5, I present estimates on a similar basis of the effect of the Child Poverty Action Group and Walley proposals (the figures for the 1968 Family Allowance increase are also included for comparison).

Table 8.5. Effect of Higher Family Allowances, Child Poverty Action Group (C.P.A.G.) Scheme and Walley Scheme on Low Income Families in Ministry of Social Security Enquiry 1966.

Families with	Below National Assistance Scale 1966 ('000's)	Raised Increase in Family Allowances of 10s. ('000's)	%	Above C.P.A.G. Proposal ('000's)	%	By Walley Proposal ('000's)	%
2 children	21	4	20	8	38	12	60
3 children	15	10	67	15	97	15	100
4 children	11	7	68	9	86	10	96
5 children	7	6	84	7	96	7	100
6 or more children	10	8	82	10	99	10	99
All families	63	35	56	48	76	54	86

Source : Calculated from *Circumstances of Families*, op. cit., Table A. 8.

Notes : These figures are not adjusted for non-response, so that the total of 63 000 does not agree with that of 70 000 given earlier.

It is assumed that the income of the families is below the level at which they begin to benefit from child tax relief (see text).

Families with 6 or more children are assumed to have an average of 6¼ children.

It is assumed that the benefits paid are the average of the scale for children aged 0–10 and 11–15.

The previous estimates were based on the assumption that the families did not have a sufficiently high income to be liable for income tax; in this case we have to make the stronger assumption that their income is below the level at which they begin to benefit from the child tax allowances. To the extent that this assumption is not satisfied, the estimates will *over*-state the benefit from the new proposals for certain families (since they under-state the loss from the abolition of child tax allowances).

---

[1] *Circumstances of Families*, op. cit.

From Table 8.5 it can be seen that both the proposed schemes would have had a greater effect on the families falling below the poverty line than the 10s. increase in Family Allowances. The Child Poverty Action Group scheme would have raised three-quarters of the families above, and the Walley proposal even more. The position of families with 2 or 3 children would be particularly improved (although it should be noted that it is here that our assumption about the families' incomes is most likely to lead us to over-state the benefit).

Unfortunately, the information from the Ministry of Social Security used in Table 8.5 is not altogether satisfactory for our purpose. The exclusion of one child families is particularly important, since one of the advantages of the new schemes would be the benefit given to low income families of this size (who do not at present receive Family Allowances). In addition the assumptions made about the income of the families may have distorted the comparison. For these reasons, I have given in Table 8.6 an alternative estimate of the effect on *all* families with children based on the Inland Revenue survey of personal incomes. The difficulties of using this source have been discussed in Chapter 2; however, most of them do not affect families with children very seriously.[1] The most important remaining difficulty is the fact that the published figures do not include National Insurance benefits. Adjustments could be made to correct for this – as was done by Prest and Stark for earlier years.[2] However, while this omission means that the figure for the total number of low income families is an over-estimate, there are no reasons to expect that it would cause serious bias in a comparison of the *relative* effects on low income families of different schemes. It may therefore be reasonable to use the unadjusted Inland Revenue figures as a basis for comparing the effectiveness of the new child benefit schemes with that of the 1968 increase in Family Allowances.

Table 8.6 shows the proportion of families with incomes below the National Assistance scale (I.A.R.) in 1966–7 that would have been raised above by the various measures. This again indicates that the new benefit schemes would have had a much greater impact than the 1968 increase in Family Allowances. The Child Poverty Action Group scheme would have raised nearly three times as many families above the poverty line, and the Walley scheme would have been even more effective.

These results relate primarily to families supported by a man in work, but we must also consider the effect of the new schemes on those who are receiving National Insurance or Supplementary Benefits. Families receiving Supplementary Benefits who are not subject to the wage stop would derive no benefit from the new schemes, since the Supplementary Benefit payment would be reduced by a corresponding amount – as in the case of the 1968 increase in Family Allowances

---

1 For example, the problem of people appearing as two separate units is unlikely to be important, as is that of school-leavers and persons dying in the course of the year.

2 *Some Aspects of Income Distribution in the U.K. Since World War II*, op. cit.

138

Those who are wage-stopped, however, would have a higher normal income when in employment as a result of the higher child benefits, so that the wage stop deduction would be smaller or eliminated altogether. Finally, those families receiving National Insurance benefits but not Supplementary Benefits would benefit to the full extent of the increase under the Child Poverty Action Group scheme, though they would gain very little from the Walley scheme.

(b) Cost of the New Child Benefit Schemes

Since the Child Poverty Action Group scheme represents an extension of the 'claw-back' policy adopted when Family Allowances were raised in 1968, it seems likely that its cost would be relatively small. The net benefit is confined to those paying less than the standard rate of income tax and as far as surtax payers are concerned there would be some net saving for the Exchequer. The Walley scheme, on the other hand, would be more generous and would leave the standard rate tax payer better off than at present. We should therefore expect that its cost would be considerably higher.

Table 8.6.   Comparison of Effect of Higher Family Allowances, Child Poverty Action Group Scheme and Walley Scheme on Families below National Assistance Scale (I.A.R.) 1966–7

Measure :	Proportion of families with incomes[a] below National Assistance scale (I.A.R.) in 1966–7 that would have been raised above by measure shown
	%
Increase of 10s. per child in Family Allowances	12
Child Poverty Action Group scheme	33
Walley scheme	48

Source :   Estimated from Inland Revenue survey of personal incomes for 1966–7 (*Report of the Commissioners of Her Majesty's Inland Revenue for the year ended 31st March 1968*, Tables 80–3).

Notes :   The National Assistance scale is that in effect until November 1966. Average rent is as estimated in Appendix B. The allowances for children were taken as the average of those for the age groups 5–10 and 11–15.

The child benefits payable under the Child Poverty Action Group and Walley schemes were taken as the average of those for the age groups 0–10 and 11–15.

It was assumed that families with 4 or more children had an average of 4½.

[a]   Incomes after income tax and National Insurance contributions (flat-rate and graduated).

139

The gross cost of the payments under the new schemes is straight-forward to calculate. Against this, we have to allow for savings on:

(i) child tax allowances

(ii) Family Allowances (allowing for the tax at present paid on them)

(iii) Supplementary Benefits and (in the case of the Walley scheme) National Insurance.

Making allowance for these savings, we come out with the following net cost for 1968–9 (for details see Appendix F):

	Child Poverty Action Group Proposal £ million	Walley Proposal £ million
Gross cost of new benefits	850	1 060
Less Saving on :-		
Child tax allowances and Family Allowances	790	790
Supplementary Benefits and National Insurance	30	65
NET COST	30	205

As anticipated, the net cost of the Child Poverty Action Group proposal would be small and it can scarcely be regarded as unmanageable. The Walley scheme, on the other hand, would have a substantial net cost – of the order of £200 million. To raise this amount of revenue would require an extra 6d.–9d. on the standard rate of income tax. This reflects the fact that his scheme is considerably more generous and the benefit is not restricted to those paying less than the standard rate of income tax. (In his estimate of the cost Walley ignored the tax paid on Family Allowances, which led him to take a rather too optimistic view).

So far we have only considered the total cost of the new schemes, but it is also important to examine the *distribution* of this cost. Under the Child Poverty Action Group scheme at least part of the extra benefit to low income families is being financed by the reduction in the benefit given to surtax payers with children. A man with 3 children (under 11) earning £7 500 a year would, for example, be worse off to the extent of some £50 a year if their proposal were to be put into force. While this is only a small amount, it does raise an important issue of principle – is it right that the burden of helping low income families with children should fall on rich families with children rather than rich bachelors or childless couples? There are, in other words, problems of horizontal as well as of vertical equity. This difficulty is recognised by the Child Poverty Action Group when they discuss the question of raising the revenue required to cover the net cost: 'any consequential increase in taxation,..., should fall mainly on single persons and childless couples rather than on families with children'.[1]

---

1 'Memorandum to the Chancellor of the Exchequer', op. cit., para. 8.

However, once we have abolished the child tax allowances, there is no way of imposing a differential tax burden!

(c) *Effect of the New Child Benefit Schemes on Work Incentives*

In Chapter 6, I argued that there were two separate aspects to work incentives — the decision whether or not to enter the labour force, and the decision about how many hours to work. It is important to keep this distinction in mind, since the new child benefit schemes would have different effects on the two decisions.

One of the arguments advanced in the campaign for Family Allowances was that they would help avoid the situation where a man could be better off receiving unemployment pay than at work. If child allowances are paid to all families and not just to those who were out of work (as was the case before the Second World War), then there will be less of an incentive for a man to remain 'voluntarily' unemployed. The same is undoubtedly true of the new child benefit proposals. We have seen that the Walley scheme would provide only limited benefit (if any) to families receiving National Insurance benefits since the child allowances given under National Insurance would be abolished. Under neither scheme would people receiving Supplementary Benefits benefit from the change (since the assistance payment would be reduced correspondingly). In this way the new schemes would reduce any tendency for voluntary unemployment, although, as I have already suggested in Chapter 6, it seems unlikely that the problem of the 'work-shy' is one of great importance.

In the case of decisions about how many hours to work, I distinguished in Chapter 6 between income effects (depending on the level of net income) and substitution effects (depending on the marginal rate of taxation). The aim of the proposed schemes is to raise the net income of families at the lower end of the income scale, so that the income effect would tend to lead them to work less (on the assumption that leisure is a normal good). At the same time, the abolition of the child tax allowances would raise the marginal tax rate for many families (at their present levels of income). It has been estimated that the April 1968 increase in Family Allowances and the accompanying adjustment in child tax relief brought a further 350 000 households within the scope of income tax at that time.[1] It also increased the number paying the standard rate. This would be true to an even greater extent of the Child Poverty Action Group and Walley proposals. For example, a family with 3 children under 11 at present (1969–70) begins to pay tax when the annual earnings of the father reach £719;[2] under the Child Poverty Action Group proposal, they would begin to pay tax at an income of £482. Moreover, they would begin to pay the standard rate of tax at £816 rather than £1 053. Both income and substitution effects would tend to work in the direction of a reduction in work effort.

---

[1] These figures were given by the Chancellor of the Exchequer in his 1968 Budget Speech.

[2] Assuming that all income earned by father and that only allowances applicable are the personal and child allowances.

141

Nonetheless, it seems unlikely that the new child benefit schemes would have a serious adverse effect on decisions about how many hours to work. The people who might be led to reduce their work effort are in the lower half of the income distribution, and as I have suggested in Chapter 6, they are less likely to be affected by changes of this kind than those higher up the income scale.[1] Secondly, while the new schemes would bring more families within the tax net, they would *reduce* the number dependent on means-tested benefits such as rate rebates which effectively involve very high marginal tax rates.

New Child Benefits — Summary

The new child benefit schemes discussed in this section can be seen as the logical extension of the 'claw-back' policy adopted by the Government when it raised Family Allowances and simultaneously cut child tax allowances in 1968. Since these proposed schemes go much further, they provide substantially more benefit to low income families than the 1968 measures. The Child Poverty Action Group scheme would raise over twice as many families above the poverty line. The Walley scheme would do even more for families where the father was in work, although those receiving National Insurance benefits would gain less.

Comparing the new benefit schemes with the 'Back to Beveridge' increase in Family Allowances discussed at the beginning of the section, we have seen that the benefits given for children after the first are less generous than the subsistence needs level advocated by Beveridge. However, for small families this would be more than offset by the benefit given for the first child in a family, and for these families the new schemes would not fall far short of the Beveridge objective of providing for the subsistence needs of children apart from the first. In addition the new schemes would help the one child family with low income which gains nothing from Family Allowances.

The Child Poverty Action Group scheme could be introduced at a relatively low budgetary cost — of the order of £30 million in 1968–9. This low cost does, however, conceal the fact that part of the benefit for low income families is being obtained at the expense of surtax payers with children, and it is questionable whether this represents an equitable distribution of the burden. The more generous Walley scheme would have a substantial net cost — estimated at £205 million in 1968–9.

Finally, it seems unlikely that the new schemes would have seriously adverse effects on work effort and if anything they would tend to discourage 'voluntary' unemployment.

2.   MINIMUM WAGE LEGISLATION

When in 1795 Samuel Whitbread brought before the House of Commons a bill to

---

[1] A surtax payer would be worse off as a result of the introduction of new child benefits, so that the income and substitution effects would in his case operate in opposite directions.

establish a minimum wage, it was rejected by Pitt the Younger on the grounds that a minimum wage would not take any account of varying family needs. He argued that[1] 'Were the minimum fixed upon the standard of a large family, it might operate as an encouragement to idleness on one part of the community, and if it were fixed on the standard of a small family, those would not enjoy the benefit of it for whose relief it was intended.'

While Pitt may have been right in rejecting a minimum wage as a complete solution to the problem, it does not follow that it might not today play an important role *in conjunction* with other measures to help large families. As we have seen, the present Family Allowances fail in two respects: the allowances themselves fall below the subsistence level advocated by Beveridge, and some people have earnings below the level required to support a family with one child. A 'Back to Beveridge' increase in the Family Allowances would deal with the first of these problems, but not with the second. The new child benefit schemes would go further towards solving the second, since they would provide benefit for the first child in a family, but an alternative solution through a minimum wage might be more successful. For this reason, I examine in this section the possibilities of minimum wage legislation – even though this does not fall strictly within the field of social security.

The Wages Councils

Before examining the possibilities of new legislation, it should be pointed out that the Government does at present through the Wages Council system enforce minimum wages in a range of industries. These Councils were first set up in 1909 following the investigations of the sweated trades by Charles Booth and others, and there are now about 60 in all covering nearly 4 million workers – or 1 in 6 of all employees. The primary purpose of the Wages Councils is to protect low paid workers by determining minimum rates of pay which are statutorily enforced. In June 1968 the minimum weekly wage in most industries fell in the narrow range £9 10s. to £10 10s., so that it can be said that they contain the germ of a national minimum wage, albeit at a very low level.

In Chapter 5, I referred to the finding of Marquand that nearly half the lowest paid industries in the 1960 earnings survey were ones in which Wages Councils were operating. Again, the reports of the Prices and Incomes Board on two further Wages Council industries – retail drapery and agriculture – showed that they both contained a high proportion of low paid workers. This suggests that the Government could make an important contribution to helping the low paid through the existing Wages Councils. An increase in minimum wage rates for all Wages Council industries, enforced through the present machinery, would benefit a substantial number of those with low earnings.

Nevertheless, an increase in the minimum rates enforced by the Wages Councils would only represent a partial solution, since many low paid workers are outside

---

1 This reference I owe to L. Jeger, 'Rathbone Re-Read', *Poverty – Journal of the Child Poverty Action Group*, Autumn 1968.

the industries covered. The evidence discussed in Chapter 5 also suggested that it would not be sufficient to extend the Councils to a few industries not at present covered. For this reason, attention has turned instead to a national minimum wage covering all industries. (A national minimum has the further advantage that the onus for special pleading would lie with the industry, in contrast to the policy of extending the Wages Councils, where each bargain would be struck separately).

A National Minimum Wage

There have been a number of recent proposals for a national minimum wage, including those of Professor H. Clegg, of J. Edmonds and G. Radice, and of the General Council of the T.U.C.[1] The topic was also discussed by the Royal Commission on Trade Unions and Employer's Associations, which recommended that the Government should review methods of protecting the low paid, including the possibility of a national minimum wage. As a result of this renewed interest, the Government appointed an Inter-Departmental Working Party to examine the consequences of introducing a national minimum wage, which produced a detailed report at the beginning of 1969.[2]

Before we can discuss the implications of a national minimum wage, we need to clarify what this would mean. Would it, for example, apply to basic wage rates or to actual earnings? Would it be based on weekly or hourly rates of pay? Would it apply equally to men and women, and what would be the position of juveniles? These questions are discussed at some length in the Working Party's report and for simplicity I shall concentrate on the type of national minimum considered by them. This would involve a minimum hourly earnings level applied to all hours worked, including overtime. It would apply to women and juveniles as well as men, although not necessarily at the same rates. Since the minimum is expressed on an hourly basis, it could also be applied to those working part-time. (There might need to be special provisions for disabled workers.)

There remains the question of the *level* of the national minimum. The figure that seems most popular is one of £15 for a 40 hour week in the case of adult men, although in several cases it is suggested that this figure should be approached gradually from an initial level of £11 or so. It is clear, however, that the level of the minimum wage must depend on the function it is intended to perform. If the object of the minimum wage is to guarantee an income at the Supplementary Benefit scale (I.A.R.) for a family with one child (while Family Allowances provide for larger families), then the level required in October 1968 would have been only £12 10s. a week — or 6s. 3d. an hour for a 40 hour week. If, on the other hand, the minimum wage is intended to play a more important role in helping

---

1 H. Clegg, 'The Case for a National Minimum Wage', *The Times*, 28 March 1967. J. Edmonds and G. Radice, *Low Pay*, Fabian Research Series Number 270. Trades Union Congress, *Economic Review 1969*.

2 Department of Employment and Productivity, *A National Minimum Wage*, Report of an Inter-Departmental Working Party (H.M.S.O., 1969).

those with low incomes (because child benefits are not adequate), then we have to consider higher figures such as that of £15 proposed by the T.U.C. For example, to reach the present Supplementary Benefit scale (I.A.R.), a man with 4 children would have to earn £14 17s. 6d. I shall therefore consider two possible levels for the minimum wage — £12 10s. and £15 — both for an adult man working a 40 hour week.[1]

In what follows, I examine first the benefit that a national minimum wage would give to people with low incomes. I then discuss the addition to labour costs that would be involved (on the assumption of no effect on employment), and finally consider the impact on employment and the measures that would be required to offset any adverse effects.[2]

Effect of Minimum Wage on People with Low Incomes

The minimum wage would either raise the earnings of low paid workers to the minimum level or else cause them to be unemployed. In the latter event, they would still gain from the minimum wage if they had previously earned less than the Supplementary Benefit scale, since the wage stop would no longer be effective (or would be very considerably reduced). By raising their normal earnings when in employment, the minimum wage would increase the incomes of low paid workers even if they became unemployed as a result.

Let us consider first the 'limited objective' minimum wage of £12 10s. intended to guarantee earnings at the Supplementary Benefit scale (I.A.R.) for a family with one child. If Family Allowances (or other child benefits) are raised to a level sufficient for the needs of children apart from the first, then clearly only those families with above-average rents would still fall below the Supplementary Benefit scale.

In the case of the more ambitious minimum wage of £15 a week the effectiveness in helping families with low incomes is more difficult to assess. If we take a minimum weekly earnings level of £15 and allow for income tax, National Insurance contributions and Family Allowances (as in October 1968), we can calculate the take-home pay that it would give for households of different sizes — see Table 8.7. Subtracting the fixed component of the Supplementary Benefit scale (column 2) then gives the maximum housing expenditure that the family could have while still remaining above the Supplementary Benefit level (column 3). Any household with rent below this amount would be above the poverty line if there were a minimum wage of £15.

From Table 8.7 it is clear that the 'maximum rent' falls quite rapidly with the number of children. This reflects the fact that present Family Allowances are

---

1 The question of the rates for women and juveniles is taken up later.

2 One problem with a minimum wage not discussed here is that of enforcement — a point that was emphasised by Professor D.J. Robertson in his evidence to the Donovan Commission. For discussion of some of the difficulties of enforcing the present Wages Council minima, see E.G.A. Armstrong, 'Minimum Wages in a Fully Employed City', *British Journal of Industrial Relations*, 1966.

Table 8.7. Effect of a National Minimum Wage of £15 per week on the
Net Income of Households of Different Sizes — October 1968

	1. Take-Home Pay with Earnings at Minimum level of £15 per week			2. Supplementary Benefit Scale (not including any rent allowance)			3. 'Maximum Rent'		
	£	s.	d.	£	s.	d.	£	s.	d.
Couple	12	10	0	7	9	0	5	1	0
Couple + 1 child	13	5	0	9	5	0	4	0	0
Couple + 2 children	14	13	0	11	0	0	3	13	0
Couple + 3 children	15	15	0	12	16	0	2	19	0
Couple + 4 children	16	15	0	14	11	0	2	4	0
Couple + 5 children	17	15	0	16	7	0	1	8	0

Notes : Take-home pay is calculated taking account of income tax, National
Insurance contributions (flat-rate and graduated), and Family Allowances.
Family Allowances are those payable after October 1968 (the child tax
allowances are accordingly reduced by £42 for children receiving
Family Allowances).

The Supplementary Benefit scale is that introduced in October 1968.

It is assumed that the Supplementary Benefit allowances for children
may be taken as the average of those for children aged 5—10 and 11—12.

'Maximum rent' shows the maximum housing expenditure that a family
earning £15 would have without falling below the Supplementary
Benefit scale. It is assumed that the household has no other source of
income besides the man's earnings.

Amounts are rounded to the nearest 1s.

less than the Supplementary Benefit scales for children. It means, however, that
for a family with 5 children a minimum wage of £15 is probably not going to be
enough. For example, the Prices and Incomes Board enquiry into the rents
charged by 20 local housing authorities showed that in January 1968 58% of the
tenants of 3-bedroomed houses had net rents (allowing for rebates) in excess of
£2, and 24% in excess of £2 10s.[1] (N.B. these figures do not allow for rates).
From the Family Expenditure Survey for 1964 we can obtain a distribution of
rents for all unfurnished accommodation (both local authority and private).[2] If we

---

[1] National Board for Prices and Income, *Increases in Rents of Local Authority
Housing*, Report No. 62 (H.M.S.O., 1968), Statistical Supplement, Table 22.

[2] Ministry of Labour, *Family Expenditure for 1964* (H.M.S.O., 1965), Table U.

adjust these figures for the increase in housing costs since then,[1] we can estimate that over a half of all tenants had rents in excess of £2 in October 1968. This is supported by the results of the Ministry of Social Security enquiry into families receiving Family Allowances, which showed that two-thirds of the families with 5 or more children where the father was in full-time work had housing expenditure of more than £2 in 1966.

Even if the minimum wage of £15 would not guarantee an income at the Supplementary Benefit level for families with 4 or more children, it would nevertheless provide considerable help to low income households. In September 1968, 8% of all adult men in full-time employment earned less than £15 a week (and 14% earned less than 7s. 6d. an hour). In addition, the minimum wage would undoubtedly lead to a substantial reduction in the number of households subject to the wage stop. According to the report by the Supplementary Benefit Commission, most of those visited in their enquiry had net earnings between £9 10s. and £11 10s. a week in 1967.[2]

In the case of both minimum wage levels we must, however, bear in mind that:

(a) a minimum wage would do nothing directly to help the self-employed.

(b) we cannot assume that everyone works a 40 hour week, and a casual worker may earn less than £15 a week even with a 7s. 6d. hourly minimum.

(c) as mentioned earlier, special provisions may have to be made for the disabled.

We may conclude, then, that a minimum wage of £12 10s. could be an effective way of helping families with only one child or no children, but that even the £15 minimum favoured by the T.U.C. would not by itself provide an adequate solution to the problems of large families. The £15 minimum wage would need therefore to be accompanied by other measures to help families with children. A minimum wage at this level would nonetheless provide considerable benefit to low income families and would reduce the number subject to the wage stop.

The Addition to Labour Costs

In so far as the minimum wage did not lead to a reduction in the demand for labour, it would cause labour costs to rise. If as a result prices rise, minimum wage legislation would come into conflict with the present prices and incomes policy, and the *real* benefit given to the low paid worker would be reduced.

In its report the Working Party presented estimates of the increases in labour costs that would follow from different minimum wage levels on the assumption that there was no effect on employment. The figures given in Table 8.8 are based on its estimates (which presumably relate to 1968, although no date is given). In its discussion of the figures, the Working Party emphasised the

---

1 Using the housing component of the retail price index.

2 *Administration of the Wage Stop*, op. cit.

Table 8.8. Increase in Labour Costs as a Result of a National
             Minimum Wage — 1968

| | Addition to total wage and salary bill % | |
| | 1. No repercussions | 2. Limited repercussions |
Hourly Rates :	%	%
MEN and YOUTHS[a]		
Minimum hourly earnings of 6s. 3d. for men (£12 10s. for a 40-hour week)	0.6	1.0
Minimum hourly earnings of 7s. 6d. for men (£15 for a 40-hour week)	1.7	2.3
ALL WORKERS[a]		
Minimum hourly earnings for men of 6s. 3d. and for women :		
4s.	0.9	1.4
5s.	1.5	2.1
6s. 3d.	3.3	3.9

Source : Estimated from *A National Minimum Wage*, op. cit., page 40.

Notes : The estimates assume that the minimum wage has no impact on
          employment or productivity.

The assumptions about repercussions are as follows :
'No repercussions' — increase strictly confined to those below
minimum level.
'Limited repercussions' — allowing for tapering increases to those
just above the minimum level. For example, in the case of men
working a 40 hour week and a minimum of 7s. 6d. an hour :

Men earning under £13 15s. would be brought up to £15
Men earning £13 15s but under £15 would receive an extra £1 5s.
Men earning £15   but under £16 5s. would receive 18s. 9d.
Men earning £16 5s. but under £17 10s. would receive 12s. 6d.
Men earning £17 10s. but under £18 15s. would receive 6s. 3d.

[a] It is assumed that the wage and salary bill for juveniles would rise
by the same proportion as that for adults of the same sex.

importance of two factors: the extent of the repercussions on those above the national minimum level, and the question of extending the minimum to cover women workers. If we consider first a minimum wage covering men and youths only, the figures in Table 8.8 suggest that the overall addition to labour costs would not be unmanageable. Under the 'limited repercussions' assumption, the cost of a 7s. 6d. an hour minimum would be around 2% of the total wage bill, which could be accommodated within the context of the Government's incomes policy, although it would mean that the increase for those workers above the minimum would have to be very much smaller in that year. This would, however, depend critically on the assumption that the repercussions can be kept to a low level and if there were to be considerable 'spill-over' to the higher paid, the addition to labour costs might be very much higher (the 'extreme' figure quoted in the report is 7.4% — although this is not of course an upper bound). Moreover, if keeping the spill-over down to a manageable level required detailed control of individual wage bargains, this would destroy one of the attractive features of a national minimum wage — that it could be applied universally without special consideration for each industry.

The problem of extending the national minimum wage to female workers is obvious enough — such a high proportion have low earnings that the addition to labour costs would be very much larger if they were included. If the national minimum were fixed at 6s. 3d. an hour and this rate were applied to women as to men, the cost would rise to four times the cost when applied to men alone. The Working Party did point out that the introduction of 'equal minima' like 'equal pay' might have to be phased over a number of years, and in the initial stages different minima might have to be applied to men and women. Even so, a minimum hourly rate of 5s. for women would more than double the addition to labour costs involved in a 'limited objective' minimum wage of £12 10s. a week.

The Effect of a Minimum Wage on Employment

Every first year economics student is taught that minimum wage legislation cannot really help the low paid worker because the final effect is for him to become unemployed rather than better paid. He is told in Samuelson, for example, that minimum wage laws 'often hurt those they are designed to help. What good does it do a Negro youth to know that an employer must pay him $1.60 per hour, if the fact that he must be paid that amount is what keeps him from getting a job?'[1] Whether or not a firm is able to pass on the increased cost in higher prices, the low paid workers would become relatively dearer and there would be an incentive for the firm to substitute other types of labour or machinery (although possibly only in the long run).

To this the student might well react by arguing out that conditions in the British labour market are very different from those in the American South and that it is characterised more by labour shortage than by the high unemployment rates

---

1 P.A. Samuelson, *Economics — An Introductory Analysis*, Seventh Edition (McGraw-Hill, 1967), p. 377.

common among young Negroes. Might not therefore a minimum wage play a positive role in the Government's policy of securing redeployment of labour? However, we have seen in Chapter 5 that there is a definite tendency for particular industries and regions to have an above-average proportion of low paid workers and as a result a minimum wage would tend to cause redundancy among those workers least likely to be absorbed into industries where labour is in short supply. We have seen that the Development Areas have a considerably higher proportion of low paid workers, and, as was pointed out by the Government's Working Party in its report, 'the introduction of a national minimum earnings level would tend to counter the effects of the Regional Employment Premium in making labour relatively cheaper to employers in Development Areas than elsewhere'.[1] Moreover, half those earning less than £15 in September 1968 were aged over 50. For them adjustment would undoubtedly be more difficult than for younger workers, and many firms would be unwilling to re-train men so near retirement age.

It may well be the case therefore that the Development Areas are our equivalent of the American South and the low paid worker over 50 the counterpart of the Negro youth. The introduction of a minimum wage may lead to unemployment among particular groups of 'vulnerable' workers. It is, however, very difficult to estimate what the size of the effect on employment is likely to be. Clearly not all of those at present earning less than the minimum wage would be thrown out of work, but we cannot make any more definite statement than this. The evidence relating to the United States Federal minimum wage is inconclusive and in any case the minimum applied there is rather different from that envisaged in this country.[2]

In order to offset any possible effect on employment, the minimum wage would need to be accompanied by measures designed to help those most affected — particularly in the form of increases in the aid given to Development Areas and in the effort devoted to industrial re-training.[3] (Of course, these additional measures might solve the problem *without* the minimum wage, but the latter is probably necessary as a catalyst). The extent of the additional measures required would depend on the level of the minimum wage to be introduced, and would naturally be less important in the case of a £12 10s. a week minimum than with the more ambitious objective of £15 a week.

---

[1] *A National Minimum Wage*, op. cit., para. 141.

[2] For references to the United States literature see H.M. Douty, 'Some Effects of the $1.00 Minimum Wage in the United States', *Economica*, 1960, and J.M. Peterson, 'Research Needs in Minimum Wage Theory' *Southern Economic Journal*, 1962.

[3] This problem is discussed in more detail by Edmonds and Radice, *Low Pay*, op. cit.

A National Minimum Wage — Summary

Pitt rejected a minimum wage because it would not provide for the needs of everyone living in poverty. The Government's Working Party appears equally to have been searching for a single all-embracing solution and they regarded as one of the major limitations of the minimum wage the fact that it would not help the retired, the unemployed or the chronic sick![1] A minimum wage clearly cannot, however, be expected to provide for the needs of all those below the poverty line, and it must be considered in conjunction with other measures to help those with low incomes.

In this section, I have considered two possible roles that a national minimum wage could play in helping people with low incomes. The first is that of helping those households that do not benefit from Family Allowances. As we have seen, the assumption underlying the Beveridge Plan that wages would be sufficient to cover the needs of these households is not necessarily valid. If a national minimum wage could guarantee a minimum level of earnings (for a 40 hour week) at the Supplementary Benefit scale (I.A.R.) for a one child family, then it would fill an important gap. It would only do so adequately, however, if measures were taken to offset any effect on the employment of particularly 'vulnerable' types of worker. (The extent of the possible effect on employment and of the compensatory measures that would be required is a subject which needs further investigation). The number of workers that would be affected by a minimum wage at this level is relatively small and it would involve only a minor addition to labour costs (on the assumption of no change in employment).

Secondly, I have discussed the possibilities of a minimum wage at the rather higher level of £15, which would be intended to help not only those with one child but also the larger families for whom the present child benefits are not adequate. Here Pitt's objection has much more force, and we have seen that even at this level it would not provide satisfactorily for the needs of larger families. Moreover, the effect on employment would be bound to be more serious and the addition to labour costs larger by a factor of 2 or 3 than in the case of a £12 10s. minimum level.

3.   SOCIAL SECURITY CONTRIBUTIONS AND THE LOW PAID WORKER

A man's take-home pay may be increased by either raising his gross earnings or reducing the amount deducted from it in income tax and social security contributions. The first of these possibilities has been discussed in the previous section, and I now consider whether the net earnings of low paid workers can be

---

[1] *A National Minimum Wage*, op. cit., para. 168.

raised by reducing the burden of social security contributions.[1]

Table 8.9. Income Tax and National Insurance Contributions Paid by a Person Earning Just Sufficient to Bring a Household to the Supplementary Benefit Level (I.A.R.) — June 1969.

Household Type :	Gross earnings required to bring household to Supplementary Benefit level (I.A.R.)			Income tax paid on these earnings			National Insurance paid on these earnings		
	£	s.	d.	£	s.	d.	£	s.	d.
Married Couple with :									
No children	10	6	0	4	10			17	10
1 child	12	6	0	—				19	9
2 children	13	5	0	—			1	0	8
3 children	14	1	0	—			1	1	8
4 children	14	17	0	—			1	2	2
6 children	16	12	0	—			1	4	0

Note : These figures are calculated on the same basis as those in Table 8.7, although the tax rates used are those in force for 1969–70.

In Table 8.9 I have shown the impact of the present (June 1969) income tax and National Insurance contributions on a person who is earning just enough to bring his family to the Supplementary Benefit level (I.A.R.). In all cases £1 or more would have been deducted from his gross earnings — even at this low level of income. This amount is quite substantial in relation to the net incomes of these households : for a family with one child it would represent nearly 10%. The deduction is largely in the form of National Insurance contributions, as families with children pay no income tax at all at this level of income (partly as a result of the concessions in the 1969 Budget). From this it appears that by reducing the burden of National Insurance contributions on low paid workers, the Government could raise their take-home pay quite considerably, and in this section I examine some of the ways in which this could be done.

The New National Superannuation Contributions

As we have seen in Chapter 7, the Government has announced its intention of abolishing the present contributions when National Superannuation is introduced

---

[1] Throughout this section I assume that the burden of the employee's contribution falls on the worker (the employer's contribution is not discussed here). This practice is followed by most writers in this field. See, for example, A.T. Peacock, *The Economics of National Insurance* (Hodge, 1952), Chapter V and J.A. Pechman, H.J. Aaron and M.K. Taussig, *Social Security : Perspectives for Reform* (The Brookings Institution, 1968).

and replacing them by wholly earnings-related contributions. Column 1 of Table 8.10 shows what the effect of the new contributions would have been if they had been in force in June 1969. Those at the bottom of the scale would have had to pay less than at present and those with earnings above £19 a week more than they do now. However, the reduction for the low paid worker is quite small. A person earning just the amount required to support a family with one child at the Supplementary Benefit level (I.A.R.) would be better off by only slightly over 3s. a week. The new National Superannuation contributions would still represent a substantial deduction from the earnings of the low paid worker.

Introducing A Minimum Exemption Level

The proposed National Superannuation contributions would replace the present regressive schedule by one which was proportional up to a certain earnings level (after which it became regressive).[1] Suppose, however, that we went further and *exempted* earnings up to a certain level, so that the contribution schedule became progressive. For the sake of illustration, we can take an exemption level of 40% of national average earnings — which in June 1969 would have been approximately £9 12s. A person would then have to pay contributions only on earnings above £9 12s. (and below the scheme's ceiling of £36).

This would, of course, require a higher rate of contributions on earnings above the exemption level. Using the information about earned income contained in the Inland Revenue report for 1966–7, we can estimate the rate of contribution that would be necessary on earnings above the exemption level to give the same total revenue from employees' contributions. This estimate is only very approximate, but it should indicate the order of magnitude (for details of the method of estimation, see Appendix G). On this basis, the rate of contributions payable on the band of earnings between 40% of the national average and the upper limit (1½ times the national average) would be of the order of 11–13% — or around double the rate proposed for National Superannuation.

Column 4 in Table 8.10 shows the effect of this exemption level on the contributions paid at different income levels. Those with low earnings would benefit a great deal from this change: the person earning just enough to keep a family with one child at the Supplementary Benefit level (I.A.R.) would now be about 13s. a week better off than at present.

Replacement of Social Security Contributions by a Surcharge on Income Tax

By introducing a minimum exemption level into the social security contribution schedule, we would be moving closer to the pattern of income tax deductions. In his 1969 Beveridge Memorial Lecture, Sir Paul Chambers went much further and argued that the social security contributions should be abolished altogether and

---

1 By 'regressive' I mean that the contribution rises less than proportionately with income. Under the proposed National Superannuation contributions, a person earning £2 000 a year in April 1968 would have paid 5.8% of his income in contributions, but a person earning £5 000 would have paid only 2.3%.

Table 8.10. Social Security Contributions – Present Contributions, Proposed National Superannuation Contributions, and Contributions with a Minimum Exemption level – June 1969.

Earnings £ per week	1. Present National Insurance Contributions[a] (at June 1969) £	s.	d.	2. Proposed National Superannuation Contributions[b] £	s.	d.	3. Difference (2–1) £	s.	d.	4. National Superannuation Contributions with an Exemption level[c] £	s.	d.	5. Difference (4–1) £	s.	d.
8		16	8		10	10	–	5	10		0	0	–	16	8
9		16	8		12	2	–	4	6			0	–	16	8
10		17	10		13	6	–	4	4		1	0	–	16	10
11		18	10		14	10	–	4	0		3	5	–	15	5
12		19	9		16	2	–	3	7		5	10	–	13	11
13	1	0	8		17	6	–	3	2		8	3	–	12	5
14	1	1	8		18	11	–	2	9		10	8	–	11	0
15	1	2	7	1	0	3	–	2	4		13	1	–	9	6
20	1	5	4	1	7	0	+	1	8	1	5	1	–	9	3
25	1	6	0	1	13	9	+	7	9	1	17	1	+	11	1
30	1	6	5	2	0	6	+	14	1	2	9	1	+ 1	2	8
40	1	6	5	2	8	7	+ 1	2	2	3	3	6	+ 1	17	1
50	1	6	5	2	8	7	+ 1	2	2	3	3	6	+ 1	17	1

Notes: a   The present National Insurance contributions include both flat rate and graduated (not contracted out).

b   At June 1969 earnings levels. The June 1969 average weekly earnings figure is estimated as approximately £24 (this only affects the upper ceiling).

c   Earnings up to 40% of national average exempt (see text) and contribution rate above this of 12% (up to ceiling of 3/2 average earnings).

154

the revenue raised by an increase in income tax.[1] He criticised the National Superannuation contributions as 'a pale, unsatisfactory and partial imitation of income tax' and pointed out that income tax is a very much more precise way of relating contributions to a person's circumstances. It takes account not only of his earnings, but also of the number of children he has and his other sources of income.

If the social security contributions were replaced by a surcharge on income tax, then for those with low incomes this would be more or less equivalent to abolishing the contributions completely, since we have seen that they pay little or no income tax. It would therefore provide a considerable benefit to those with low earnings — much more so than the new contributions proposed for National Superannuation.

There are however two objections to this proposal of Sir Paul Chambers. Firstly, the surcharge on income tax required to provide the same level of revenue would be quite substantial. I have estimated that in 1968–9 the surcharge required to give the same revenue as the *employees'* contributions under the proposed National Superannuation scheme would have been approximately 3s. 6d. in the £ on the standard rate of income tax. This would represent a very substantial increase in the marginal tax rate faced by those in the upper part of the income scale. If one believes that income taxation has an adverse effect on the incentive to work of those at the top, then an increase of this order would be very difficult to accept (rather strangely, the question of the effect on incentives was not discussed by Sir Paul Chambers in his Lecture).

The second objection to the abolition of social security contributions is that it would destroy the 'contributory' basis of the scheme — an aspect on which Beveridge laid great stress (as did the Government in its White Paper on National Superannuation). In order to assess the strength of this objection, we have to decide exactly what is entailed by the 'contributory principle'. The interpretation which seems most in accord with the view of Beveridge is that the social security scheme should be *neutral* as far as the distribution of income is concerned — everyone should receive what in some sense 'they had paid for'.[2] There are two principal arguments for maintaining the contribution principle as interpreted in this way. Firstly, people are said to prefer to receive benefits in this form: in Beveridge's words 'benefit in return for contributions, rather than free allowances from the State, is what the people of Britain desire.'[3] Secondly, to the extent that people see a relationship between the contributions they pay and the benefits that they receive, any possible disincentive effect of the contributions will be reduced.[4]

---

1 *Forward from Beveridge*, Beveridge Memorial Lecture 1969, op. cit.

2 See, for example, *Social Insurance and Allied Services*, op. cit., para. 273.

3 ibid., para. 21.

4 They will then be seen as compulsory saving rather than as a pure tax.

For Beveridge, the contribution principle required that contributions and benefits be flat-rate. Although this did not necessarily guarantee neutrality *between* generations, it did (in the case of pensions at least) ensure that *people of the same age* received the same amount and paid the same contribution. With the introduction of earnings-related schemes, the concept of neutrality becomes more complicated, but it could be argued that this condition is satisfied in the case of the graduated pension — since £1 of contributions earns the same pension whoever pays it. Under National Superannuation, however, this would no longer be true : £1 contributed by a person with low earnings would give more additional pension than £1 contributed by someone higher up the scale. The proposed scheme does, therefore, entail a major element of redistribution.

The important question is whether the changes in social security contributions discussed here would represent any further departure from the contributory principle than the proposed National Superannuation scheme. As far as the introduction of an exemption level into the contribution formula is concerned, there seems really to be very little effective difference. On the other hand, the complete abolition of the contributions suggested by Sir Paul Chambers would represent an important change. This lies not in the abolition of the contributions *per se* (since the surcharge on income tax would also be called a 'contribution') but in the fact that a person's pension could no longer be tied directly to contributions. For the amount actually paid by a person in income tax will depend on a whole range of factors (how many children he has, whether he has a mortgage or life insurance, etc.) and his pension could certainly not be based on this.[1] If contributions were financed through a surcharge on income tax, the pension would have to be divorced from a person's contribution record and this would undoubtedly weaken the link with 'insurance'.

New Social Security Contributions — Summary

The present National Insurance contributions represent a substantial deduction from the earnings of low paid workers, and for a man earning just enough to bring a one child family to the Supplementary Benefit scale (I.A.R.) they amount to 10% of his net income.

The contributions proposed for the new National Superannuation scheme would fall less heavily on the low paid worker, but would still be considerable even for a person earning only £10 a week. The burden could, however, be substantially reduced by the introduction of a minimum exemption level for contributions.

The alternative solution of abolishing contributions and financing the scheme through a surcharge on income tax would be even more effective in helping those with low incomes, but would involve a major change in the nature of the insurance scheme in so far as benefits could no longer be tied to contributions. The required surcharge on the standard rate would also be very high — 3s. 6d. in the £.

---

1 If it were, then we should have such anomalies as a married man receiving a smaller pension than a single person with the same income over his lifetime. Sir Paul Chambers, of course, would prefer the pension to be flat-rate in any event.

9 Negative Income Taxation and Social Dividend Schemes

The last few years have seen growing interest in the possibilities of solving the problem of poverty through some type of 'negative income tax' scheme. Interest in this has been particularly strong in the United States,[1] where over a thousand economists signed a petition in its support in 1968 — demonstrating a remarkable degree of unanimity for the economics profession! However, while the term 'negative income tax' is of recent origin, the basic principle is far from being new. The rudiments of the idea were present in the Speenhamland system of giving relief adopted in 1795, and very similar schemes were discussed in Britain over twenty years ago under the title of a 'social dividend'.

In view of the similarity of principle, I have brought together in this chapter the discussion of two schemes of this type, although they have in fact quite different objectives. The first is a negative income tax scheme[2] which has been proposed for this country by Professor D.S. Lees to help low income families with children, and which can be viewed as an alternative to the schemes for new child benefits considered in the previous chapter. The second section is concerned with the more ambitious social dividend schemes which aim to provide a single comprehensive solution to the problem of poverty — covering not just one group of the population but all those with low incomes.

1. A PROPOSED NEGATIVE INCOME TAX FOR FAMILIES

The basic idea of negative income taxation is to extend the tax schedule below the present exemption levels so that people whose incomes fall below these levels will not merely pay no tax but will receive a supplementary payment. In other words, whereas under the present income tax a person either pays tax or he does not, with a negative income tax there would be a third possibility — that the Inland Revenue paid him.

---

1 For references to the proposals put forward in the United States, see C. Green, *Negative Taxes and the Poverty Problem* (The Brookings Institution, 1967).

2 In this field the names multiply even faster than the schemes. For the connoisseurs, I have followed Green (op. cit.) in confining the term 'negative income tax' to schemes based on the present income tax exemption levels. The more radical schemes involving major changes in the present income tax are referred to as 'social dividend' schemes.

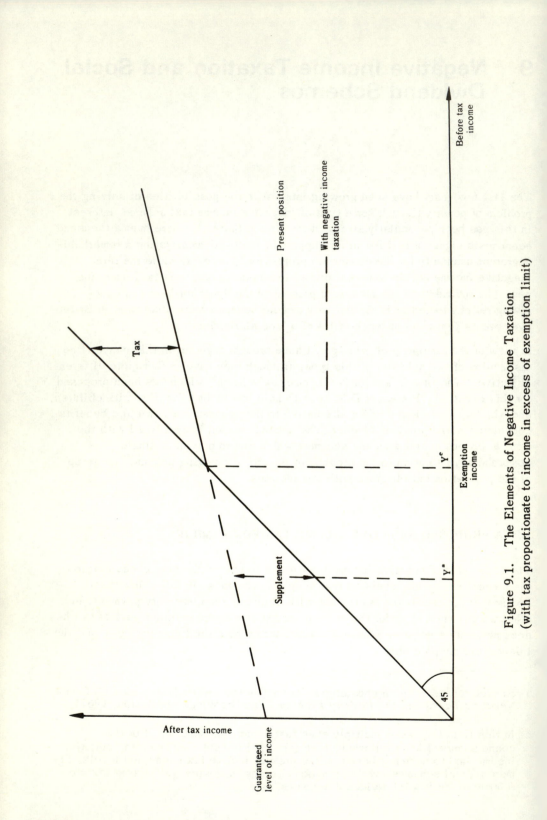

Figure 9.1. The Elements of Negative Income Taxation
(with tax proportionate to income in excess of exemption limit)

The elements of the scheme are illustrated in Figure 9.1 for the simple case of a tax proportionate to income in excess of an exemption limit. If a person's income is above the exemption level, Y^e, he pays tax just as at present; if, however, it is below Y^e he receives a supplement proportionate to the gap between his income and the exemption level. The size of the supplement is determined by the negative tax rate, t, so that at the income level Y^a he receives a supplement of $t\,(Y^e - Y^a)$. The tax rate t and the exemption level of income Y^e together determine the guaranteed level of after-tax income $(t\,Y^e)$ which a person receives if he has no other source of income. The negative income tax can in fact be interpreted as providing a guaranteed level of income and then taxing any other income received until the supplement is extinguished. (This is of course the same in principle as the income supplement scheme for old people discussed in Chapter 7).

The proponents of negative income taxation have pointed to the fact that people with low incomes do not receive the full benefit from the allowances provided under the present income tax.[1] As we have seen in Chapter 8, this is particularly true of the allowances for children, which give little or no benefit to families with low incomes. A negative income tax, on the other hand, would mean that all families with children gained from the allowances. A family with an income below the level at which it begins to pay tax would receive a negative tax supplement which increased with the level of the child allowance. This has led to the suggestion by Professor D.S. Lees that more help could be given to low income families through replacing the present Family Allowances by a negative income tax covering all families with children.[2] In the rest of this section, I examine some of the implications of this proposal. (It should be emphasised at the outset that the negative income tax would apply only to income tax payers with dependent children).

The negative income tax proposed by Lees would operate in the way described above: all income tax payers with children whose incomes fell short of their total tax allowances would receive a supplement equal to 50% of the difference. A family whose tax allowances (personal, child, earned income allowances etc.) totalled £900 but whose income was only £600, would receive a supplement of £150.

The effect of this scheme with the present income tax allowances is illustrated for a family with 3 children in Figure 9.2.[3] On the assumptions described in the

1 Cf. M. Friedman, *Capitalism and Freedom* (University of Chicago Press, 1962) and R. Lampman, 'Approaches to the Reduction of Poverty', *American Economic Review*, May 1965.

2 D.S. Lees, 'Poor Families and Fiscal Reform', *Lloyds Bank Review*, October 1967.

3 Figure 9.2 is drawn on the basis of the income tax allowances in force for 1969–70. These allowances have been increased since Lees proposed his scheme in 1967, so that the supplement is higher than that suggested by his calculations.

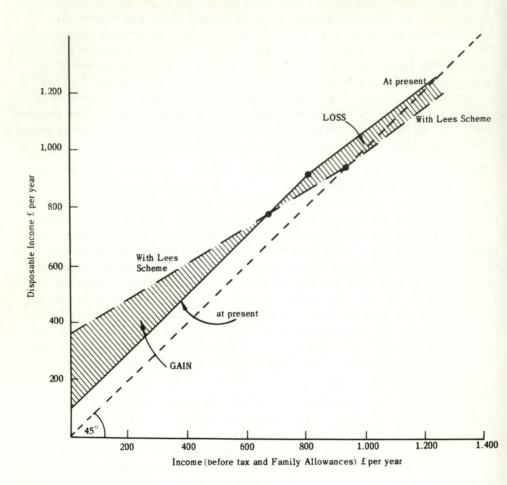

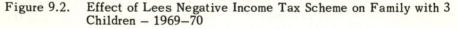

Figure 9.2.   Effect of Lees Negative Income Tax Scheme on Family with 3
              Children — 1969—70

Note: This figure is drawn on the following assumptions:
  (1) The only deductions for tax purposes are the personal and child allow-
      ances and earned income relief.
  (2) All income is earned by the father.
  (3) In the case of the Lees scheme, the child allowances are those before
      allowing the 1969—70 reduction for children receiving Family Allowance
  (4) All children are aged under 11.
  (5) That the effective rate of tax applied to earned income under the Lees
      scheme is 38.9% — see footnote 1, page 161.

notes to this figure, this family would receive a negative tax supplement if its income fell below £926 a year. A family with an income of £500 would receive a supplement of £166 per year and a family with an income of £700 would receive £88.[1] Against this supplement must be set the loss from the abolition of Family Allowances, which in 1969—70 are worth £99 to this family if it pays no income tax. In all, such a family would gain from the Lees proposal if its income apart from Family Allowances is at present below £672 — or if its total income is below £771.

In his article Lees only sketched his proposal in broad terms, and there are a number of important gaps. He did not specify, for example, how income was to be defined for the purpose of negative income taxation, or over what period it was to be assessed; he did not discuss how unearned income was to be treated, or what deductions and allowances would be permitted. Without these details it is difficult to examine the consequences of his proposals and in order to do so I have filled in some of the features which he left undiscussed. In doing this I have assumed that the negative tax would have to be integrated as far as possible with the existing income tax if it were to be administratively feasible. This means that the definition of income, the period of assessment, and so on, would be the same as under the present income tax. I have also assumed that it would operate as far as possible through the P.A.Y.E. system: where an employee was entitled to a supplement, this would be added to his earnings by the employer, who would in turn deduct it from the tax forwarded to the Inland Revenue.

Although integration of the negative income tax with the present 'positive' tax system might bring it nearer to administrative feasibility, this has a number of important implications which should not be overlooked. Some of the most obvious are outlined below:

(i) in its period of assessment, the income tax is very different from the present social security provisions, which are based on a weekly period. This has important implications for those whose earnings fluctuate a great deal from week to week.

(ii) under the present income tax, National Insurance and Supplementary Benefits are not taxable and would not, therefore, be counted for negative tax purposes. This point will be discussed further below.

(iii) under the income tax, relief is given for such things as life insurance and mortgage interest and these would therefore increase the negative tax supplement to those below the exemption level.

(iv) since the self-employed are not in general covered by P.A.Y.E., their

---

1 In the calculations given by Lees, he bases the negative tax supplement on the tax allowances including the earned income relief allowed on its *actual earnings*. This means that where the family's income is all earned, the negative tax rate is only $\frac{7}{9} \times 50\% = 39\%$. In other words, if the father earns £200 more, the exemption level will go up $\frac{2}{9} \times £200 = £44$, and the negative supplement will fall by 50% of (£200 − £44) = £78.

negative income tax supplement would have to be based on the previous
year's earnings and could not be adjusted quickly for changes in earnings.

Implications of the Lees Scheme

The discussion of the implications of the Lees scheme follows the same pattern
as that of the child benefit schemes in Chapter 8. The first part deals with the
effect of the scheme on low income families, the second with the probable cost
and the third with the effect on work incentives. As a further factor in the case
of the negative income tax scheme, we have also to consider the question of its
administration (which did not raise any problems in the case of the new child
benefit schemes).

(a) *Effectiveness of Lees Scheme in Helping Low Income Families*

In the case of a family with 3 children, Figure 9.2 showed that in 1969–70 the
Lees scheme would benefit all families with incomes below £771. On the other
hand, families with incomes above this level would be worse off since they would
lose the Family Allowances and receive less (or nothing) from the negative tax
supplement. Since the Supplementary Benefit level (I.A.R.) would be £725,[1] this
means that the benefit from the Lees scheme would be confined to families below,
or only slightly above, the poverty line.

Table 9.1 shows the effect of the Lees scheme for families of different sizes on
the basis of the assumptions described in detail in the notes. The first column
gives the 'exemption level' of income at which the family would cease to receive
negative tax supplements. The second column shows the income at which the
family would cease to benefit overall from the introduction of the Lees scheme
(allowing for the loss of Family Allowances). This income level may be compared
with the Supplementary Benefit scale (I.A.R.) shown in column 3. The last column
in Table 9.1 shows the gross earnings at which the negative tax supplement would
be just sufficient to raise the family to the Supplementary Benefit scale (I.A.R.).

From Table 9.1, it is apparent that the introduction of the Lees scheme would be
a very efficient way of redistributing income from those above the poverty line to
those below it. In each case the income at which a person would cease to gain
from the change is very close to the Supplementary Benefit scale (I.A.R.). With
the Lees scheme, the money at present spent on Family Allowances would in
effect be taken away from those above the poverty line and given to those below.
In this way, it promises to be an effective way of helping those families with
low incomes at little additional cost, since the increased benefit to those at the
bottom is financed to a considerable extent by those above the poverty line.

The question of cost will be discussed below, but it should be noted that, unlike
the child benefit schemes discussed in Chapter 8, the burden of helping low
income families would fall more or less evenly on families above the poverty

---

[1] Assuming that two children are aged under 5 and one between 5 and 10.

Table 9.1.   Effect of Replacing Family Allowances by the Lees Negative Income Tax Scheme – 1969–70

	1	2	3	4
Number of Children in Family	Income Tax 'Exemption level'	Total present income below which Lees scheme gives higher income	Supplementary Benefit scale (I.A.R.)[a]	Earnings at which supplement sufficient to raise family to S.B. scale (I.A.R.)[b]
1	646	646	594	645
2	810	736	686	690
3	974	818	778	740
4	1 138	900	870	790
5	1 302	982	962	830
6	1 466	1 064	1 054	880

Notes: This table is based on the same assumptions as Figure 9.2, except with regard to the ages of children.

In calculating the child tax allowances, the average of the rates for children aged under 11 and aged 11–15 is used. In the case of the Supplementary Benefit scale, the allowance was based on the average for children aged 5–10 and 11–12.

a   The Supplementary Benefit Scale is that in force in June 1969.

b   *Gross* earnings (allowing for National Insurance contributions and income tax) and rounded to nearest £5.

line – including those only a little above.[1] This is brought out in Figure 9.2. A family with 3 children with an income only £2 above the Supplementary Benefit scale (I.A.R.) would lose 10s. a week as a result of the introduction of the Lees scheme. The Lees scheme would therefore mean a reduction in income for families who, although above the poverty line, are far from well off. (In fact, when we allow for National Insurance contributions, the take-home pay of these families may be *less* than the Supplementary Benefit scale (I.A.R.)).

Table 9.1 also suggests that the negative tax supplement would be relatively less generous to large families than to small families: a man with 2 children would have to earn £13 5s a week to reach the Supplementary Benefit level, but a man with 6 children would need to earn £16 16s a week. The additional negative tax supplement for an extra child in a family would be 50% of the child tax allowance, which in the case of a child under 11 would be £1 2s – or little more than the present Family Allowance for the third and subsequent children. As we have seen in Chapter 8, the present Family Allowances fall a long way short of the Beveridge objective of meeting the subsistence needs of all children apart from the first. In the case of the Lees scheme, one must take into account the fact that the negative tax supplement would be paid for the first child, but even so the total supplement for large families would probably fall below that payable with Family Allowances increased to a 'Back to Beveridge' level.

As in the case of the child benefit schemes, I have used the Inland Revenue survey of personal incomes to estimate the effect of the introduction of the Lees scheme on low income families. (Since the benefit to a family depends critically on its level of income, it is not possible to use the results of the Ministry of Social Security enquiry). As pointed out in the previous chapter, the absolute figures for the numbers below the poverty line would be misleading (because National Insurance and other benefits are excluded from income), but the Inland Revenue survey may nonetheless provide a reasonable basis for comparing the relative effectiveness of the different schemes.

Table 9.2 is based on the Inland Revenue survey of personal incomes for 1966–7, and shows what the effect of the Lees scheme would have been if it had replaced the Family Allowances then in force. For comparison, I have included the corresponding figures for a 10s increase in Family Allowances and for the new child benefit schemes (as given in Table 8.6). The Lees scheme would have been considerably more effective in helping raise families above the National Assistance scale (I.A.R.) than the 10s increase in Family Allowances – principally because of the benefit given to families with 1 child. It would, however, have been slightly less effective than the Child Poverty Action Group

---

[1] It should be noted that the loss from the abolition of the Family Allowances to those at present paying income tax would be partly offset by the restoration of the child tax allowances to their pre-1968–9 level. The overall loss for a standard rate tax payer would be £18 per child for third and subsequent children. For a surtax-payer the loss would of course be smaller than this – and he may in fact come out rather better than someone just above the poverty line!

scheme and considerably less so than the Walley scheme.

So far we have discussed the effect of the Lees scheme on the assumption that the father is in work, but we must also consider what would happen if he became sick or unemployed. As we have seen, neither National Insurance nor Supplementary Benefits are at present treated as taxable income. If we take first of all the (unlikely) case of a man's being unemployed or sick for the whole of the tax year, then he would be assessed for negative income tax purposes as having no income and would receive a 'full' supplement equal to 50% of his total allowances. This supplement, together with National Insurance benefit, would raise him comfortably above the Supplementary Benefit scale unless he had very high rent.

It has, however, been suggested by Mr. Douglas Houghton that the National Insurance benefits should be brought within the P.A.Y.E. system and taxed as other income.[1] He argues that this could be done by making the Ministry of Social Security the 'employer' of someone who was sick or unemployed, so that they deducted tax from the benefit as due. If this were done (as seems inevitable if a negative income tax were to be introduced), then the benefit from the Lees scheme to families where the father was sick or unemployed would be considerably smaller and would not in general be enough to raise a person to the Supplementary Benefit scale (I.A.R.), so that the need for Supplementary Benefits would remain. When we allow for the more realistic case of a person's being unemployed or sick for part of the year, we must take account of the fact that the annual income tax assessment assumes a greater degree of averaging than is allowed for in the weekly Supplementary Benefits assessment.[2] Finally, the Lees scheme, like the child benefit schemes, would lead to a substantial reduction in the number of families subject to the wage stop — since the normal income of the family when the father was at work would be increased.

(b) *The Cost of the Lees Scheme*

In his article, Lees presented a minimum and a maximum estimate of the cost of his scheme for the year 1964—5 of £75 million and £118 million respectively (before allowing for the saving on Family Allowances). He concludes that 'even on our maximum assumption, which is almost certain to be an over-statement, the cost of a negative income tax is considerably less than that of present family

---

1 D. Houghton, *Paying for the Social Services*, Occasional Paper 16 (Second Edition, Institute of Economic Affairs, 1968), p. 29.

2 The negative tax supplement received by a person when sick or unemployed would depend on his earnings in the earlier part of the year. If these had been above the exemption level, the negative tax supplement (including tax refunds) might be quite small. We should note also that there would be the reverse of the usual income tax 'averaging' problem: a person might do better if he was sick for one tax year and worked the next than if he was sick for six months in both.

allowances'.[1]

Table 9.2.   Estimated Effect of Lees Scheme on Low Income Families —
Comparison with 1968 Increase in Family Allowances and New
Child Benefit Schemes

Measure:	Proportion of families with incomes below National Assistance scale (I.A.R.) in 1966—7 that would have been raised above by measure shown %
Increase of 10s per child in Family Allowances	12
Child Poverty Action Group scheme	33
Walley scheme	48
Lees scheme	30

See notes to Table 8.6.

This prediction of a substantial net *saving* from his scheme is rather optimistic. In calculating the net cost of the scheme, Lees uses the Inland Revenue survey of personal incomes to estimate the cost of the negative tax supplements and then compares this with the *gross* cost of Family Allowances (£150 in 1964—5). It is, however, the *net* rather than the *gross* cost of Family Allowances that should be used in making the comparison, and account must be taken of the income tax that is at present paid on them. The tax paid may be estimated at £35 million,[2] so that it would make a significant difference. On this basis, there would still be a net saving on the minimum asumption, but it would be considerably smaller, and on the maximum assumption the scheme would just about break even. (It should be borne in mind, however, that we have not taken account of the saving on Supplementary Benefits.)

From this it appears that the Lees scheme could be introduced at virtually no budgetary cost and possibly with some saving. This is achieved by reducing the benefit paid to families with children above the poverty line. As with the new child benefit schemes, it is open to the objection that the burden of helping those with low incomes would fall on the rich with children and not on those

---

1 *Poor Families and Fiscal Reform,* op. cit., p. 14. The minimum estimate is based on the assumption that all children are aged less than 11, the maximum estimate on the assumption that they are all over 11 (and under 16).

2 This estimate is based on the Inland Revenue survey of personal incomes. It may at first sight appear rather high, but it should be borne in mind that abolishing Family Allowances increases the number eligible for negative tax supplements. (Lees estimated the cost of his scheme on the basis of incomes *including Family Allowances*). The figure given for the tax paid on Family Allowances includes this increase in negative tax supplements.

without children. With the Lees scheme, this objection is more serious, since, as we have seen, it is not just surtax payers who would be worse off and families with children not far above the poverty line would have a substantial reduction in their net income. This could be offset by adjustments elsewhere in the tax system, but the scheme would then look very different.

(c) *Effect on Work Incentives*

As in the case of the child benefit schemes, we must distinguish two separate aspects of the incentives question: decisions about whether or not to enter the labour force, and decisions about the number of hours to work.

The effect of the Lees scheme on the first of these decisions would clearly depend on whether there was any change in the treatment of National Insurance and other benefits for income tax purposes. However, this would primarily affect the size rather than the direction of the effect, for even if these benefits were included as taxable income, a person would still receive a larger negative tax supplement when out of work (the size of the supplement rises as his income falls). In this respect, therefore, the Lees scheme — unlike the child benefit schemes — would tend to have an adverse effect on decisions about whether to enter the labour force.

Turning to the effect on the number of hours worked (or intensity of work effort), it is clear that for most families the Lees scheme would reduce their net income without changing their marginal tax rate. We should therefore expect them to work more (on the assumption that leisure is a normal good), although it seems unlikely that this effect is of much importance. For the minority of families who gain from the scheme, however, the effect is likely to be in the opposite direction. These families would be better off — by a considerable amount in some cases — and would face a very much higher marginal tax rate than at present. Families with incomes below the exemption level would face an effective tax rate of 7s 9d in the £ — or considerably higher than the present standard rate of income tax on earned income (6s 5d).

Although this would only relate to a minority of families (around 10–15%) and although we have seen in Chapter 6 that high marginal tax rates may be less of a disincentive at the lower end of the income scale, this increase in the marginal tax rate is certainly too high to be ignored. Lees himself dismisses the possibility that his scheme might lead to any reduction in work effort with the comment that 'the effects on the incentive to work are unlikely to be marked with a negative income tax rate of 50%'.[1] However, he provides no support for this view, and as we have seen in Chapter 6 the available evidence does not allow us to draw any such definite conclusions about the size of the disincentive effect.

Professor Kaim-Caudle has pointed out in his criticism of the Lees scheme that it cannot be viewed in isolation from the means-tested benefits at present

---

1 *Poor Families and Fiscal Reform*, op. cit., p. 11.

provided.[1] In support of this he cites the (probably extreme) case of a man who for every £1 increase in his earnings would lose 5s rate rebate and 3s 4d rent rebate, and have to pay social security contributions (1s 4d under the proposed National Superannuation scheme). If a 39% negative income tax rate were then to be introduced on top of this, his marginal tax rate would be over 17s in the £. The response to this might be that the negative income tax would allow these means-tested benefits to be replaced. This, however, would involve a considerable reduction in the benefit given to many low income families (who might well be worse off) and would make nonsense of the estimates of its effectiveness given above. Moreover any attempt to compensate for the loss of these benefits by increasing the negative tax supplement would be self-defeating, since this could only be achieved by raising the negative tax rate.[2]

(d) *Administration*

In the case of the new child benefit schemes, no problems of administration would arise, since the new benefits could be administered through the existing Family Allowance machinery. The same is not true, however, of the negative income tax, which raises a number of serious administrative problems. These problems might in fact be soluble if the scheme were fully integrated with the P.A.Y.E. system, but this would, as we have seen earlier, limit the effectiveness of the scheme (for example in helping the self-employed), and would add considerably to the costs of administration. It would mean that all those families now relieved from tax by the allowances would fall within the Inland Revenue net. Moreover, the problem of enforcement would be increased by the higher marginal tax rates: the stakes would now be higher on both sides.

As we have seen, Lees did not fill out the details of his proposed scheme and did not discuss the way in which it was to be administered. This invited the charge by Professor Townsend that 'none of the proposals for negative income tax have been made with direct reference to the *actual* circumstances of a cross-section of even ten or 20 households in poverty' and that they were 'abstract and indeed vague economic exercises'.[3] He goes on to list some of the most obvious problems.

Clearly this is an important question but I do not feel that it would be fruitful to discuss it at greater length here. This reflects not only my personal lack of expertise, but also the fact that the information required to assess the feasibility of a negative income tax is simply not available. It seems out of the question to make any realistic estimate of the likely costs of its administration. The

1 P.R. Kaim-Caudle, 'Selectivity in Family Allowances' in *Social Services for all*? Part One, Fabian Tract 382. See also P.R. Kaim-Caudle, 'Selectivity and the Social Services', *Lloyds Bank Review*, April 1969.

2 The adoption of a non-proportional tax schedule might ease the problem.

3 P. Townsend, 'The difficulties of negative income tax', in *Social Services for all*? Part Four, Fabian Tract 385.

difficulties are well illustrated by the recent debate on 'selectivity' and 'universality' in which the discussion has been characterised by such assertions as 'Equipment is at last available which could, if required, quite cheaply bring the personal taxation and welfare services of the whole nation up to date every day',[1] and that 'the computer code number proposal is not, and never can be, the answer to the problem of child poverty.'[2] Where exactly between these two extremes the truth lies can only be discovered by a detailed examination of the problems — preferably by a body able to call evidence from the Government departments to whom the administration of the scheme would fall.

The Lees Negative Income Tax — Summary

A negative income tax of the type suggested by Professor Lees would do a great deal to help families with children who fall below the poverty line. It would do considerably more than the 1968 increase in Family Allowances, although it would not be quite as effective as the new child benefit schemes discussed in Chapter 8. The effect on families where the father was out of work would depend on the treatment of National Insurance and other benefits under the negative income tax. If these were to be taxed as other income, the scheme would not eliminate the need for Supplementary Benefits among these families. It would, however, substantially reduce the number subject to the wage stop.

The replacement of Family Allowances by the negative income tax would involve virtually no budgetary cost (although Lees' claim that it would bring a considerable net saving is not borne out). This would be achieved however, by reducing the benefit given to the majority of families with children, many of whom are themselves not far above the poverty line.

There are two important uncertainties with regard to the effect of the scheme proposed by Lees. The first concerns the effect on work incentives. The scheme would lead to a substantial increase in the marginal tax rate faced by the bottom 10–15% of the families in the income distribution. Whether this is likely to have a serious effect on work effort is, however, not known. The second unknown is the cost of administering the scheme and indeed whether its operation would in fact be feasible at all.

2.   A SOCIAL DIVIDEND FOR ALL?

The negative income tax scheme discussed in Section 1 was directed at one particular group of the population and had one specific objective — helping low income families with children. In this section, I examine a much more radical

---

1   B. Rhys Williams, *The New Social Contract* (Conservative Political Centre, 1967).

2   R.M. Titmuss, *Commitment to Welfare* (George Allen and Unwin, 1968), Chapter X.

proposal — to merge the present social security and income tax systems into a single social dividend scheme. Under this scheme, the present social security benefits would be abolished and replaced by a social dividend payable to everyone. The revenue required to finance the scheme and to replace the present income tax would be raised by a proportional tax on all income.

A comprehensive scheme of this type would, it is claimed, provide everyone (whether in work or not) with a guaranteed minimum income, and would eliminate the need for special provisions to help particular categories. Moreover, it would fill the gaps in the present social security system, providing a solution to the problems we have considered in earlier chapters. It has recently been argued by C.V. Brown and D.A. Dawson, for example, that [1]

> 'A guaranteed income for everyone in the country could at a stroke eliminate the hard core of real poverty that remains in Britain. *Everyone* would be entitled to it and *everyone* would receive it. Poverty due to ignorance, ineligibility or pride leading to not claiming present benefits would be eliminated. The present system of benefits from numerous agencies using different and sometimes conflicting criteria would end.'

The second principal advantage claimed for the social dividend scheme is that it would improve work incentives. It would provide more encouragement for people at present receiving state benefits to re-enter the labour force, and would, it is argued, allow the marginal tax rate to be reduced over a wide range of income. Thus, Brown and Dawson conclude that 'this would appear to be one of those all too rare occasions when the dictates of equity and efficiency point in the same direction'.

The proposals of Brown and Dawson are the most recent in a long line of social dividend schemes. The idea is in fact primarily associated with the name of Lady Rhys Williams, who first put forward a scheme of this type in 1942. She subsequently produced a number of revised versions of the scheme, which was discussed by the Royal Commission on the Taxation of Profits and Income in 1954, together with similar proposals by the Liberal Party, Professor J.E. Meade, Sir Paul Chambers and A.T. Haynes and R.J. Kirton.[2]

In this section I consider one particular version of a social dividend scheme — based on the first of the Rhys Williams proposals, which presented the principal features of the social dividend in their starkest form. She did not describe this

---

[1] Brown and Dawson, *Personal Taxation, Incentives and Tax Reform*, op. cit., p. 79.

[2] Lady Juliet Rhys Williams, *Something to Look Forward To* (MacDonald, 1943). For references to the other schemes, see the memorandum submitted on this subject by the Board of Inland Revenue to the Royal Commission on the Taxation of Profits and Income, Minutes of Evidence, Third Day. See also, A.T. Peacock, *The Economics of National Insurance*, op. cit., Ch. 7, B. Rhys Williams, *The New Social Contract*, op. cit., and H.S. Booker, 'Lady Rhys Williams' Proposals for the Amalgamation of Direct Taxation with Social Insurance, *Economic Journal*, 1946.

scheme in great detail, but I think that it is fair to say that the version considered here embodies the spirit of her proposal. (The changes that have taken place since 1942 have, of course, necessitated some modification of the details). I shall first describe the main elements of the scheme, and then consider its impact on the distribution of income and on work incentives. I have however postponed discussion of the conclusions to be drawn until Chapter 10.

A Social Dividend Scheme

The principal elements of the scheme discussed here are:

(a) Payment of a weekly *social dividend* to all men, women and children at the present Supplementary Benefit scale rates (including an average allowance for housing expenditure).

(b) Abolition of the present Family Allowances, National Insurance benefits, and Supplementary Benefits.

(c) Abolition of employees' National Insurance contributions, income tax and surtax.

(d) Finance of the social dividend payments, and replacement of the revenue at present raised through income tax, by a proportional tax on all income (except the social dividend).[1]

Proportional Tax Rate Required under Social Dividend Scheme

The effectiveness of the social dividend — both in redistributing income and in improving work incentives — depends crucially on the level of the proportional tax that would be required to finance the social dividend and to replace the present direct taxes. It is, however, very difficult to estimate the tax rate required with any precision.[2]

Calculation of the gross cost of the social dividend payments is reasonably straight-forward, although it still requires a number of assumptions (see the notes to Table 9.3). The gross cost, together with that of the major categories, is shown

---

1 This scheme is rather different from that proposed by Brown and Dawson, which is closer to the later 'compromise' versions of the Rhys Williams scheme. They would pay differential rates of social dividend to those who were sick, unemployed, disabled, widowed, or over 65 — so that the insurance benefits would remain in a watered-down form. The social dividend for people outside these groups would be considerably below the Supplementary Benefit scale. Their scheme would be financed by a direct tax of 32½% up to £4 000 (with higher rates above, but the top being only 42½%), by a value-added tax at 11% (although Purchase Tax would be abolished), and by a wealth tax. They would also abolish *all* current grants from the Government (not just the social security benefits) and housing subsidies.

2 This is well illustrated by the disagreement between the Liberal Party and the Inland Revenue about the rate of tax required to finance the former's proposal submitted to the Royal Commission on Taxation of Profits and Income. See the memorandum of the Board of Inland Revenue, op. cit.

Table 9.3. Revenue Required under Social Dividend Scheme — Estimate for 1967

	£ million 1967	
1. Gross Cost of Social Dividend		
13.6m. married couples	5 880	
9.9m. single householders	2 880	
4.3m. single non-householders	610	
13.7m. children	1 120	
		10 490
2. Present Revenue		
income and surtax [a]	4 042	
employees' National Insurance contributions [b]	942	
		4 984
3. Saving on Present Benefits [c]		
National Insurance	– 2 085	
Supplementary Benefits	– 392	
Family Allowances	– 161	
		– 2 638
TOTAL REVENUE REQUIRED		12 836

Notes: These estimates are based on the total population of the United Kingdom (mid-year estimate) in 1967 (*Annual Abstract of Statistics*, 1968, Table 11). The Supplementary Benefit rates are those in force in June 1967 and include average rent as estimated in Appendix B (except for children where a 3s allowance per child for rent is included). All those over 65 are assumed to receive long-term addition, those below are assumed not to. It is assumed that all those aged 16—20 are unmarried and non-householders and that all those single persons over 21 are householders. The number of married couples is estimated on the basis of the 1966 sample census (*Annual Abstract of Statistics*, 1968, Table 13).

[a] United Kingdom taxes on income plus additions to tax reserves from 1968 Blue Book, Table 22.

[b] National insurance and health contributions (Blue Book, Table 22) less employers contributions (Blue Book, Table 25).

[c] Blue Book, Table 41.

in the first item of Table 9.3 (it should be noted that the social dividend rates vary with age for children and that they are higher for people over 65 — who are assumed to receive the long-term addition). To this gross cost we must add the present revenue of income and surtax and the employees' National Insurance contributions (item 2 in Table 9.3). If finally we subtract the cost of the present National Insurance, Supplementary Benefits and Family Allowances, we arrive at the total amount that would have to be raised to meet the budgetary cost of the scheme — £12 800 million.

The difficulties arise when we try to estimate the revenue from a proportional tax on all income. One approach would be to take the total personal income as at present assessed for income tax. This source would not, however, cover those people with incomes below the effective exemption limit (£275 in 1966–7), who would be taxed under the social dividend scheme. From the Blue Book, we can obtain an estimate of the total income of all persons including those with incomes between £50 and £275 on an Inland Revenue basis for 1966.[1] If we take this figure, subtract the social security benefits no longer paid under the social dividend scheme, and assume a 4% rise in incomes between 1966 and 1967, we arrive at a total taxable income of some £25 000 million in 1967. This would mean a tax rate of 51.7% — or, in a pre-decimal age, 10s 4d in the £.

A quite different approach to estimating the rate of tax required has been used by Brown and Dawson, and before them by Lady Rhys Williams, Professor Peacock and others. This is based on the total personal income recorded in the Blue Book. From this they subtract income in kind, imputed income, and current grants from public authorities, and then treat the remainder as the base for the proportional tax under the social dividend scheme.[2] Following the same approach for 1967, we arrive at a total taxable personal income of £27 579 million.[3] This is some £2 500 million higher than the figure reached above, and it would mean a significantly lower tax rate — 9s 4d in the £.

The difference between these two figures can largely be explained by the inclusion in the Brown-Dawson estimate of income which is not at present subject to tax. This includes in particular the income of charities, interest on National Savings, capital allowances for the self-employed, and employees' contributions to superannuation funds. Part of the difference can be explained by the inclusion of those with incomes below £50 in the Brown-Dawson estimate, but the amount

---

[1] Central Statistical Office, *National Income and Expenditure 1968* (H.M.S.O., 1968). Referred to below as the Blue Book.

[2] They also allow for current transfers to charities from companies, the adjustment for life insurance and superannuation funds, and add back interest paid. For a further discussion of their approach, see Appendix H.

[3] This figure does not include interest paid as part of the tax base, since in the scheme discussed here it is not envisaged that the present relief on mortgage interest would be withdrawn, and interest on loans for business purposes would not be taxed in any event.

involved can only be small. It should also be noted that inclusion of income below this level reflects a touching degree of faith in the ability of the Inland Revenue to collect tax from all sources.

It seems reasonable to assume that much of the income included in the Brown-Dawson estimate but not in the Inland Revenue-based figure would not in fact be covered by the proportional tax (for further discussion, see Appendix H), so that the tax rate required would be nearer the upper rather than the lower of the two figures. However, the reconciliation of the two estimates is clearly a subject that requires further examination, and in some cases requires more detailed specification of the social dividend scheme.

However, whichever of the two estimates is the more accurate, the rate of tax required is very high by present standards. Even the lower figure is nearly half as high again as the present standard rate on earned income. Lady Rhys Williams herself suggested that this high rate of tax could be reduced by introducing a supplementary tax on incomes above a certain level and the same procedure was adopted by Brown and Dawson. The additional rate of tax introduced by them is, however, very low (only 10%), and would not allow any substantial reduction in the general rate. For this reason, I shall concentrate here on the simple case of a purely proportional tax.

Finally, we must bear in mind that the calculation of the tax rate presented above is a purely budgetary one, in which considerations of the effect on the level of demand have played no part. This is clearly of great importance — although with a change of this magnitude it is very difficult to predict the effect with any accuracy. One important factor, however, is the effect of the scheme on the distribution of income — a subject to which I now turn.

Effect of Social Dividend on the Distribution of Income

In examining the redistributive effect of the scheme, it is important to distinguish those at present receiving social security benefits from those that are not.

(a) *Those not at Present Receiving Social Security Benefits*

With the introduction of the social dividend, people in this group would gain to the extent of the dividend and (in the case of those in work) from no longer paying National Insurance contributions, but they would in general pay a higher average rate of tax.[1] From the structure of the scheme, it is clear that those who would derive a *net benefit* would be those in the lower part of the income distribution and those at the very top. Those at the lower end would not pay enough extra tax to offset the gain from the social dividend; while for the top surtax payers, the average rate of tax would in fact be significantly lower than at present.

---

1 It should be noted that the scheme discussed here, unlike the proposals of Brown and Dawson and others, would not abolish current grants from the Government apart from social security and would not abolish housing subsidies.

Table 9.4 shows the impact of the scheme on a family with 3 children on the basis of two different assumptions about the tax rate required. This shows that the family would benefit if its income was £1 900 or less even with the higher rate of tax. The low paid worker would benefit very substantially: a person with an income at present of £600 a year would gain over £7 a week. This may be compared with a benefit of £2 17s a week from the Walley scheme and £1 9s a week from the Lees negative income tax proposal. People at the very top (over £10 000) would also gain considerably — which would not be the case with the other schemes. The table also brings out the sensitivity of the results to the exact rate of tax required. With a tax rate of 9s 4d, a family with an income of £2 000 a year would gain by £84, but if the rate were 10s 4d, they would be worse off by £15 — or a difference of nearly £2 a week.

The results of Table 9.4 suggest that the scheme would give a net benefit to the majority of families with 3 children where the father is in work. Similar calculations for families of different sizes presented in Table 9.5 (on the basis of a 10s tax rate) suggest rather surprisingly that the same is true of other tax units. According to these figures a single person would derive a net benefit from the introduction of the scheme if his income is at present below £1 150 and a married couple with no children would gain if their income is now less than £1 700.

These results do in fact suggest that the social dividend scheme would provide a net benefit to more than half of the population and this apparent generosity is very puzzling. To quote Professor Hicks' comment on the table given in the Liberal Party submission to the Royal Commission on Taxation,[1]

'It does seem very extraordinary that there are so many pluses in the last column and so few minuses. One knows that the number of people who get the big pluses, ..., is quite small and that helps to explain it; nevertheless, I think that one is right in saying that there are not enough minuses to balance the pluses in the last column and something therefore needs to be explained, because this is essentially a re-distributive scheme, ..., and therefore, on balance, somebody must lose for somebody else to gain.'

Cross-examination of the Liberal Party representatives failed to produce any very satisfactory explanation of this paradox. In the same way, I have no simple solution to offer, although it must, I think, be largely accounted for by the following factors:

(a) As already noted, the method of calculating the tax required for the earlier schemes (including that of the Liberal Party) included income which would probably not be liable for tax, and the tax rate used was therefore too optimistic.

(b) The calculations shown in Tables 9.4 and 9.5 of the present net income took no account of tax allowances apart from the personal and child allowances.

---

1 Minutes of Evidence of the Royal Commission on the Taxation of Profits and Income, Third Day, Question 444.

Table 9.4. Effect of Social Dividend Scheme for Family with 3 Children (Aged 4, 8, 12) where Father in work — 1967

| Present | | With Social Dividend [c] | | | |
| | | Tax at 9s 4d | | Tax at 10s 4d | |
Gross Income [a]	Net Income [b]	Net Income	Gain over present	Net Income	Gain over present
600	559	972	+413	944	+385
800	748	1 078	+330	1 040	+292
1 000	930	1 186	+256	1 138	+208
1 250	1 122	1 318	+196	1 258	+136
1 500	1 295	1 452	+157	1 379	+84
1 750	1 465	1 585	+119	1 500	+35
2 000	1 635	1 719	+84	1 620	−15
2 500	1 975	1 985	+10	1 861	−114
3 000	2 314	2 252	−62	2 104	−210
5 000	3 627	3 317	−310	3 172	−455
10 000	6 014	5 992	−22	5 494	−520
12 000	6 541	7 052	+511	6 692	+151

Notes: a Income including Family Allowances.

b After income tax and National Insurance contributions. It is assumed that all income is earned by the father and that the only allowances against tax are the personal and child allowances.

c At the Supplementary Benefit scale in force in June 1967 and including average rent as estimated in Appendix B (except for children where a 3s allowance per child for rent is included).

However, the wife's earned income allowance, the dependent relative allowance, the life insurance relief, etc. all provide substantial benefit to present income and surtax payers. If we assume for example that the married couple with no children derived their incomes equally from the earnings of the husband and the wife, then they would cease to gain from the social dividend at an income of around £1 200 a year rather than £1 700 a year. (Although the assumption in these calculations that all income was earned would work in the opposite direction).

(c) These calculations relate only to those in work, and since some of those receiving National Insurance benefits or Supplementary Benefits may be worse off as a result of the scheme (see below), there may be a net transfer from those out of work.

In order to make some allowance for the first two factors, I have made an alternative estimate based on a tax rate of 10s 4d and using information from the Inland Revenue survey of personal incomes to calculate the allowances for wife's earned income, dependent relatives, and life insurance. The resulting figures for

Table 9.5. Effect of Social Dividend Scheme on Households of Different Sizes – 1967

| Present gross income (£ per year) | Gain from introduction of social dividend (with 10s tax rate) | | | | | |
	Single person	Married couple without children	Married couple with 1 child	Married couple with 2 children	Married couple with 4 children
600	86	198	260	340	494
800	54	155	206	255	404
1 000	25	124	160	202	309
1 250	– 19	80	117	145	213
1 500	– 62	36	73	101	149
1 750	– 107	– 9	28	56	104
2 000	– 152	– 53	– 17	11	59
3 000	– 331	– 232	– 197	– 169	– 121

See the notes to Table 9.4. The social dividend rates for children are taken as the average of those for the group 5–10 and 11–15.

the calendar year 1967 are shown in Table 9.6. (In each case the tax and social dividend are calculated on the average number of wives, children, dependants, etc.). This shows that on average those with incomes up to £1 200 would benefit from the scheme — as well as those in the highest income group. If we add up the figures in the last column, this gives a *net* benefit to the tax payers as a whole of £200 million — which must either come from those not included here (e.g. pensioners at present covered by the age exemption) or else reflect the fact that even the tax rate of 10s 4d would be too low.

(b) *Those at Present Receiving Social Security Benefits*

The social dividend would replace all the present social security benefits — Retirement Pensions, sickness and unemployment benefit, widows' benefits, industrial injury benefits, and so on. At the same time, Supplementary Benefits would be abolished. For people at present receiving these benefits, therefore, the net gain from the introduction of the scheme would be very much smaller than for those in work. For example, the net gain to a single person receiving the flat-rate unemployment benefit would have been £1 8s. in 1967. To examine the effect in more detail we must consider separately those receiving Supplementary Benefits and those dependant solely on National Insurance.

We may begin with the case of pensioners not receiving Supplementary Benefits, for whom the effect of the social dividend would be rather similar to that of the income supplement scheme discussed in Chapter 7. A pensioner would receive a pension at the Supplementary Benefit level (I.A.R.), which would represent a substantial increase over the present pension. At the same time, he would be taxed at a rate of (approximately) 50% on other income that he received — occupational pensions, earnings etc. However, unlike the situation with the income supplement scheme, this rate of tax would continue after the income level was reached at which he was no better off than at present and pensioners with incomes above this level would be considerably worse off than now as a result of the social dividend. In 1967, a single pensioner would have ceased to benefit from the introduction of the social dividend if his income (apart from the pension) was over £200 a year. In other words, there would be pensioners not far above the poverty line who would be adversely affected by the scheme. Moreover, none of the present additions to the flat-rate pension — such as the graduated pension or the addition for deferred retirement — would continue to be paid. Although we have seen that these are only small amounts, their loss would reduce still further the benefit given to old people by the social dividend.

The position of those below pension age receiving unemployment or sickness benefit or the widows' benefits (apart from widows' allowances)[1] would be similar to that of pensioners. The social dividend would be paid at the

---

[1] *Widows' allowances* are paid for the first 26 weeks of widowhood. After that, a widow may qualify for a *widow's pension* or a *widowed mother's allowance* if she has dependent children or is over 50. These long-term benefits are at a lower rate than the initial widow's allowance.

Table 9.6.   Estimate of Gain from Social Dividend in 1967 on Basis of Inland
Revenue Survey of Personal Incomes

Average gross income in 1967 £ a year	Average gain from introduction of social dividend £ a year	Number of persons ('000's)	Total Gain (2 × 3) £ million
307	170	342	58
348	141	764	108
401	120	875	105
454	105	878	92
507	88	900	79
588	78	1 716	134
696	64	1 684	108
862	60	1 762	106
910	49	1 784	87
1 016	33	1 704	56
1 122	14	1 599	22
1 230	− 9	1 434	− 13
1 336	− 30	1 191	− 36
1 440	− 56	1 000	− 56
1 550	− 84	767	− 64
1 721	− 122	1 285	− 157
1 991	− 173	670	− 116
2 360	− 231	495	− 114
2 920	− 312	229	− 71
3 660	− 383	214	− 82
4 800	− 522	103	− 54
5 820	− 566	60	− 34
7 330	− 549	57	− 31
9 540	− 399	28	− 11
18 280	+ 1 982	41	+ 81

Notes: Estimated on the basis of the Inland Revenue survey of personal incomes
for 1965–6, with an adjustment for the increase in incomes between then
and 1967.

The social dividend was calculated in the same way as for Tables 9.4
and 9.5.

A uniform allowance of £35 was made for National Insurance contributions.

Supplementary Benefit level (I.A.R.), which is significantly higher than the present flat-rate insurance benefits. However, in this case the loss of the earnings-related supplement would be more important and a person at present receiving this might be considerably worse off. For example, a man (with 3 children) earning £24 a week when in work would in 1967 have received a National Insurance benefit including the earnings-related supplement (and Family Allowances) of £14 19s 6d, but under the social dividend he would have received only £12 18s. The same is true of other categories of National Insurance benefit — industrial injury benefits and widows' allowances — which are at present set at a higher level than the flat rate benefit for sickness, unemployment etc. People receiving these benefits would in general be worse off under the social dividend. Finally, we should note that the grants at present paid for maternity and death would also be discontinued.

The discussion above related to the people not now receiving Supplementary Benefits. For a person now on Supplementary Benefits the benefit from the social dividend would be smaller and he might well be worse off. The scheme as envisaged above would replace the present assistance payments by the social dividend at the Supplementary Benefit level *including average rent*. A person receiving assistance who had no other source of income would therefore be worse off than at present if he had above-average rent or other exceptional needs. On the other hand, those at present subject to the wage stop would gain even if they had above-average rent — since the social dividend would raise their normal take-home pay when in work.

Effect of Social Dividend on Distribution of Income — Conclusions

From this examination of the redistributive effect of the social dividend scheme, we can see that it would provide considerable benefit to those in the lower half of the income distribution not now receiving social security benefits. Those below the poverty line would gain a great deal — more than with the new child benefit schemes and with the Lees negative income tax proposal. At the same time, those at the very top of the income distribution would also benefit from the introduction of the social dividend — since the tax rate would be very much lower than the present top surtax rates.

Those at present receiving social security benefits would however gain rather less from the social dividend scheme and might well lose as a result of its introduction. Those receiving Supplementary Benefits would be worse off if their rent was above the average allowed for in the social dividend and if they had no other income. The social dividend would be less than the National Insurance benefits now payable for industrial injuries, widows' allowances, and (in many cases) earnings-related sickness, unemployment or widows' benefits. Pensioners and others with income apart from National Insurance would now face a tax rate of 50%, and the 'break-even' point would not be far above the poverty line.

Finally, we should note that while the social dividend would, as claimed by Brown and Dawson, provide a guaranteed minimum income for everyone, this guarantee would not provide for individual housing expenditure. This means that to ensure that everyone reached the Supplementary Benefit standard, there would need to be a means-tested supplementary allowance to cover those with above-average rent or else the scheme would have to be accompanied by a radical change in the present housing policy.

Effect of Social Dividend Scheme on Work Incentives

The proponents of the social dividend principle, from Lady Rhys Williams to the present day, have laid great stress on the beneficial effect of the scheme on work incentives: the first part of *Something to Look Forward To* was entitled 'The Problem of the Motive for Labour', and Brown and Dawson put forward their proposal after a long discussion of the effect of the present income tax on work effort.

As in the discussion of earlier schemes, we must distinguish between decisions about whether or not to work and decisions about the number of hours worked. Lady Rhys Williams herself seemed to be primarily concerned with the first of these problems. Writing at the time of the Beveridge Plan, she argued that the benefits proposed would 'have the effect of undermining the will to work of the lower-paid workers to a probably serious and possibly dangerous degree. Not only will the idle get as much from the State as will the industrious workers, they will get a great deal more.'[1]

With the social dividend, the situation would be different, and a man would always receive more from working than if he were unemployed. As a result, the introduction of a social dividend today might be expected to provide more incentive for people to enter the labour force and to reduce the problem of the 'workshy'. However, the discussion of this problem in Chapter 6 suggested that it is very much a figment of popular imagination, and that the number of able-bodied people remaining 'voluntarily' unemployed is extremely small. From the evidence discussed there, it did not appear that the National Insurance scheme has led to the dire consequences predicted by Lady Rhys Williams in 1943.

The effect of the scheme on hours worked would depend on its impact on a person's net income and on his marginal tax rate (the tax paid on an additional £1 of income). In Chapter 6 we saw that a higher net income tends to lead a person to work less (if leisure is a normal good), and that a higher marginal tax rate has (other things being equal) the same effect. In Figure 9.3 I have shown (in stylised form) the effect of replacing the present provisions by a social dividend with a proportional rate of tax. From this we can deduce that in the first range of income people would be under pressure to reduce their work effort — since both income and substitution effects operate in that direction. In the third range, on the other hand, both effects operate in the direction of increased work effort. In the second and fourth ranges, the net effect is indeterminate.

The overall effect of the social dividend scheme on hours worked would depend

---

[1] *Something to Look Forward To*, op. cit., p. 141.

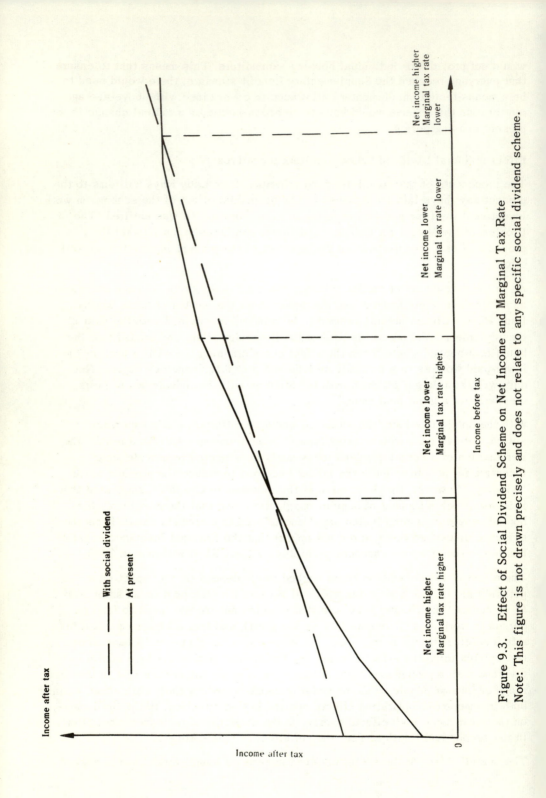

Figure 9.3. Effect of Social Dividend Scheme on Net Income and Marginal Tax Rate
Note: This figure is not drawn precisely and does not relate to any specific social dividend scheme.

on the number of people in each of these ranges. The first range consists of those at the lower end of the income distribution who would gain from the introduction of the scheme, and as we have seen earlier this would be true of a large number of people. Moreover the rise — both in net income and in the marginal tax rate — would be considerable. Comparing the effect therefore with that of the new child benefit schemes and the Lees proposal, the social dividend would result in a much larger increase in the marginal tax rate at the lower end of the scale, and would affect many more workers. Although it is not possible to assess the quantitative effect on work effort, it seems likely that the disincentive effect would be larger than with either of these schemes. We must, however, take account of fact that at the bottom of the income scale there would be a reduction in the number subject to means-tested benefits such as rent and rate rebates (which involve high marginal tax rates).

Against this, we have to set any increase in work effort by those in the third group — which is in fact the one to which Brown and Dawson devote most attention. These people are those who now face a marginal tax rate in excess of that required under the social dividend — i.e. they must be surtax payers — but do not have sufficient income to gain from the social dividend. The number in this group must however be very small — in 1966–7 the total number of persons assessed for surtax was less than 2% of the total number of persons within the purview of the income tax.[1]

Effect of Social Dividend Scheme on Work Incentives — Conclusions

This analysis does not therefore support the view that the social dividend would unambiguously lead to an improvement in work incentives. It would make 'voluntary' unemployment less attractive, but this does not in fact appear to be a major problem. When we consider the effect on working hours (or work intensity), then only a small minority fall in the range where an increase in work effort seems most likely. A very much larger number of people in the lower half of the income distribution could in fact be led to work less. Although I have argued earlier that the effect on those at the lower end of the scale is likely to be less marked than among those more free to adjust their individual work effort, the increase in the marginal tax would be very large. In order to get round this problem, Brown and Dawson suggest that 'If this were thought to be a major stumbling block to the adoption of the plan it would be possible to change the rates so as to leave the lowest income group in about the same position as at present'. But this of course would defeat the objective of redistributing income towards low income families and would still leave the problem of the marginal tax rate being higher.

---

1 Brown and Dawson stress the fact that the rate of direct tax required to finance their scheme would be no higher than the present standard rate on earned income, but it would be accompanied by a value added tax at the rate of 11%, and, as they themselves point out, this may also be expected to have an effect on work incentives.

Finally, there is the argument by Brown and Dawson that 'the most important effect on incentives of a radical reform such as the one above would result from killing off the myth that Britain is more heavily taxed than she really is'. While the problem of tax myths is clearly an important one, there are other ways of exploding them besides a radical change in the tax structure! We could, for example, adopt the simpler suggestion they make of calling 6s 5d the 'standard rate' and having a 1s 10d surcharge for unearned income.

10 Conclusions – For and Against

'A pamphlet on the Poor Laws generally contains some little piece of favourite nonsense, by which we are told this enormous evil may be perfectly cured. The first gentleman recommends little gardens; the second cows; the third village shops; the fourth a spade; the fifth Dr. Bell, and so forth. Every man rushes to the press with his small morsel of imbecility; and is not easy till he sees his impertinence stitched in blue covers'.

Sydney Smith, Edinburgh Review, 1820[1]

The title of this concluding chapter has been chosen to emphasise the fact that the aim of this study has not been to advocate any one particular change in Government policy, still less to produce a blue-print for reforming the social security system. Instead, I have tried to provide an impartial analysis of the advantages and disadvantages of various proposals in a way that will provide a background for decisions about what ought to be done.

The aim of this chapter is not therefore to put forward any particular 'piece of favourite nonsense', but rather to bring together the results of Part II and summarise them in a way that makes clear the essential choices to be made. In doing this, I first discuss two possible comprehensive solutions to the problem of poverty – through a social dividend and through a 'Back to Beveridge' policy. I then consider in Section 2 the alternative 'piecemeal' approach to the problem of adopting specific measures to help particular groups. Finally, Section 3 contains a number of concluding reflections.

1 A COMPREHENSIVE SOLUTION?

In the course of this study I have considered two policies which, although very different in form, can be described as 'comprehensive' solutions to the problems of poverty. The first is the social dividend scheme examined in Chapter 9, which would replace the present 'partial' measures – National Insurance, Family Allowances, and Supplementary Benefits – by a single benefit providing a guaranteed minimum income for everyone. The second solution – a 'Back to Beveridge' policy – is not one that I have discussed as an entity, but has been used as a yardstick when evaluating proposals for partial reforms.

The Social Dividend

The logic of the social dividend is very attractive: the objective of providing a guaranteed minimum income to everyone could be fulfilled through one single

---

1 This reference I owe to J.R. Poynter, *Society and Pauperism*, op. cit., p. 330. ('Dr. Bell' was the proponent of a system of education based on self-instruction.)

scheme — covering the old, the sick and unemployed, those with large families, those with low earnings, the disabled, the fatherless, and so on. There would be no problem of people's not receiving the benefits to which they were entitled; and the scheme would allow the present array of partial measures to be abolished with consequent administrative savings.

The social dividend would, therefore, provide a minimum floor to incomes — in the scheme discussed in Chapter 9, at the Supplementary Benefit level (including average rent) — and in this way would help those people whose incomes at present are below the poverty line. As we saw in Chapter 9, it would provide particular benefit to those who are in poverty even though they are in full-time work, and they would gain considerably more than from the partial reforms discussed in Chapter 8. Those people at present receiving the flat-rate National Insurance benefits would also gain from the introduction of the scheme, and a pensioner household with no other income would receive an increase (in June 1969) of some £2 a week.

Despite these attractive features, closer examination of the social dividend scheme reveals a number of serious problems. Firstly, the benefit provided under the scheme is at a uniform rate for all, the only distinctions being those between children of different ages and householders and non-householders, and individual circumstances would not be taken into account. As noted earlier, this means that some people would receive less in the form of the social dividend than they receive under the present Supplementary Benefits — particularly where they have high housing expenditure or exceptional needs. If the object is to ensure that no one falls below the present Supplementary Benefit scale of requirements, there would still be need for a means-tested scheme to provide for those with high rent, etc. In other words, the social dividend would greatly reduce the need for Supplementary Benefits, but would not allow it to be abolished altogether.

Secondly, the proponents of the social dividend scheme have not taken full account of the problems involved in the abolition of the National Insurance scheme. Although the social dividend considered in Chapter 9 would be higher than the present flat-rate National Insurance benefit, there would be a number of National Insurance recipients who would be worse off as a result of the reform. This applies especially to those receiving industrial injury benefits, widows' allowances and the earnings-related supplements to unemployment, sickness and widows' benefits. A number of other benefits would also be abolished — including the addition to the flat-rate pension for deferred retirement, the graduated pension, and the death and maternity grants. Even apart from questions about the importance of the 'insurance principle', it is not clear that the present National Insurance provisions should be dismantled and replaced by a uniform (and in some cases lower) benefit. This problem is recognised at one point by Brown and Dawson, who say that 'particular groups (e.g. the disabled) could be singled out for better (or worse) treatment',[1] but this is precisely what the present National Insurance system is trying to do.

---

[1] *Personal Taxation, Incentives and Tax Reform*, op. cit., p. 87.

The third problem of the social dividend scheme relates to the question of work incentives. One of the claims made by Brown and Dawson and others is that the new scheme would have a beneficial effect on incentives. The analysis in Chapter 9 did not bear out this claim, and it seemed possible that on balance the outcome might be a reduction in work effort.

The effects of the social dividend would not, of course, be limited to helping those at the bottom of the income distribution, and the scheme would have profound consequences for those higher up the scale. Most importantly, it would benefit those at the very top at the expense of those lower down — the tax burden on the top surtax payers would be reduced. For Brown and Dawson, this is one of the attractions of the scheme, but not everybody would agree with this view. Not only would the income tax system become less progressive, but also a number of 'refinements' such as the earned income relief would be lost. These problems could be overcome through the introduction of a supplementary tax, by taxing earned income at a different rate, and so on, but then we should more or less be back where we started.

A further problem concerns the possible saving on administration, on which Lady Rhys Williams laid great store. The proportional rate of tax on all income, together with the abolition of all special benefits, certainly suggests a considerable saving on administrative costs. Brown and Dawson similarly suggest that 'the greater simplicity of the system should free resources at present necessitated because the tax and benefit system is so complex'. [1] At the same time, there would be an increase in the number liable for tax, since none would be exempt, and the responsibility of ensuring that all small incomes were covered would increase the work of the Inland Revenue. Moreover, with a tax rate of the order of 50%, there would be a much increased incentive to evade or avoid tax at the lower end of the income distribution. Brown and Dawson refer to the fact that 'high income individuals would no longer have the same incentive to search for tax loopholes', but take no account of the reverse effect at the other end, where there would certainly be scope for evasion if not avoidance. In this connection, it must be remembered that their estimates of the tax rate required rested on the assumption that the Inland Revenue would be successful in collecting all the tax due. Finally, we are not as in 1942 planning for 'Reconstruction', and the dismantling of the system now in operation and replacing it by the social dividend would represent a considerable burden on our legislative and administrative resources.

On closer examination, therefore, the social dividend scheme appears rather less attractive, and there are a number of major problems which should be considered very carefully before we embark on such a major reform of our social security and tax system. Some of the problems might be overcome by adopting a 'compromise' version of the scheme — retaining the National Insurance benefits at a lower rate and re-introducing surtax. However, as was pointed out by Professor Hague when

---

1 ibid., p. 96.

reviewing the last of the Rhys Williams schemes,[1] 'the essential simplicity of the original scheme, which was its great attraction, would now vanish. Some income tax allowances would remain, the tax rate would rise for incomes over £600 and there would still be much work for the National Insurance and Assistance staffs'.[2]

A 'Back to Beveridge' Policy

For Beveridge, the abolition of want required 'a double re-distribution of income, through social insurance and by family needs'.[3] In Chapter 7, I discussed the effect of raising the Retirement Pension to the 'subsistence' level recommended by Beveridge — or the Supplementary Benefit scale (including average rent); similarly, in Chapter 8, I considered the possibility of increasing Family Allowances to the level of the Supplementary Benefit allowances for children. If we were also to increase the other flat-rate National Insurance benefits, then these measures taken together can be said to represent a 'Back to Beveridge' policy for dealing with poverty.

The effect of this policy would in many ways be similar to that of the social dividend scheme. It would provide considerable benefits to those receiving National Insurance benefits but not Supplementary Benefits, and would greatly reduce (although not eliminate) the need for Supplementary Benefits. People in work who had 2 or more children would gain from the higher Family Allowances, and everyone would be brought up to the poverty line provided they earned enough to support a family with 1 child at the Supplementary Benefit level. The only loophole would be where a man's earnings did in fact fall below this level, since Beveridge did not recognise the existence of this problem and therefore made no provision for it.

The 'Back to Beveridge' policy would not involve any change in the income tax system, and the scheme would be financed through the existing taxes and National Insurance contributions. The revenue that would have to be raised is set out in Table 10.1, which shows the net cost of the increases in National Insurance benefits and Family Allowances (allowing for the income tax paid on Family Allowances and Retirement Pensions, for the saving on Supplementary Benefits and including the cost of extending Retirement Pensions to those not at present covered). From this it is clear that the net cost of a 'Back to Beveridge' policy would be considerable — of the order of £750 million. Raising this revenue

---

1 D.C. Hague, review of Lady Rhys Williams, *Taxation and Incentive*, in *Economica*, 1953.

2 A much more satisfactory compromise would be a scheme similar to those proposed for the United States by Professor Tobin and others (see for example J. Tobin, J.A. Pechman, and P.M. Mieszkowski, 'Is a Negative Income Tax Practical?', *The Yale Law Journal*, 1967). This scheme would overlap to some extent with the present income tax, but would leave it basically unchanged.

3 *Social Insurance and Allied Services*, op. cit., para. 11.

Table 10.1.   Cost of a 'Back to Beveridge' Policy — 1969—70

	£ million
Gross Cost:	
Retirement Pensions[a]	725
Other National Insurance benefits [b]	175
Family Allowances[c]	295
Saving on Supplementary Benefits[d]	− 285
Income tax paid on Family Allowances and Retirement Pensions[e]	− 155
NET COST	755

Notes: [a] Including cost of extending Retirement Pensions to those not at present
covered. For details of estimate, see Appendix E.

[b] Unemployment and sickness benefit, widows' benefits (excluding
widows' allowances and widows' basic pensions). These are assumed
to be raised to the Supplementary Benefit level (I.A.R.) for adults and
the first child in a family (other children would be covered by Family
Allowances and there would be a saving as far as they were concerned).
It is assumed that half those sick or widowed would have been eligible
for the long-term addition but that none of the unemployed would have
been The cost is estimated on the basis of the total number receiving
these benefits in 1968 (*Annual Report of the Department of Health and
Social Security*, 1968, p. 352) and the average number of children in
1966—68 (ibid., p. 296).

[c] Based on the number of children receiving Family Allowances in
December 1968 (ibid., p. 352).

[d] The method of estimating the saving on Supplementary Pensions has
been described in Appendix E. A similar approach is adopted in the
case of Supplementary Allowances, although it is necessary to
distinguish between those receiving National Insurance benefits and
those who are not.

[e] Estimated by the method described in Appendix E (Retirement
Pensions) and Appendix F (Family Allowances).

through National Insurance contributions and income tax (on the assumption that
the Exchequer bore the whole cost of Family Allowances and a third of that of the
National Insurance benefits, with the remainder being shared equally between
employer and employee) would require 1s. 3d. on the standard rate and an increase
of 3s. in the flat-rate contribution for an adult man. If the whole cost were to be
financed through an increase in income tax (a procedure which would not have
met with the approval of Beveridge), then the standard rate would have to rise by
around 2s. 3d.

The high cost of the 'Back to Beveridge' policy arises, of course, because the

increased benefits have to be paid to all: the increase in Retirement Pensions or
Family Allowances would benefit the well-to-do as well as those below the
poverty line. This is not true, however, of the partial reforms that I have
discussed (such as the income supplement for old people or the new child benefits)
which limit the benefit to those at the lower end of the income scale. These partial
schemes may, therefore, best be seen as means for achieving the 'Back to
Beveridge' objective at a lower cost.

2. THE PIECEMEAL APPROACH

In this section, I examine the scope for a series of partial measures directed at
the problems of particular groups, within the framework of the objective of
ensuring a minimum income for everyone.

Old People

Old people make up one of the single largest groups below the poverty line. In
1965, some 40% of Retirement Pensioners had incomes which were not sufficient
to bring them to the National Assistance scale and of these a substantial
proportion did not claim assistance.

The Government's proposed National Superannuation scheme aims to deal with
this problem by ensuring that the state pension itself is sufficient to guarantee a
minimum standard of living – through the introduction of earnings-related
pensions for those not covered by occupational schemes. In Chapter 7, I showed
that when in full operation the scheme would guarantee a pension at the
Supplementary Benefit level (including average rent) to nearly all old people
providing that the Government raised pensions in payment in line with increases
in national average earnings. Less than 1% of men would still receive less than
this amount, although the position for women dependent on their own earnings
record would be less satisfactory. The National Superannuation scheme would,
of course, cost considerably more than the 'Back to Beveridge' policy: the
better-off pensioner would not simply receive the same pension, but would receive
more. However, the Government apparently feels that the earnings related nature
of the benefits allows this revenue to be raised with less difficulty than would
be the case with the smaller amount required for an increase in flat-rate benefits.

There would, however, be a long transition period before National Superannuation
became fully effective, during which the pensions of a large number of old
people – those already retired and those retiring before 1992 – would remain
below the Supplementary Benefit level (I.A.R.). Even by 1990, there would still
be over a third with pensions below this level – though a number of these would
have other income which brought them above the poverty line. Although the
National Superannuation scheme would do a great deal to help the pensioners of
the next century, it could not therefore solve the problems of the immediate future.

From the White Paper on National Superannuation, it appears that the Government
intends the problems of the transition period to be met by the Supplementary

Benefit scheme. However, the analysis of Chapter 4 suggested that this confidence may be misplaced — while Supplementary Benefits may be more effective than National Assistance, many people are still not claiming the assistance to which they are entitled.

The problem of poverty among old people will therefore remain with us for the next twenty or thirty years unless further measures are taken. If we reject the 'Back to Beveridge' increase in flat-rate Retirement Pensions as too expensive, then the most promising alternative is the income supplement scheme proposed by Mrs. Wedderburn and examined in detail in Chapter 7.

This scheme would raise the flat-rate pension for all old people to the Supplementary Benefit level (I.A.R.) and then tax other income at the rate of 10s. in the £. This would reduce the net cost to less than 60% of the 'Back to Beveridge' increase. It would however mean that a very large proportion of pensioners would have to start filing tax returns with consequent administrative and personal costs. The operation of the scheme through the present income tax system would also lead to inflexibility and a pensioner faced by a fall in income might suffer considerable hardship before the Inland Revenue could adjust the supplement. Finally, the 10s. in the £ tax rate might lead to some reduction in the incentive for pensioners to take up part-time work, although if the government were really concerned about this it could do something about the present earnings rule for Retirement Pensioners.

Families with Children

I have examined two types of scheme to help low income families with children. The first type includes the proposals of the Child Poverty Action Group and Sir John Walley, both of which would replace the present Family Allowances and child tax allowances by a single child benefit. The second type of scheme would also abolish Family Allowances, but would retain the child tax allowances in a negative income tax scheme — as suggested by Professor Lees.

In the case of the first type of scheme, we have seen that the benefits given for all children but the first are less generous than the subsistence level advocated by Beveridge. This is, however, more than compensated for in all except the largest families by the fact that the benefit would be payable in respect of the first child. The Child Poverty Action Group and Walley schemes would do a great deal to help low income families and would raise a large proportion above the poverty line. Moreover, since the benefit from the increase would be limited (with the Child Poverty Action Group scheme at least) to those at present paying less than the standard rate of income tax, the schemes could be introduced at a very low cost.

The second scheme — the Lees negative income tax — could also be introduced at a low cost and possibly with some saving to the Exchequer. It too would provide considerable benefit to families with children below the poverty line. This benefit would, however, be partly achieved at the expense of those not far above the poverty line, who would lose their present Family Allowances and would gain less or nothing from the negative income tax supplement. (The contrast between the two types of scheme is exemplified by the fact that the Lees scheme would reduce the income of families who would *gain* from the Child Poverty Action Group proposal). We have also seen that there are two potential problems with the negative income tax that have not been satisfactorily resolved — the question of its administrative feasibility and the possible adverse effect on work incentives.

Low Earners

One loophole in the 'Back to Beveridge' policy as a comprehensive solution is the fact that some people have earnings which are less than adequate for a family with only 1 child. An increase in Family Allowances would need, therefore, to be accompanied by some measure to help people with low earnings. In Chapter 8, I discussed two such measures — minimum wage legislation and new social security contributions.

A general method of raising the take-home pay of those with low earnings would be to reduce the burden of National Insurance contributions. The proposed National Superannuation contributions would be a step in this direction, but, as we have seen, their effect would be only limited. A much more effective measure would be the introduction of a lower exemption limit in the contribution schedule, so that contributions were only paid on earnings above a certain level. Still greater benefit would be given by totally abolishing the contributions and raising the revenue through a surcharge on income tax. This would, however, entail a more serious departure from the present system and would weaken still further the already tenuous links with 'insurance'.

A more specific reform would be the introduction of a national minimum wage at a level sufficient to guarantee a net income at the Supplementary Benefit level (including average rent) for a family with 1 child. In June 1969 this would have meant minimum weekly earnings (for a 40 hour week) of around £12 10s. Provided that adequate measures were taken to offset any effect on the employment of particularly 'vulnerable' workers, this could be of substantial benefit to those with low earnings and would (in conjunction with higher Family Allowances) eliminate the need for the wage stop. Moreover, the addition to labour costs would be relatively small. The case for a minimum wage at a higher level is less compelling, however, since the effect on employment and labour costs would be much more serious and even a £15 minimum would not by itself provide for the needs of all those in work who fall below the poverty line.

Partial Reforms — Conclusions

A combination of partial measures — an income supplement scheme for pensioners, new child benefits and a minimum wage of £12 10s. a week — could therefore fulfil the same objectives as the 'Back to Beveridge' policy at a lower overall cost, and would in fact do more to help those with no children or only 1 child. This lower cost would, however, to some extent be achieved by sacrificing other objectives. The income supplement scheme would involve all pensioners in filing a tax return, and to this extent it would represent a means-tested benefit; the new child benefits would affect the tax burden for richer people as between families and bachelors; and the minimum wage would require supporting measures to offset any effect on employment.

3. CONCLUDING COMMENTS

The Need for an Overall View

In this discussion of possible reforms, I have stressed the importance of viewing the problem of poverty as a whole so that the measures are considered in conjunction rather than as single, alternative solutions.

The need for this overall view is well illustrated by the recent report on a national minimum wage, which concludes that 'a national minimum is likely to be a less efficient means of relieving poverty than selective social benefits related to individual needs'.[1] As I emphasised in Chapter 8, this totally ignores the possibility that the minimum wage might have an important role to play if it were combined with 'selective social benefits'.

There are many other examples of the importance of this inter-relationship: National Superannuation must be considered in terms not only of the benefits provided to old people but also with a view to the burden of contributions on low paid workers; the abolition of child tax relief under the new child benefit schemes would affect the proposal to replace social security contributions by a surcharge on income tax; reforms which affect the marginal tax rate faced by those with low incomes must be examined in the light of the myriad of means-tested benefits at present provided by local authorities.

The Supplementary Benefit Scale and Individual Needs

In this study I have accepted as the poverty standard to be applied the Government's own definition of the minimum standard of living — the Supplementary Benefit scale. This poverty standard includes therefore allowances for particular expenditure by the individual household: most importantly housing, but also for exceptional needs (such as special diet or extra fuel for old people).

The mechanism which allows these special needs to be met is the detailed assessment of each individual case by the Supplementary Benefit Commission. It seems likely, however, that much of the stigma associated with Supplementary Benefits derives from a dislike of this detailed assessment. On the other hand, under a system which would provide benefit without stigma, such as the 'Back to Beveridge' National Insurance provisions or a social dividend scheme, the benefit could not be adjusted to each person's individual needs. The increased Retirement Pensions or the social dividend would only be paid at the

---

[1] *A National Minimum Wage*, op. cit., para. 170.

Supplementary Benefit scale (including average rent), and this might well be less than a person is entitled to under the present Supplementary Benefits if he has above-average rent or exceptional needs. Something akin to the Heisenberg Uncertainty Principle is at work. If we provide a detailed assessment of individual needs to ensure that everyone is above the poverty line, then people are deterred from claiming, but if we administer the scheme in such a way that people are willing to apply, then we cannot make any very precise adjustment for their needs.

The Need for More Information

Throughout this study, I have emphasised the lack of information about the circumstances of people with low incomes. This has affected not only the examination of the present situation but also the assessment of proposals for reform.

The need for more information was particularly apparent in Chapter 2, where I reviewed the available evidence about poverty in this country. Despite the pioneering work of Professors Abel-Smith and Townsend and other writers, we still lack a satisfactory overall picture of the relationship between incomes and needs (on the Supplementary Benefit or any other standard). This information can really only be provided by a national survey of poverty — similar perhaps to the enquiries carried out by the Government into the circumstances of Retirement Pensioners and families receiving Family Allowances, but covering the whole population and not just people in particular categories. If this were not possible, a second-best would be an up-to-date analysis of the Family Expenditure Survey data on the lines of *The Poor and the Poorest*. Since the sample size has now been increased, the expenditure survey might provide a great deal more useful information, although it would clearly help if it could be planned with this subsidiary object in mind.

The discussion of particular reforms also revealed other important areas about which our knowledge was seriously deficient. These included such questions as the effect of different schemes on work incentives, the effect of a national minimum wage on employment, and the administrative feasibility of a negative income tax.

Finally, I should stress that because of these major gaps in our knowledge, the conclusions reached in this study should be regarded as purely tentative and they will undoubtedly need to be re-examined in the light of further information that becomes available.

A Royal Commission on Poverty?

In the past few years we have been inundated with reports of Royal Commissions — the Public Schools, Donovan, Maud, Todd and so on. For this reason, the suggestion of yet another commission is made with great reluctance. There are, however, a number of important reasons why a Royal Commission on Poverty could perform an extremely valuable function. I have stressed the serious need for more

194

information about the present circumstances of those with low incomes, and the importance of viewing the problem as a whole. A Royal Commission with broad terms of reference would be able to provide both. It would be able to call evidence (Government departments could for example be examined on the administrative feasibility of different schemes) and would provide the natural framework for a new national survey of poverty. In this it would resemble the current Swedish Royal Commission on Low Income Groups, which is carrying out a wide programme of research. It would be able to consider measures in conjunction and (it is hoped) draw up a coherent and co-ordinated strategy. Finally, the establishment of a Royal Commission would help draw to the problem of poverty the attention which it undoubtedly deserves.

Appendices

APPENDIX A Child Allowances, National Insurance, and Supplementary Benefits (as in force in June 1969)

This appendix provides a brief description of the principal features of the social security system in Britain as in force in June 1969. I have made no attempt to be comprehensive and the description should not be taken as applicable in every individual case. For further details, the reader is referred to the Department of Health and Social Security. (Two convenient sources are its publications *Everybody's Guide to Social Security* (H.M.S.O., 1968) and the *Annual Report of the Department of Health and Social Security for 1968*, Part II, Appendix II).

I ALLOWANCES FOR CHILDREN

Financial aid is provided to families with children in two principal forms: Family Allowances and child tax allowances.

1. Family Allowances

Family Allowances are paid to families with two or more children below the age limits, at the rate of 18s. for the second child and £1 for the third and all subsequent children. The age limits are 15 for children who leave school at that age, 16 for certain incapacitated children and 19 for children who remain at school or college, or who are apprentices with low earnings. The allowances are taxable as earned income.

2. Child Tax Allowances

Under both income and surtax, there are allowances against taxable income for dependent children. For the tax year 1969–70, these allowances are at the rate of £115 for each child not over 11, £140 for children over 11 and not over 16, and £165 for children over 16 receiving full-time education, although there is a reduction of £42 in the personal tax allowance for each child receiving Family Allowances. This means that a family with 3 children under 11 will effectively receive a tax allowance of £115 for the first child and £73 each for the second and third children. (Where a child has a separate income of its own exceeding £115, the income tax allowance is reduced by the excess).

II NATIONAL INSURANCE

The National Insurance scheme provides benefits for retirement, unemployment, sickness, widowhood, maternity, death and orphanhood. These benefits are given subject to contribution conditions. I have given below a brief outline of the first three benefits and of the National Insurance contributions:

1. Retirement Pensions

The Flat-Rate Pension

The standard flat-rate Retirement Pension is paid at the rate of £4 10s. a week to all old people who satisfy the contribution conditions and are *either* over the minimum retirement age (65 for men, 60 for women) *and* have retired from regular work *or* over the age of 70 (65 for a woman). In other words, the pension is a *retirement* pension for those not more than 5 years over the minimum retirement age, but an *old age* pension for those over 70 (65 for women). 'Retirement' means that a person is no longer in regular employment, but does not preclude occasional or part-time work. This 'retirement condition' is enforced through the earnings rule — see below. It is possible for a person to cancel retirement and return to work (but not more than once).

The contribution conditions are:

 (i) a person must have paid at least 156 contributions of any class.

 (ii) he must have paid or been credited with an average of 50 flat-rate contributions per year between age 16 and the last complete contribution year before age 65 (60). If the average falls below this, then the pension is paid at a reduced rate. A minimum average of 13 is required, below which no pension is payable at all.

Most people qualify for the full pension: at 31 December 1966 only 5.5% of Retirement Pensioners received less than the full rate.

A married woman can receive a pension in her own right if she satisfies the retirement and certain special contribution conditions. Alternatively she can qualify for a reduced pension on her husband's insurance if her husband is a Retirement Pensioner at the rate of £2 16s. a week. Where the wife of a Retirement Pensioner does not qualify for a pension (e.g. because she is under 60), then the husband can claim a dependant's allowance at the same rate of £2 16s.

The condition that a person can only receive the pension between 65 and 70 (60 and 65 for a woman) if he has retired is enforced through the *earnings rule*. Under this rule, the pension is reduced if the person earns more than £6 10s. a week. It is reduced at the rate of 6d. for every 1s. of earnings between £6 10s. and £8 10s. and by 1s. for every 1s. above £8 10s. A wife's pension (other than the dependant's allowance) is reduced similarly if she earns over £6 10s. a week.

People who do not retire at the minimum age qualify for increases in their pensions at the rate of an increase of 1s. in the weekly rate of pension for every 9 flat rate contributions which they pay after the minimum retirement age in respect of employment or self employment.

198

Graduated Pension

In addition to the flat rate pension, a person who has paid graduated contributions receives a graduated pension. The amount received depends on the number of 'units' earned since the scheme was introduced in April 1961. Each £7 10s. which a man pays in graduated contributions (£9 for a woman) earns him one unit — or a 6d a week addition to his pension (apart from the first unit for which only half this amount has to be paid). (The cost of a unit is higher for women because they qualify for the pension five years earlier).

It is possible for an employer to contract employees out of the graduated scheme if he satisfies the Registrar of Non-participating Employments that they are covered by an adequate occupational pension scheme. (N.B. the decision to contract-out is the employer's and not the employees'). However since 1966 additional graduated contributions have been payable (with no contracting out) to cover the earning-related short-term benefits and these contributions earn pension rights, so that all employees retiring after 1966 receive some graduated pension even if they are contracted out of the main scheme.

The widow of a man who has paid graduated contributions will (when she retires) get a graduated addition equal to one half the graduated pension which her husband had earned or was drawing when he died.

2. Unemployment and Sickness Benefits

Flat-Rate Unemployment Benefit

The standard flat-rate unemployment benefit is payable, at the rate of £4 10s. to people satisfying the contribution and other conditions, for up to 312 days (i.e. twelve months excluding Sundays) in any period of interruption of employment (after 3 waiting days). For this purpose, spells of unemployment and sickness not separated by 13 weeks count as a single period of interruption of employment. After benefit has been paid for 312 days, it cannot be drawn again until the person has returned to work and paid at least 13 contributions as an employed person.

To be entitled for the benefit, a person must be unemployed and capable of, and available for, employment. He may be disqualified for up to 6 weeks if he leaves a job without just cause or loses it through misconduct, or if he refuses a suitable job without just cause.

The benefit includes provision for payment of allowances for dependent adults and children at the rate of £2 16s. for an adult and £1 8s. (including the Family Allowance) for a child.

Flat-Rate Sickness Benefit

To receive sickness benefit, a person must satisfy the contribution conditions and show that he is incapable of work 'by reason of some specific disease or bodily or mental disablement'. This is usually done by submitting a doctor's medical certificate.

The benefit may be paid for an unlimited period providing incapacity for work continues. (A limit of 312 days applies however where a certain minimum number of contributions have not been paid since entry into insurance).

The benefit is paid at the same rate as unemployment benefit (including allowances for dependants).

Earnings-related Supplement to Sickness and Unemployment Benefits

An earnings-related supplement can be payable to anyone between 18 and the minimum retirement age who is entitled to flat-rate sickness or unemployment benefit and who has reckonable earnings in excess of £450 in the relevant tax year. It is payable after 12 waiting days for up to 156 days (i.e. six months excluding Sundays).

The amount of the supplement is one-third of the person's average weekly earnings between £9 and £30, provided that the total benefit, including the flat-rate benefit (with the dependants' allowances), does not exceed 85% of his average weekly earnings. Average weekly earnings are taken as one-fiftieth of the gross annual earnings, broadly those taxed under P.A.Y.E. in the last complete income tax year before the start of the period of interruption of employment.

3. Contributions

Flat-Rate Contributions

In general, all people below the retirement age who are not in full-time education are liable for flat-rate contributions, the main exception being married women, who may choose whether or not to contribute. The rate depends on the age, sex and class (employed, self-employed and non-employed) of the person. It also depends on whether the employee is contracted out of the graduated pension scheme: if he is contracted out, then the flat-rate contribution is higher. Contributions are paid both by the employee and the employer. Those who are in receipt of sickness or unemployment benefit are credited with contributions for each complete week during which benefit is paid.

Graduated Contributions

Those adult employees earning more than £9 who are not contracted out of the graduated pension scheme pay additional contributions at the rate of 4¾% on weekly earnings between £9 and £18 and ½% on earnings between £18 and £30 (for employees paid monthly there are corresponding rates).

Those who are contracted out of the graduated scheme pay graduated contributions at the lower rate of ½% on weekly earnings between £9 and £30.

In both cases the employer pays a contribution equal to that of the employee.

200

III SUPPLEMENTARY BENEFITS

Supplementary Benefits are payable to those people aged 16 and over not in full-time work whose resources are insufficient to meet their requirements as defined by the regulations. Persons of pensionable age and over are entitled to a *supplementary pension* and those below pension age to a *supplementary allowance*. The scheme is administered by the Supplementary Benefits Commission as part of the Department of Health and Social Security.

The amount of benefit is broadly the amount by which a person's requirements exceed his resources (the calculation of these is described below). The resources and requirements of a couple are aggregated, together with those of any dependent children living with them. In general, those in full-time work or undergoing full-time education are excluded, as are those involved in a trade dispute (although in this case benefit may be paid for the requirements of any dependants). Where a person eligible for a supplementary allowance is able to work he will normally be required to register at an Employment Exchange as a condition of receiving the allowance.

Calculation of Requirements

There is a fixed scale laying down the basic requirements of married couples, single householders, children (according to age) etc. – see page 18.

In addition to this scale, there is a long-term addition payable to those receiving supplementary pensions and those who have received the supplementary allowance continuously for two years. The long term addition is not payable whilst the basic allowance is paid on condition of registration at the Employment Exchange and neither do such periods count towards the qualifying period of two years. There are also certain other exceptions for people in hospital or resident in accommodation provided under Part III of the National Assistance Act, 1948.

Where the person claiming benefit is a householder, his requirements are increased by the net rent payable 'or such part of it as is considered reasonable in the circumstances'. 'Net rent' is defined as the rent payable for one week *plus* the weekly amount of general and water rates and, for owner-occupiers, mortgage interest and an allowance for insurance and repairs.

Calculation of Resources

In assessing the income of the claimant, the following types of income are taken into account in full: the main National Insurance pension and benefits, Family Allowances and maintenance payments. However, certain amounts of income apart from these can be 'disregarded':

(i) *Earnings* £2 of net weekly earnings (after allowing for reasonable expenses) are disregarded, except in the case of persons required to register for employment when it is £1. This disregard is personal in that a separate disregard applies to the claimant, his wife and any dependent children (£1 in the case of children).

(ii) *Disablement Pensions* Up to £2 is disregarded of the total of war and industrial disablement pensions, workmen's compensation, and certain amounts of war or industrial widow's pensions.

(iii) *Other Income* Up to £1 of other income (e.g. superannuation, sick pay or annuities) can be disregarded, provided that the overall amount disregarded under (ii) and (iii) does not exceed £2 a week.

In assessing resources, capital assets apart from an owner-occupied house are taken into account if they exceed £300. All capital above £300 is treated as equivalent to a weekly income of 1*s.* a week for each complete £25 between £300 and £800 and 2*s.* 6*d.* a week for each £25 thereafter. (Any actual income from the capital being disregarded). This imputed income is treated as other income for the purposes of the disregard (iii), so that a person with no other income to be disregarded under (ii) and (iii) can have up to £800 actually ignored.

Additions for Exceptional Expenses

The amount of benefit arrived at by deducting resources from requirements may be increased where there are exceptional expenses, such as for a special diet, extra heating or domestic assistance. In deciding whether to increase the amount paid, the long term addition of 10*s.* is taken into account, so that only where these expenses exceed 10*s.* is any further provision made. In addition, any disregarded income over 10*s.* is also taken into account before any exceptional allowance is made.

Adjustment to Normal Earnings — 'Wage Stop'

Where a person is required to register at an Employment Exchange, the allowance is restricted so that his total income when out of work is no greater than it would be if he were in full-time work in his normal occupation. This restriction may also be imposed in cases of short-term sickness.

APPENDIX B — Calculation of 'Average' Rent included in Supplementary Benefit Scale (I.A.R.)

The method used was to estimate the rent paid by different households in 1967 on the basis of the Family Expenditure Survey and the Ministry of Social Security Annual Report for 1967, and then to extrapolate this to other years on the basis of the average amount of rent paid by those receiving National Assistance.

The 1967 Family Expenditure Survey gives total housing expenditure for different household types and income levels — as shown in Table B.1. The Annual Report of the Ministry of Social Security gives the average net rent paid by households receiving Supplementary Benefits, and this is shown in the last column of Table B.1.

Table B.1. Housing Expenditure by Household Type — 1967

| | Family Expenditure Survey 1967 Income Range | | | Average for Households Receiving Supplementary Benefits |
	Below £6	£6–£10	£10–£20	
	£ s.	£ s.	£ s.	£ s.
Household Type:				
Single Person	1 3	1 18	2 4	1 11
Couple	–	1 10	2 7	1 15
Couple and –				
1 child	–	–	2 1	
2 children	–	–	2 3	2 9
3 or more children	–	–	1 17	

Source: *Family Expenditure Survey*, Tables 3–7, and *Annual Report of Ministry of Social Security 1967*, page 29.

Notes: The amounts are given to the nearest shilling.

In the case of the Family Expenditure Survey, the figure for owner-occupiers includes an imputed rent.

For want of any better criterion, I have in the case of single persons and couples taken the average of the Ministry of Social Security figure and that for the lowest income group in the Family Expenditure Survey. This gives figures of around £1 7s. for a single person and £1 12s. for a couple. In the case of families, it has been pointed out by a number of writers (see, for example, A.M. Henderson,

'The Cost of a Family', *Review of Economic Studies*, 1950) that there is a tendency for housing costs not to increase with the number of children and I have therefore taken the figure of £2 for all families with children regardless of size.

In order to obtain corresponding figures for earlier years, I have assumed that housing expenditure varied over time in the same way as the average rent paid by those receiving National Assistance (as published in the *Annual Reports of the National Assistance Board*). (To obtain figures for 1968 and 1969, I have assumed the same increase as that shown by the retail price index for housing). The resulting figures for selected years are shown in Table B.2.

Table B.2.   'Average' Rent, 1948–69 (rounded to the nearest 6*d.*)

Year	Single Person			Married couple			Married couple with children		
	£	*s.*	*d.*	£	*s.*	*d.*	£	*s.*	*d.*
1948		8	6		10	0		12	0
1955		10	6		12	6		16	0
1960		16	6		19	6	1	4	6
1963	1	1	0	1	5	0	1	11	0
1965	1	4	0	1	8	6	1	16	0
1966	1	5	6	1	10	0	1	18	0
1967	1	7	0	1	12	0	2	0	0
April 1968	1	8	0	1	13	6	2	1	6
June 1969	1	10	0	1	15	0	2	4	0

These figures agree quite closely with those used by other writers for similar purposes. For example, M.F.W. Hemming ('Social Security in Britain and Certain Other Countries', *National Institute Economic Review*, August 1965) uses the following figures for 1965 – £1 4*s.* for a single person, £1 7*s.* 6*d.* for a couple, and £1 16*s.* for a family with children. Similarly, Gough and Stark ('Low Incomes in the United Kingdom, 1954, 1959 and 1963', *The Manchester School*, June 1968) use the average rent paid by the National Assistance Board and assume that rent payments do not increase after the addition of the first child. The resulting figures for 1963 are very similar to those used above.

APPENDIX C   Estimate of the Number of People with Low Incomes from the Family Expenditure Survey 1967

The basis for the estimate is the distribution of households by gross weekly income and household composition given by the 1967 Family Expenditure Survey. This information is given in Table 24 of the published report, but the income ranges in this table are rather too broad for our purposes (the bottom two are 'Under £6' and '£6 but under £8'). However, the Department of Employment and Productivity very kindly provided more detailed figures for the lowest income groups, which were used in making the estimate.

Two important features of the estimate have been noted in the text: it is on a *household* basis, and we have to assume that every household had an average level of housing expenditure (as described in Appendix B). A number of other assumptions were made:

(a) *Entitlement to Long-term Addition* In the case of single persons and couples, there were obviously a high proportion of pensioners at the lower end of the income distribution, who would have been entitled to the long-term addition. I assumed that this was true of 75% — on the basis that 77% of single persons (71% of couples) with incomes below £6 were over 65 and that 70% of their income (62% for couples) came from pensions. I did not allow for any other households being eligible for the long-term addition, and since some undoubtedly would have been (e.g. widows with children), this will tend to under-state the number with low incomes.

(b) *Families with Children* It was assumed that the allowance for children could be taken as the average of those for the age groups 5 to 10 and 11 to 15. It was assumed that families with '4 or more children' had an average of 4½.

(c) *Assumptions about Household Composition* In determining the assistance scale that should be applied to a household, there were a number of cases where some assumption had to be made about its precise composition. In this I followed the procedure of Abel-Smith and Townsend (*The Poor and the Poorest*, Appendix I) as far as possible. I also used the information about household composition provided in Table 17 of the Family Expenditure Survey. For example, in the case of the category 'Three adults and one or more children', I took the average number of children shown in Table 17 and applied this to the combined category in Table 24. In the case of 'All other households' (both with and without children), I took the average of the groups that could be identified from Table 17 and assumed that those not identifiable (2.6% of the households in the sample) did not fall below the poverty line.

(d) *Housing Expenditure* The assumptions about housing expenditure for those household types not covered in Appendix B are set out below:

	£	s.	d.
3 adults	2	0	0
3 adults and children	2	8	0
4 adults	2	8	0
4 adults and children	2	15	0
1 adult and children	1	12	0

On the basis of these assumptions, we can then estimate how many households would have fallen below the Supplementary Benefit scale as it was from the beginning of 1967 up to 30th October 1967. This gives the results shown in Table C.1.

Table C.1. Estimated number in sample with Income below Supplementary Benefit Scale (I.A.R.)

Household Composition	Households	Persons
Single Person	183	183
Couple	92	184
Couple with 1 child	3	9
Couple with 2 children	8	32
Couple with 3 children	11	55
Couple with 4 or more children	22	143
3 Adults	3	9
3 Adults with one or more children	3	18
4 Adults	1	4
All other	38	134
TOTAL below Supplementary Benefit level (I.A.R.)	364	771
% of total in Family Expenditure Survey	4.9%	3.5%

In order to make an approximate extrapolation of these estimates to the whole population, the figures from the Survey were blown up by a factor of $\dfrac{55\,068\,000}{22\,135}$ — i.e. by the ratio of the United Kingdom population in June 1967 to the total number of persons in the Family Expenditure Survey.

Finally, it should be noted that there are a number of reasons why this estimate is likely to under-state the number of people living in households below the Supplementary Benefit scale (I.A.R.) — apart from those discussed in the text.

The Supplementary Benefit scale used is that in force before 30 October 1967, and if we had taken the scale that came into operation at that date, the number falling below would have been noticeably higher. Similarly, the assumptions made about household composition and about entitlement to the long-term addition were both on the conservative side and probably led us to under-state the number falling below.

APPENDIX D   The Effects of Introducing Supplementary Benefits — Detailed Analysis

The arrangement of this appendix follows the same pattern as adopted in the text: the first section deals with estimating the effect of increases in the assistance scale, and the second with the effect of introducing Supplementary Benefits.

I.   THE 'DEMAND' FOR NATIONAL ASSISTANCE

The aim of this section is to discuss the regression equations presented in the text and to examine the influence of other explanatory factors. All the equations referred to (together with those given in the main text) are set out in Table D.1.

(a) Adjustment for Late-Age Entrants

In the text I discussed briefly the problem of the late-age entrants to the National Insurance scheme who qualified for Retirement Pension in July 1958. As explained there, these people were almost certainly less likely to claim National Assistance than those already receiving the pension.

Suppose that we denote by α the proportion of Retirement Pensioners excluding late-age entrants who received National Assistance and by α^1 the corresponding proportion for late-age entrants. Let P denote the total number of Retirement Pensioner households and P^1 the number of late-age entrant households. Then after July 1958 the proportion of Retirement Pensioner households receiving National Assistance will fall from α to

$$\frac{\alpha(P - P^1) + \alpha^1 P^1}{P} = \alpha - (\alpha - \alpha^1)\frac{P^1}{P}$$

P was approximately 4 400 000 and P^1 290 000 (in terms of households), so that if we take $\alpha = 0.23$ and (as an extreme case) $\alpha^1 = 0$, the proportion receiving National Assistance would fall by around 1.5%. If we consider the years after 1958, then P^1/P would have fallen (as P rose) and α^1 probably increased, so that the effect could have been expected to die away.

In order to allow for these factors, two terms were included in equation (2) (and subsequent equations):

D – a dummy variable from 1958 on, to capture the initial effect.

T – a time trend beginning in 1959, to allow for the effect dying away over time.

Table D.1. Regression Equations used to Explain Proportion of Retirement
Pensioner Households Receiving National Assistance — 1951–65

Number of Equation		$\bar{R}^2$ and D.W. (Durbin–Watson statistic)
(1)	$Y = 24.4 \left(\dfrac{NA}{RP}\right) - 0.6$ (4.6)　　　(4.5)	$\bar{R}^2 = 0.64$ D.W. $= 1.13$
(2)	$Y = 20.1 \left(\dfrac{NA}{RP}\right) + 4.0 - 1.7D + 0.3T$ (4.9)　　　(5.1)　(0.7)　(0.1)	$\bar{R}^2 = 0.74$ D.W. $= 1.18$
(3)	$Y = 24.1 \left(\dfrac{NA}{RP}\right) \quad - 1.5D + 0.3T$ (0.3)　　　　　(0.6)　(0.1)	$\bar{R}^2 = 0.74$ D.W. $= 1.26$
(4)	$Y = 18.3 \left(\dfrac{NA + AR}{RP}\right) - 2.2D + 0.3T$ (0.2)　　　　　(0.6)　(0.1)	$\bar{R}^2 = 0.72$ D.W. $= 1.21$
(5)	$Y = 24.4 \left(\dfrac{NA}{RP}\right) \quad - 1.2D + 0.2T - 13.7X$ (0.3)　　　　　(0.5)　(0.1)　(5.5)	$\bar{R}^2 = 0.81$ D.W. $= 0.75$
(6)	$Y = 25.1 \left(\dfrac{NA}{RP}\right) \quad - 0.9D + 0.2T - 0.7U$ (1.1)　　　　　(0.8)　(0.1)　(0.7)	$\bar{R}^2 = 0.72$ D.W. $= 1.21$

Using National Assistance Rates and Retirement Pension for Married Couple:

(7)	$Y = 23.6 \left(\dfrac{NA'}{RP'}\right) \quad - 2.5D + 0.4T$ (0.2)　　　　　(0.6)　(0.1)	$\bar{R}^2 = 0.78$ D.W. $= 1.64$

Using quarterly data 1954^{I}–1966^{III}

(8)	$\bar{Y} = 20.3 \left(\dfrac{NA}{RP}\right) \quad - 1.8D + 0.2T$ (0.1)　　　　　(0.2)　(0.04)	$\bar{R}^2 = 0.87$ D.W. $= 1.10$

NOTATION

Variable	Definition
Y	Percentage of Retirement Pensioner households receiving National Assistance in December of each year.
$\bar{Y}$	Ratio of Retirement Pensioner households receiving National Assistance to total Retirement Pensioners in March, June, September and December of each year.
$\left(\dfrac{NA}{RP}\right)$	Ratio of National Assistance scale (not including housing expenditure) to Retirement Pension for a single person.

Table D.1. Regression Equations used to Explain Proportion of Retirement
Pensioner Households Receiving National Assistance – 1951–65

NOTATION (cont.)

Variable	Definition
$\left(\dfrac{NA'}{RP'}\right)$	ditto for a married couple
D	Dummy variable 1958–65 (or 1958^{III} to 1966^{III} in the case of equation (8))
T	Number of years since 1958 (since 1958^{III} in the case of equation (8))
X	$= \Delta\left(\dfrac{NA}{RP}\right)$ for $\Delta NA > \Delta RP$
	$= 0$ otherwise
U	Unemployment rate (%) in United Kingdom in December.

From equation (2) it can be seen that D is of the order of magnitude expected if $\alpha^1 = 0$ (1.7 against 1.5) and that the effect would have died away completely by 1965.

(b) Constant Term

In neither equation (1) nor equation (2) is the constant term significant (at 5% level). Since there are no grounds for expecting it to be significant (we really have little idea what would happen if $(NA/RP) = 0$), I have therefore dropped it from the remaining equations. Equation (3) is of the same form as equation (2) but without the constant. The coefficient of (NA/RP) is increased but not substantially, and the fit is unaffected.

(c) Allowance for Average Rent

In equations (1) and (2), the National Assistance scale was used without any allowance for housing expenditure. Equation (4) shows the result of using the National Assistance scale (I.A.R.) – as defined in Appendix B. The coefficient of this term is reduced in comparison with equation (3). The overall fit is slightly worse.

(d) Delayed Response to Increases in the Assistance Scale

No allowance has been made for any delays in adjusting to changes in the assistance scale and in the pension rates. While the National Assistance Board would stop paying assistance at once to those who were no longer eligible because of an increase in the pension, the reverse is almost certainly not true and it may be quite a long time before people realised that they were eligible for National Assistance as a result of an increase in the scale. For this reason

210

I have included in equation (5) a term (X) which for those years when the National Assistance scale *increased* relative to the Retirement Pension was equal to the increase in (NA/RP) (in other years it was zero).

This coefficient was significantly different from zero at the 5% level and suggested that as a result of delays only about half the effect of an increase in the assistance scale would be felt in the first year. The overall fit was improved (although the Durbin-Watson statistic was less satisfactory).

(e) Employment Opportunities

It is possible that the opportunities for employment for old people may affect the proportion receiving assistance: if a man can supplement his pension by part-time work, then he will not go to the National Assistance Board. As a test of this hypothesis, the level of unemployment was introduced in equation (6). The coefficient of U was both insignificant and of the 'wrong' sign, which suggests that employment opportunities are not an important factor. Since we have seen that only a minority of Retirement Pensioners had earnings of any kind in June 1965 (when unemployment was as low as 1.2%), this is not perhaps surprising.

(f) Using Rates for a Married Couple

Equation (7) shows the result of using the rates for a married couple rather than a single person as in equation (3). The fit is marginally better, although the coefficient of D is probably rather too high.

(g) Using Quarterly Data

Equations (1) to (7) have been based on figures for December of each year. Quarterly figures are available for the number of Retirement Pensioner households receiving National Assistance, but there are no figures on this basis for the total number of Retirement Pensioner households. If, however, we take as the variable to be explained the ratio of *households* receiving assistance to the total number of *people* receiving Retirement Pensions, then we can estimate a quarterly equation for the period $1954^{I}-1966^{III}$ – see equation (8). (The quarters relate to the ends of March, June, September and December). This equation gives a very good fit for this period.

In interpreting the coefficients of this equation, it must be borne in mind that the denominator of the left hand side is larger than in equations (1) to (7). In fact, the predictions obtained from this equation are very similar to those from the earlier equations. If we take an increase of 8s. in the National Assistance scale in December 1965 (as discussed in the text), then equation (8) predicts an increase of 130,000 compared with the figure of 120,000 obtained using equation (1).

Finally, I should note that there is one factor that I have not taken into account in these equations: for the years 1957–60 a number of people receiving widows' pensions were classified by the National Assistance Board as receiving Retirement Pensions (see *Report of the National Assistance Board for the Year Ended 31st December 1961*, (H.M.S.O., 1962), p. 8). I have made no allowance for this, but the overall effect is very small.

II.   THE EFFECT OF INTRODUCING SUPPLEMENTARY BENEFITS

This section has two purposes: to explain in more detail the points made in the main text, and to compare the predictions obtained from the different equations discussed in Section I of this appendix.

(a) Discretionary Additions

As was explained in the text, part of the increase in the assistance scale in November 1966 was intended to replace the discretionary additions paid under National Assistance (although people with special needs in excess of the long-term addition may still receive extra payments covering the excess). This meant that the effective increase for a person previously receiving discretionary additions (73% of Retirement Pensioners in December 1965) was less than the amount shown in Table 4.1.

In order to correct for this factor, we may make an alternative estimate based on the average amount received in the form of discretionary additions. The 1965 Annual Report of the National Assistance Board showed that the average discretionary addition for a Retirement Pensioner household in December 1965 was 10s. 1d. However, this included an average 6s. addition for extra fuel, which was then paid from November to April only — so that the average addition over the full year was 7s. 1d. Moreover, this was the average per person receiving any addition, and if we average over all pensioner households, then it came to just over 5s.

The estimates presented in Tables 4.3, 4.4 and D.2. were based on an effective increase in the assistance scale of 5s. less than the amounts shown in Table 4.1 (i.e. allowing for the average discretionary addition just derived). There are two reasons why this seems likely to be a conservative estimate:

(i)   The critical question is not the *average* discretionary addition but the amount that would have been received by households on the 'margin' of qualifying for assistance — since these are the people who would be affected. There are good reasons to expect that the 'marginal' household would not have been eligible for additions equal to the average. The additions are paid to cover 'special needs' for which only a certain proportion of the pensioner population would qualify, and these people would have been likely to be receiving National Assistance anyway.

(ii) A person previously receiving an addition in excess of the long-term addition (9s. in November 1966) would not lose the whole discretionary addition, but only 9s. of it, so that again taking the average would be too high.

212

(b) Delayed Response

As we have seen, there is a tendency for the response to increases in the assistance scale to be delayed and equation (5) suggested that the increase in the proportion receiving assistance in the first year may be half the final increase. On this basis, we should not have predicted such a large increase in 1966 – see the results set out in Table D.2. However, by November 1967 the predicted effect is at the same level as that from equation (1); so that the delay really only concerns the figure for 1966.

(c) More Generous Disregards

In the text, I referred to the more generous provisions for disregarding income and saving introduced in November 1966. This change, which could equally well have taken place under National Assistance (as in fact happened in 1959), would have increased the number eligible for assistance.

As far as income was concerned, the changes raised the limits up to which various amounts could be disregarded: for example, the overall limit for income other than earnings was raised from £1 10s. to £2. The provisions for savings are rather more complicated and it is difficult to make a direct comparison of the disregards before and after November 1966. However, it seems fairly clear that the change would have increased the number eligible. For example, National Assistance was not payable if a person had savings in excess of £600 (apart from an owner-occupied house and the special treatment of 'war savings'), but this upper limit was discontinued in the Supplementary Benefits scheme.

It is virtually impossible to estimate the effect that these changes would have had on the proportion receiving assistance. However, it is interesting to note that of the 300,000 'new' beneficiaries in November 1966 (i.e. those who had not received National Assistance in recent years), nearly 50,000 had savings in excess of the National Assistance limit of £600 (Ministry of Social Security, *Annual Report for 1966*, Table 6.4).

(d) A Comparison of the Predictions Obtained from Different Equations

The predictions obtained from different equations are set out in Table D.2. (equations (4) and (6) are omitted since it appeared that neither housing expenditure nor employment opportunities contributed much to the explanation of changes in the proportion receiving assistance).

From this it appears that the results are broadly in line with those from equation (1). If we look at the results with an allowance for discretionary additions for the increase between December 1965 and November 1968, then these all support the statement in the text that 'between a half and two thirds of the increase' was attributable to the higher assistance scale.

213

Table D.2. Predicted Increase in Number Receiving Assistance 1965–8

Equation used	Predicted increase expressed as % of actual increase		
	Dec. 1965–Dec. 1966	Dec. 1965–Nov. 1967	Dec. 1965–Nov. 1968
	%	%	%
(1)	68	60	83
(2)	57	53	74
(3)	67	60	83
(5)	35	61	72
(7)	50	43	66
(8)	71	63	86
With Allowance for Discretionary Additions			
(1)	47	39	64
(2)	39	36	58
(3)	47	39	65
(5)	26	40	54
(7)	37	35	55
(8)	48	41	67

Notes: For those equations including an adjustment for late-age entrants, it was assumed that this effect had fully died away by 1965.

In predicting the values for November 1967 and 1968, the equations were used without adjustment.

APPENDIX E   Cost of New Pension Proposals

I   'BACK TO BEVERIDGE' INCREASE

In the text the gross cost of this increase for tax year 1969–70 was given as approximately £650 million (N.B. this was on the basis of the pre-November 1969 rates). From this we must subtract the income tax paid on the higher pensions and the saving on Supplementary Benefits. We must also allow for the cost of extending Retirement Pensions to those at present too old to qualify.

(a) Income Tax

The basis for the estimate of the income tax paid on the higher pensions is the Inland Revenue survey of personal incomes for 1966–7. This gives the distribution of income tax units receiving Retirement Pensions by income ranges (for married couples and single persons separately). Using this distribution and making a number of assumptions, we can estimate the increase in tax liability resulting from the pension increase. The assumptions are of necessity rather crude, but the order of magnitude should be about right.

The assumptions made were as follows:

(i) It is assumed that the only allowances applicable are the personal allowances and the special exemption for the aged. Disregarding other allowances (such as for dependent relatives) causes the tax paid to be over-stated.

(ii) It is assumed that all income is earned, which will cause the tax paid to be under-stated (since some will undoubtedly receive investment income not covered by age relief). Although in view of the age relief and the fact that occupational pensions are treated as earned income, this may not be too important.

(iii) The effect of the general increase in income between 1966–7 and 1969–70 has been approximated by multiplying everyone's income by a factor of 1.15.

(b) Saving on Supplementary Benefits

The total annual cost of Supplementary Pensions at the rates applying at the end of 1968 was estimated at £225 million by the Department of Health and Social Security (*Annual Report for 1968*, page 235). Allowing for a 10% increase between end-1968 and the year 1969–70, this gives a total of £250 million.

However, Supplementary Pensions would still be paid to those with above-average rents or exceptional needs. Making a rough allowance for these on the basis of the figures for November 1967, we obtain a net saving of £205 million.

(c) Cost of Extending Retirement Pension to Those Too Old to Qualify

According to the Ministry of Pensions and National Insurance enquiry, there were some 480,000 people in this category in June 1965 (*Financial and other circumstances of Retirement Pensioners,* op. cit., Table I.1). If we assume that by 1969—70 this number had fallen to 400,000, then we can calculate the gross cost of paying them Retirement Pensions (at the Supplementary Benefit level (I.A.R.)) as £125 million (assuming that three quarters were single persons). The saving on Supplementary Benefits from this group (which is quite substantial) has already been included under (b). No attempt was made to estimate the tax paid on these pensions.

II INCOME SUPPLEMENT SCHEME

One method of estimating the cost of the income supplement scheme would be to follow the approach adopted with the 'Back to Beveridge' increase using the Inland Revenue survey of personal incomes. If we do this, we arrive at an estimated net cost of some £340 million. However, the Inland Revenue survey excludes many of those pensioners who have some other source of income besides the Retirement Pension but not sufficient to be liable for tax. For this reason, the figure given will over-state the true cost (since it takes no account of the 50% tax paid on other income by those not covered in the survey).

I have therefore adopted the alternative approach of using the information about incomes given in the 1965 Ministry enquiry (*Financial and other circumstances of Retirement Pensioners*, op. cit., Table BR.1). I have estimated from this the cost of the same *percentage* increase in the Retirement Pension (with the 50% tax rate on other income), and have then up-dated this to 1969-70. The resulting figure was £295 million. This includes the cost of extending the Retirement Pension to those not at present covered and assumes that they would receive the full income supplement; to this extent the estimate will still over-state the true cost.

APPENDIX F   Cost of New Child Benefit Schemes

In order to arrive at the net cost of the Child Poverty Action Group (C.P.A.G.) and Walley schemes, we have to estimate:

(i) the gross cost of the benefits

(ii) the saving on child tax relief

(iii) the saving on Family Allowances (allowing for the tax at present paid on them)

(iv) the saving on Supplementary Benefits and National Insurance (in the case of the Walley scheme)

Each of the components is discussed in turn:

(i) We have to decide first which children would be eligible. It is not clear whether the new schemes follow the present Inland Revenue approach of taking an upper income limit, or the Family Allowance method of including all children under 15 plus children at school after this age and apprentices with low earnings. The estimate given here is in fact based on a hybrid of these definitions, since the figures required to make a consistent estimate are not available. The total number of children is made up of the total of children in families receiving Family Allowances (including the first child) plus the number of 1 child families reported by the Inland Revenue survey of personal incomes. The sources for these figures are the Annual Report of the Ministry of Social Security 1966 (Table 7) and the Inland Revenue survey of personal incomes for 1966–7. The figures relate to December 1965 and the year 1966–7 respectively and are adjusted to give an estimated total for 1968–9. (The number of children in families receiving Family Allowances is also adjusted to an United Kingdom basis).

The rates of benefit were taken as the average of those for the age groups 0–10 and 11–15.

(ii) The estimate of the saving from abolishing the present child tax relief is based on the 1965–6 survey of personal incomes by the Inland Revenue, updated for the rise in personal incomes between then and 1968–9 (with a special adjustment for the increase in Family Allowances). In doing this I was given considerable help by Professor R.J. Ball and Dr. R. Agarwala of the London Business School, who made available to me a computer program for analysing the impact of different tax changes using the Inland Revenue survey.

The estimates are based on the 25 income groups given by the Inland Revenue and

217

the distribution by these groups of families of different sizes (Tables 117–120 in the Annual Report for the year ended March 31st 1967). For each group, the following variables have been calculated: average income, average earned income, average number of dependents (excluding children), the proportion of wives earning and their average earnings. These variables are the averages for the whole income group – not broken down by family size. On this basis the total tax and surtax liability for each income group is calculated applying the usual income tax rules. In doing this the child tax allowance is taken as the average of that for children aged under 11 and for children aged 11–15. It is assumed that families with 4 or more children had exactly 4.

The total tax liability has been calculated for 4 different situations:

A. With Family Allowances and child tax allowances as there were in force in 1968–9 (with child tax allowance reduced by £36 for children attracting Family Allowances).

B. With Family Allowances as in 1968–9 but child tax allowance abolished.

C. With no Family Allowances or child tax allowances.

D. With Family Allowances as in 1968–9 and child tax allowances not reduced for children attracting Family Allowances.

The results are as follows (for income and surtax combined):

	£ million
B–A	590
C–A	500
B–D	675

The first figure (B–A) gives the cost of the child tax allowances in force in 1968–9. This is lower than the official quoted figure of £675 million. However, the third figure (B–D) comes out to exactly £675 million, which suggests that the official figure refers to the cost of child tax allowances without taking account of the reduction for children attracting Family Allowances.

(iii) The gross expenditure on Family Allowances is estimated by extrapolating the figures for the number of children receiving allowances from those given for December 1967 (Annual Report of Ministry of Social Security 1967, Table 60). (These figures are also adjusted to an United Kingdom basis). The resulting gross cost is £290 million.

The method of calculating the income tax payable on these allowances has been described under (ii). The combined saving on child tax relief and Family Allowances is given by:-

Gross cost of Family Allowances + C – A
= £790 million

(iv) The saving on Supplementary Benefits is estimated on the basis of the proportions of families of different sizes receiving Supplementary Benefits in November 1967 (*Annual Report of Ministry of Social Security 1967*, Table 32) taking account of the 1968 increase in Family Allowances.

The saving on National Insurance benefits is estimated on the basis of the information provided in Table 23 in *Annual Report of Ministry of Social Security 1966.*

These estimates are only very approximate.

APPENDIX G New Social Security Contributions — Estimated Rates Required to Yield Same Revenue

In Chapter 8 (Section 3), I discussed two variations on the proposed contributions for the National Superannuation scheme: the introduction of a minimum exemption level, and the replacement of the contributions by a surcharge on income tax. In both cases I gave an estimate of the rates of contribution/surcharge that would have been required to give the same total revenue as the proposed National Superannuation contributions in 1968–9.

In this appendix I describe the method of estimating the revenue from the proposed National Superannuation contributions and from the two alternative proposals. The estimates are in all cases only very approximate and are intended only as a guide to the orders of magnitude.

(a) Revenue from National Superannuation Contributions

The revenue is estimated using the distribution of Schedule E income (wages, salaries, Forces pay, occupational pensions etc.) for 1966–7 given in Table 44 of the Inland Revenue Report for 1968. These figures are up-dated to 1968–9 on the basis of the change in average earnings (of adult male manual workers in manufacturing and certain other industries).

This source does not allow a very precise estimate since it includes income which would not be liable for contributions (e.g. occupational pensions) and may have excluded income which would have been covered. An approximate adjustment is made for the most important factor — occupational pensions. (Retirement Pensions and Family Allowances were already excluded).

The resulting figure for the total revenue from National Superannuation contributions for 1968–9 is in fact very close to the figure given by the Government Actuary for 1972–3 (calculated at April 1968 earnings levels): £1,900 millions as against £1,941 million.

(b) Required Rate of Contribution with an Exemption Level

This is calculated on the same basis as (a). The two figures given in the text relate to alternative assumptions about occupational pensions. The lower figure assumes that all the income from this source was below 40% of average earnings, the higher is based on the assumption that occupational pensions were distributed uniformly over the whole range. (The former assumption seems the most realistic.)

(c) Surcharge on Income Tax

The surcharge required is calculated using the Inland Revenue Survey of personal incomes as described in Appendix F but adapted to cover the whole population not just families with children.

APPENDIX H   The Tax Base for a Social Dividend

In this appendix I discuss very briefly some of the detailed problems in estimating the tax rate required to finance a social dividend scheme of the type described in Chapter 9. It might be felt that the discussion of details is out of place at this stage, and that it is the principles of the scheme that should be our primary concern. However, we have seen in Chapter 9 that the effect of the social dividend – both on the distribution of income and on work incentives – depends critically on the rate of tax that would be required.

I have tried here to raise some of the more obvious problems, but there are undoubtedly many others that I have not covered. The discussion is therefore far from exhaustive, and, as I have emphasised in the text, this subject is one that requires examination in greater depth before we can reach any final conclusions.

I   THE BROWN–DAWSON APPROACH

Table H.1.   Taxable Personal Income derived from National Income Accounts

	£ million	
	1966[a]	1967
Total Personal Income	32,018	33,435
plus interest paid[b]	+ 670	+ 725
less imputed income and income in kind	– 1,885	– 2,044
current transfers to charities from companies	– 30	– 32
current grants from public authorities	– 2,975	– 3,352
adjustment for life insurance	– 409	– 428
'Taxable personal income'	27,389	28,304

Source: *National Income and Expenditure 1968*, Table 25.

Notes: (a) These figures differ from those given by Brown and Dawson on account of revisions in the national accounts.

(b) Brown and Dawson included interest paid in the tax base. This has not been done in the text, since in the scheme discussed there it is not envisaged that the relief on mortgage interest would be withdrawn.

Brown and Dawson (*Personal Taxation, Incentives and Tax Reform,* op. cit.) approach the problem by taking the national accounts figure for total personal income and then making a number of adjustments. Figures corresponding to theirs for 1966 and 1967 are shown in Table H.1.

II   PROBLEMS WITH THE BROWN–DAWSON APPROACH

As mentioned in the text, there are a number of questions that must be raised in relation to the approach adopted by Brown and Dawson (and by earlier writers), including the following:

(a)   *Capital Allowances for the Self-Employed*   The figure given for income from self-emplyment is before providing for depreciation and stock appreciation. Since capital allowances would presumably continue under the social dividend, this would reduce taxable income below the figure shown.

(b) *Superannuation and Life Insurance*   The rationale of Brown and Dawson's treatment of these institutions is far from obvious. They include pensions and other benefits in personal income, and make no deduction for contributions by employees or individual premiums; at the same time, they subtract the item 'adjustment for life insurance' (contributions of employers *plus* rent, dividends and interest *less* pensions and other benefits paid). On this basis the taxable income is considerably higher than with the present treatment.

(c) *Non-Taxable Income*   The figure given by Brown and Dawson includes certain items of income which are at present non-taxable and would presumably remain so under the social dividend. This includes the income of charities (Brown and Dawson only allowed for the transfers from companies), the dividend of co-operative societies, and interest paid on National Savings.

(d) *Building Societies*   The estimate by Brown and Dawson assumes that the present concessions to building societies would be withdrawn. If they were to be retained, the tax revenue would be lower (the present composite rate is 6*s*. 5*d*. in the £).

(*e*) *Tax Evasion*   The Brown–Dawson estimate is based on an optimistic view of the ability of the Inland Revenue to collect the tax due from all sources. The national accounts figure for income from self-employment includes, for example, 'an arbitrary addition' for income undetected by the Inland Revenue (Central Statistical Office, *National Accounts Statistics – Sources and Methods,* (H.M.S.O., 1968). p. 145).

III   AN ALTERNATIVE APPROACH

In the text, I gave an alternative estimate of the tax base for a social dividend scheme. This was derived from National Income and Expenditure, 1968, op. cit. Table 26, by taking the total income classified by ranges and subtracting the social security benefits that would no longer be paid and making an allowance for scholarships and other educational grants. The resulting figure for 1966 was of the order of £24,100 — or only 88% of the figure reached on the Brown—Dawson approach.

This estimate differs from that of Brown and Dawson in that it treats superannuation funds and annuities in the same way as the present income tax, provides for capital allowances for the self-employed, excludes the non-taxable income referred to above. It does not, however, treat building societies in the same way as at present, since the interest *net of tax* is included. (It also includes some items of income in kind). Finally, it excludes incomes of persons receiving less than £50 a year, but this is unlikely to be very important, and on balance it seems probable that this estimate is more nearly 'correct' than that of Brown and Dawson.